THE BE

FÉNELON

SPIRITUAL LETTERS / MAXIMS OF THE SAINTS / CHRISTIAN COUNSEL

THE BEST OF FÉNELON

SPIRITUAL LETTERS / MAXIMS OF THE SAINTS / CHRISTIAN COUNSEL

FRANCOIS DE SALIGNAC DE LA MOTHE-FÉNELON

REVISED & UPDATED BY
HAROLD J. CHADWICK

Bridge-Logos *Publishers*

Gainesville, Florida 32614 USA

All Scripture quotations are from the *King James Version* of the Bible unless otherwise indicated.

Scripture quotations marked NKJV are from the *New King James Version* of the Bible. Copyright © 1979, 1980, 1982 by Thomas Nelson, Inc., Publishers. Used by permission.

The Best of Fénelon
Copyright ©2002
by Francois de Salignac de La Mothe-Fénelon
Edited by: Harold Chadwick
Library of Congress Catalog Number: Pending
International Standard Book Number: 0-88270-893-7

Published by
Bridge-Logos *Publishers*
P.O. Box 141630
Gainesville, FL 32614
www.bridgelogos.com

Table of Contents

Introduction

In 17th century France, Francois de Salignac de la Mothe-Fénelon, Roman Catholic Archbishop of Cambray, was among a prominent trio of believers who adhered to a set of doctrines that were at that time considered by the Roman Catholic Church to be controversial and even heretical.

The Quietist doctrines stressed the importance of detachment from the things of this world and focused, instead, on the inner spiritual life and on perfect love for Christ. Fr. Miguel de Molinos, a Roman Catholic priest, originated these doctrines, or perhaps Fr. Molinos only revived these teachings during this period in church history.

Fr. Molinos wrote his views in his work titled, *The Spiritual Guide*, which was well received by many who read it, including Pope Innocent XI. Fr. Molinos' teachings also become the subject of the writings of Archbishop Fénelon and of Jeanne Marie Bouvier de la Mothe Guyon, an artistocrat with no ecclesiastical ties.

Fr. Molinos corresponded with Mme. Guyon during his incarceration, and she wrote a book on how to experience union with God through inner prayer. The book was at that time titled, *A Short and Very Easy Method of Prayer*. In one town, an enthusiastic Frenchman distributed 1,500 copies of Mme. Guyon's book from door to door. In another town, an incensed church official from Rome forcibly removed 300 copies from Roman Catholic homes and burned the books.

Despite or perhaps because of the popularity of these doctrines, in 1665, the machinations of church politics led to Fr. Molinos' imprisonment as a heretic. And many of his followers were also imprisoned at that time.

Fr. Molinos was eventually sentenced by church inquisitors to life in prison. He was several times tortured, and he finally broke down and signed a confession, admitting that he had done wrong. Because of the severity of his torments and his age, in 1696, Fr. Molinas died in prison; he was sixty-eight.

In 1695, under the orders of Louis XIV, Mme. Guyon was tried for heresy and sentenced to seven years in prison. For the first year, she was kept in the state prison in Vincennes, a city east of Paris in north-central France. Then, on August 28, 1696, she was confined in a monastery in Vaugirard, near Paris. Two years later, in September 1698, she was transferred to the infamous French Bastille in Paris. During her four-year-long imprisonment at the Bastille, she was in solitary confinement. And the damp, unheated, and poorly ventilated cell where she was confined so weakened her always-frail constitution that she remained in ill health for the rest of her life.

In 1702, she was released. But Louis XIV banished her for life to Blois, a large city one hundred miles southwest of Paris, on the Loire River. Mme. Guyon was warned that if she ever left the city, she would be returned immediately to the Bastille for the rest of her life. She remained in Blois until her death on June 9, 1717, at the age of sixty-nine.

During the fifteen years of her banishment in Blois, thousands traveled from all over Europe to listen to her teachings on the inner life and to receive spiritual counsel from her. One of those whom she often counseled, both in person before she was jailed and by letter during and after her incarceration, was Archbishop Fénelon, popularly known as just Fénelon.

From Mme. Guyon's letters and his personal conversations with her, Fénelon learned about the contemplative life. The two were staunch friends for twenty-five years. And although one of Mme. Guyon's chief persecutors, Bishop Jacques Benigne Bossuet, had been a friend and mentor to Fénelon, Fénelon remained loyal to Mme. Guyon throughout her persecution. "It would be infamous weakness in me to speak doubtfully in relation to her character in order to free myself from oppression," Fénelon wrote.

In 1697, Fénelon wrote *The Maxims of the Saints*, which expressed his views on the contemplative life. Although he did not mention Mme. Guyon's name in this book, it was obvious to all who knew of this controversy that Fénelon wrote *The Maxims of the Saints* as a defense of Mme. Guyon's teachings.

Bishop Bossuet immediately attacked *The Maxims of the Saints* as inconsistent with Christian teachings. The two prelates appealed to Rome to settle the argument, and Bossuet won. In 1699, Pope Innocent XII condemned parts of Fénelon's book.

Soon after, despite Fénelon's prominent position in the court of Louis XIV, the king sided with Bishop Bossuet and exiled Fénelon to his diocese. Fénelon remained there for the rest of his life. He had formerly lived and worked among royalty and was himself an aristocrat and a high-ranking cleric, but in the local church where he was assigned, he earned a reputation as an ideal pastor.

As you read Fenelon's writings and perhaps also practice what he and his spiritual compatriots taught, consider their cost and the cost to the hundreds of other Christians of their time who believed in these teachings and who were persecuted on account of their beliefs.

Their experience of the inner life and the accompanying perfect love enabled them to overcome adversities, remain abandoned to the will of God and love their enemies with the love of God.

The teachings in this book will do the same for you — if you have eyes with which to see, ears with which to hear, and a heart with which to believe.

Harold Chadwick

Bridge-Logos Senior Editor

SECTION I

THE WRITINGS OF FÉNELON

SPIRITUAL LETTERS / CHRISTIAN COUNSEL / MAXIMS OF THE SAINTS

FÉNELON

Spiritual Letters

And I have declared unto them thy name and will
declare it; that the love wherewith thou hast loved
me, may be in them and I in them. (John 17:26)

The letters in this collection were written by Fénelon—
François De Salignac de La Mothe Fénelon, the Archbishop of
Cambray, France—during the 17th century. As archbishop,
Fénelon became the spiritual advisor to a number of people
who were sincerely and earnestly seeking the deeper spiritual
life. Many of them were from the court of Louis XIV, which
was not noted for its morality, and was devoted to a religion that
concerned itself more with external religious rituals than with
true internal religion of the heart.

In his letters, Fénelon urged his readers to abandon
themselves to God and seek perfect love and inner perfection.

It cannot be said with certainty that any of the letters in this collection were written to Mme. Jeanne Guyon, who was a contemporary of his, and with whom he often exchanged correspondence. But much of her teachings and the direction of her search for the deeper inner spiritual life are in keeping with what Fénelon wrote in these letters.[1]

Letter 1
The advantage of humiliation

I pray often to God that He would keep you in the hollow of His hand.

The most essential point is lowliness. It is profitable for all things, for it produces a teachable spirit that makes everything easy.

You would be more guilty than many others if you made any resistance to God on this point.

You have received abundant light and grace on the necessity of becoming like a little child, and no one else has had an experience more fitting to humiliate the heart and destroy self-confidence.

The great profit to be derived from an experience of our weakness, is to render us lowly and obedient. May the Lord keep you!

Letter 2
How to bear suffering
in a way to preserve our peace

As to our friend, I pray to God to bestow upon him a simplicity that will give him peace. When we are faithful in instantly dropping all superfluous and restless reflections,— which arise from a self-love as different as possible from charity,— we will be set in a large place even in the midst of the straight and narrow path. We will be in the pure liberty and innocent peace of the children of God, without being found lacking anything toward God or people.

I apply to myself the same counsel that I give to others, and am well persuaded that I must seek my own peace in the same direction. My heart is now suffering. But it is the life of self that causes us pain. What is dead does not suffer.

If we were dead [to self], and our life were hid with Christ in God,[2] we would no longer perceive those pains in spirit that now afflict us. We would not only bear bodily sufferings with composure, but also, spiritual affliction.

By spiritual affliction, I mean trouble that is sent upon the soul and is not caused by its own actions. The disturbances created by a restless activity, however,—in which the soul adds to the cross imposed by the hand of God, and burdens itself by an agitated resistance and an unwillingness to suffer,—are only experienced because of the remaining life of self.

A cross that comes purely from God and is cordially welcomed without any self-reflective acts is at once painful and peaceful. But a cross that is unwillingly received and repelled by the life of nature is doubly severe—the internal resistance is harder to bear than the cross itself. If we recognize the hand of God and make no opposition in our will, we have comfort in our affliction. Happy, indeed, are these who can bear their sufferings in the enjoyment of this simple peace and perfect submission to the will of God! Nothing so shortens and soothes our pains as this spirit of nonresistance.

But we generally want to bargain with God. We would like at least to impose the limits and see the end of our sufferings. That same obstinate and hidden hold of life, which renders the cross necessary, causes us to reject it in part by a secret resistance that impairs its virtue. So we have to go over the same ground again and again. Because of this we suffer greatly, but to very little purpose.

The Lord deliver us from falling into that state of soul in which crosses are of no benefit to us! God loves a cheerful giver, according to St. Paul.[3] Ah! what must be His love to those who submit themselves to the entire extent of His crucifying will in a cheerful and absolute abandonment!

Letter 3
The beauty of the cross

I cannot but wonder at the virtue that lies in suffering—we are worth nothing without the cross. I tremble and am in an agony while it lasts, and all my conviction of its remedial effects vanish under the pain. But when it is over, I look back at it with admiration, and am ashamed that I bore it so poorly. This experience of my foolishness is a deep lesson of wisdom to me.

Whatever may be the state of your sick friend, and whatever the issue of her disease, she is blessed in being so quiet under the hand of God. If she die, she dies to the Lord. If she live, she lives to Him. Either the cross or death, says St. Theresa.[4]

Nothing is beyond the necessity of the cross but the established kingdom of God. When we bear the cross in love, it is His kingdom begun, with which we must remain satisfied while it is His pleasure. You have need of the cross as well as I. The faithful Giver of every good gift[5] distributes them to each of us with His own hand—blessed be His name! Ah! How good it is to be chastened for our profit![6]

Letter 4
The death of self

I cannot express to you, my dear sister, how deeply I sympathize with your afflictions. But my grief is not unmixed with consolation. God loves you, since He does not spare you, but lays upon you the cross of Jesus Christ.

Whatever light or feeling we may possess is a delusion if it does not lead us the real and constant practice of dying to self. We cannot die without suffering, neither can we be said to be dead while there is still any part in us that is alive. That death with which God blesses the soul pierces even to the dividing asunder of soul and spirit, and of the joints and marrow.[7]

He who sees in us what we cannot see knows full well where the blow should fall. He takes away that which we are most reluctant to give up. Pain is only felt where there is life, and where there is life is just the place where death is needed. Our Father wastes no time by cutting into parts that are already dead. If He sought to continue life, He would do so; but He seeks to destroy, and this He can only accomplish by cutting into that which is quick and living.[8]

You need not expect Him to attack those gross and wicked desires that you renounced forever, when you gave yourself to Christ. Instead, He will undoubtedly prove you by destroying your liberty of soul and by depriving you of your most spiritual consolations.

Should you resist? Ah! No! Suffer all things! This death must be voluntary, and can only be accomplished to that extent to which you are willing it should be. To resist death, and repel its advances, is not being willing to die. Give up voluntarily to the good pleasure of God all the things you rely upon, even the most spiritual ones, whenever He seems to want to take them from you.

Don't be fearful, O you of little faith![9] Are you afraid that He may not be able to supply from Himself the counsel and comfort of others that He takes away from you? But why does He take it away except to supply it from Himself, and to purify you by the painful lesson?

I see that every way is closed to you, and that God means to accomplish His work in you by cutting off every human resource. He is a jealous God.[10] He is not willing that you should credit to anyone else but Him what He is about to perform in you. Give yourself up to His plans—be led by His providences wherever He is leading you.

Beware how you seek aid from people, when God forbids it—they can only give you what He gives them for you. Why should you be troubled that you can no longer drink from the river when you are led to the everlasting spring itself from which its waters flow?

Letter 5
Peace lies in simplicity and obedience

Cultivate peace. Be deaf to your too prolific imagination. Its great activity not only injures the health of your body, but puts dryness into your soul. You consume yourself to no purpose. Peace and interior sweetness are destroyed by your restlessness. Do you think God can speak in those soft and tender accents that melt the soul, when you create such tumult within yourself by the continual agitation of your thoughts? Be quiet, and He will soon be heard. Have only one thing on your conscience—to be conscientiously obedient.

You ask for consolation, but you do not perceive that you have been led to the brink of the fountain and you refuse to drink. Peace and consolation are only to be found in simple obedience. Be faithful in obeying without concern for your misgivings, and you will soon find that the rivers of living water will flow according to the promise. You will receive according to the measure of your faith. Much, if you believe much. Nothing, if you believe nothing—and continue to listen to your empty imaginations.

You dishonor true love by assuming that it is rightfully anxious about the trifles that continually occupy your attention. True love goes straight to God in pure simplicity. Satan is transformed into an angel of light,[11] and assumes the beautiful form of a conscientious love and a tender conscience. But you should know from experience the trouble and danger into which he will lead you by your strong concerns. Everything depends upon your faithfulness in repelling his first advances.

If you become trustful and simple in your desires, I think you will have been more pleasing to God than if you had suffered a hundred martyrdoms. Turn all your anxieties toward your delay in offering a sacrifice so right in the sight of God. Can true love hesitate when it is required to please its well-beloved?

Letter 6
The true source of peace
is in the surrender of the will

Remain in peace. Your fire of devotion does not depend upon yourself. All that lies in your power is the direction of your will. Give that up to God without reservation.

The important question is not how much you enjoy religion, but whether you will whatever God wills.

Humbly confess your faults. Be detached from the world, and abandoned to God. Love Him more than yourself, and His glory more than your life.

The least you can do is to desire and ask for such a love. God will then love you and put His peace in your heart.

Letter 7
True good is only reached by abandonment

Evil is changed into good when it is received in patience through the love of God. Good is changed into evil when we become attached to it through the love of self.

True good lies only in detachment and abandonment to God. You are now in the trial. Put yourself confidently and without reserve into His hand.

What would I not sacrifice to see you once more restored in body, but heartily sick of the love of the world!

Attachment to ourselves is a thousand times more infectious

than a contagious poison, for it contains the venom of self.

I pray for you with all my heart.

Letter 8
Knowledge puffs up; charity edifies

I am happy to hear of your frame of mind, and to find you communicating in simplicity everything that takes place within you. Never hesitate to write me about whatever you think God requires [you to do so].[12]

It is not at all surprising that you have a sort of jealous ambition to advance in the spiritual life, and to be intimate with persons of distinction who are pious. Such things are by nature very flattering to our self-love, and it eagerly seeks them.

But we should not strive to gratify such an ambition by making great progress in the religious life, and by cultivating the acquaintance of persons high in honor. Our aim should be to die to the flattering delights of self-love by becoming humble and in love with obscurity and contempt and to have a single eye to God.

We may hear about perfection without end,—and become perfectly familiar with its language,—and yet be as far from its attainment as ever. Our great aim should be to be deaf to self, to listen to God in silence, to renounce every vanity, and to devote ourselves to solid virtue.

Let us speak but little and do much, without a thought as to whether we are observed or not.

God will teach you more than the most experienced Christians, and better than all the books that the world has ever seen.

But what is your object in such an eager chase after knowledge? Are you not aware that all we need is to be poor in spirit,[13] and to know nothing but Christ and Him crucified?[14] "Knowledge puffeth up, but charity edifieth."[15] Be content, then, with charity alone.

Do you believe that it is possible that the love of God,—and the abandonment of self for His sake,—is only to be reached through acquiring so much knowledge? You have already more than you use, and need further illuminations much less than the practice of what you already know.

O how deceived we are when we suppose we are advancing because our vain curiosity is gratified by the enlightenment of our intellect! Be humble, and do not expect the gifts of God to come from people.

Letter 9
We are not to choose the manner in which our blessings will be bestowed

You know what God requires of you—will you refuse? You perceive that your resistance to the drawings of His grace arises solely from self-love. So will you allow the refinements of pride, and the most clever inventions of self, to reject the mercies of God?

You who have so many concerns in relation to passing thoughts, which are involuntary and therefore innocent, who confess so many things that should instead be dismissed at once, have you no concerns about your long-continued resistance to the Holy Spirit—simply because He has not seen fit to confer the benefits you desire by a channel that was flattering to your self-love?

What does it matter if you received the gifts of grace as beggars receive bread? The gifts themselves would be neither less pure nor less precious. Your heart would only be the more worthy of God, if by its humility and annihilation it attracted the relief that He was disposed to send. Is this the way you put off self? Is this the view that pure faith takes of the instrument of God? Is it thus that you die to the life of self within?

To what purpose are your readings about pure love, and your frequent devotions? How can you read what condemns the very depths of your soul? You are influenced not only by self-interest, but by the persuasions of pride, when you reject the gifts of God because they do not come in a shape to suit your taste.

How can you pray? What is the language of God in the depths of your soul? He asks nothing but death, and you desire nothing but life. How can you put up to Him a prayer for His grace,—with a restriction that He shall only send it by a channel demanding no sacrifice on your part, but ministering to the gratification of your carnal pride?

Letter 10
The discovery and death of self

Yes, I joyfully consent that you call me your father! I am so and will be always. On your part there only needs to be a full and confident persuasion of it, which will come when your heart is enlarged. Self-love now shuts it up. We are in a strait[16] place, indeed, when we are enclosed in self. But when we emerge from that prison,—and enter into the immensity of God and the liberty of His children,—we are set at large.

I am rejoiced to find that God has reduced you to a state of weakness. Your self-love can neither be convinced nor vanquished by any other means. It always finds secret resources and impenetrable retreats in your courage and ingenuity. It was hidden from your eyes, while it fed upon the subtle poison of an apparent generosity, by which you constantly sacrificed yourself for others. God has forced it to cry aloud, to come forth into open day, and display its excessive jealousy.

O how painful, but how useful, are these seasons of

weakness? While any self-love remains, we are afraid of its being revealed. But so long as the least symptom of it lurks in the most secret recesses of the heart, God pursues it and, by some infinitely merciful blow, forces it into the light.

The poison then becomes the remedy. Self-love, pushed to extremity, discovers itself in all its deformity by a strong feeling of despair, and dissipates the flattering illusions of a complete life. God sets before your eyes your idol—self. You behold it, and cannot turn your eyes away. And since you no longer have power over yourself, you cannot keep the sight from others.

Thus to exhibit self-love without its mask is the most humiliating punishment that can be inflicted. We no longer see it as being wise, discreet, polite, self-possessed, and courageous in sacrificing itself for others. It is no longer the self-love whose nourishment consisted in the belief that it had need of nothing and in the persuasion that its greatness and generosity deserved a different name.

It is the selfishness of a silly child, screaming at the loss of an apple. But it is far more tormenting, for it also weeps from rage that it has wept. It cannot be still, and refuses all comfort, because its poisonous character has been detected. It now sees itself as foolish, rude, and impertinent, and is forced to look its own frightful countenance in the face. It says with Job: "For the thing which I greatly feared is come upon me, and that which I was afraid of is come unto me."[17] For precisely that which it most fears is the most necessary means of its destruction.

We have no need that God should attack in us what has neither life nor sensibility. It is only the living that must die, and all the rest is nothing. This, then, is what you needed—to behold a self-love convinced, sensitive, gross, and tangible. And now all you have to do is be quietly willing to look at it as it is. The moment you can do this, it will have disappeared.

You ask for a remedy, that you may get well. You do not need to be cured, but to be slain. Do not seek impatiently for a remedy, but let death come. Be careful, however, lest a certain courageous resolve to avail yourself of no remedy be itself a remedy in disguise, and give aid and comfort to this cursed life. Seek no consolation for self-love, and do not conceal the disease. Reveal everything in simplicity and holiness, and then permit yourself to die.

But this is not to be accomplished by any exertion of strength. Weakness has become your only possession. All strength is out of place; it only serves to render the agony longer and more distressing. If you expire from exhaustion, you will die so much the quicker and less violently. A dying life must of necessity be painful.

Stimulants are a cruelty to the sufferer on the wheel. He only longs for the fatal blow, not food, nor sustenance. If it were possible to weaken him and hasten his death, we would lessen his sufferings. But we can do nothing. Only the hand that tied him to his torture can deliver him from the remains of suffering life.

Ask, then, neither remedies, sustenance, nor death. To ask death is impatience. To ask food or remedies is to prolong our agony. What, then, shall we do?

Let it alone—seek nothing, hold to nothing. Confess everything, not as a means of consolation, but through humility and desire to yield.

Look to me not as a source of life, but as a means of death. Just as an instrument of life would belie its purpose if it did not minister to life, so an instrument of death would be falsely named if, in lieu of slaying, it kept alive.

Let me then be—or at least seem to you to be—hard, unfeeling, indifferent, pitiless, wearied, annoyed, and contemptuous. God knows how far it is from the truth, but he permits it all to appear. And I shall be much more serviceable to you in this false and imaginary character than by my affection and real assistance. For the point is not how you are to be sustained and kept alive, but how you are to lose all and die.

Letter 11
The sight of our imperfections
should not take away our peace

There is something very hidden and very deceptive in your suffering. While you seem to yourself to be wholly occupied with the glory of God, in your innermost soul, it is self alone that causes all your trouble.

You do, indeed, desire that God should be glorified. But you desire that He should be glorified by means of your perfection, and you thus cherish the sentiments of self-love. It is simply a refined pretext for dwelling in self.

If you would truly derive profit from the discovery of your imperfections, neither justify nor condemn [yourself] on their account. Instead, quietly lay them before God, conforming your will to His in all things that you cannot understand, and remaining at peace. For peace is the order of God for every condition,—no matter what it is.

There is, in fact, a peace of conscience that sinners themselves should enjoy when awakened to repentance. Their suffering should be peaceful and mingled with consolation.

Remember the beautiful word that once delighted you,— that the Lord was not in noise and confusion, but in the still, small, voice.[18]

Letter 12
Living by the cross and by faith

Everything [for me] is a cross. I have no joy but bitterness. But the heaviest cross must be borne in peace.

19

At times it can neither be borne nor dragged. We can only fall down beneath it, overwhelmed and exhausted.

I pray that God may spare you as much as possible in allocating your suffering. It is our daily bread [by which we are spiritually fed and developed]. God alone knows how much we need.

We must live with faith in the means of death. [And we must be] confident, though we do not see, that God, with secret compassion, proportions our trials [in keeping with] the unperceived assistance that He administers within [us].[19]

This life of faith is the most penetrating of all deaths.

Letter 13
Despair at our imperfection
is a greater obstacle than the imperfection itself

Do not be concerned about your defects. Love without ceasing; and you will be much forgiven, because you have loved much.[20]

We are apt to seek the delights and selfish supports of love, rather than love itself. We deceive ourselves even in supposing we are endeavoring to love, when we are only trying to see that we love.

We are more occupied with the love, says St. Francis of Sales,[21] than with the Well-Beloved. If He were our only object, we would be all taken up with Him. But when we are employed in obtaining an assurance of His love, we are still in a measure busy with self.

Our defects, regarded in peace and in the spirit of love, are instantly consumed by love itself. But considered in the light of self, they make us restless; and interrupt the presence of God and the exercise of perfect love.

The chagrin we feel at our own defects is ordinarily a greater fault than the original defect itself.

You are wholly taken up with the lesser of the two faults, like a person whom I have just seen, who, after reading the life of one of the saints, was so enraged at his own comparative imperfection that he entirely abandoned the idea of living a devoted life.

I judge [the degree] of your fidelity by your peace and liberty of soul. The more peaceful and enlarged your heart, the nearer you seem to be to God.

Letter 14
Pure faith sees God alone

Do not be anxious about the future. [Such anxiety] is opposed to grace. When God sends you consolation, regard Him only in it, enjoy it day by day as the Israelites received their manna, and do not endeavor to lay it up in store.

There are two peculiarities of pure faith: It sees God alone under all the imperfect wrappings that conceal Him, and it holds the soul incessantly in suspense. We are kept constantly in the air, without being allowed to touch a foot to solid ground.

The comfort of the present instant will be wholly inappropriate to the next. We must let God act with the most perfect freedom, in whatever belongs to Him, and think only of being faithful in all that depends upon ourselves.

This momentary dependence,—this darkness and this peace of the soul, under the utter uncertainty of the future,—is a true martyrdom, which takes place silently and without any stir. It is death by a slow fire. And the end comes so imperceptibly and internally, that it is often almost as much hidden from the sufferer, as from those who are unacquainted with that person's state.

When God removes His gifts from you, He knows how and when to replace them, either by others or by Himself. He can raise up children from the very stones.[22] Eat then your daily bread without thought for the morrow: "sufficient unto the day is the evil thereof."[23]

Tomorrow will take thought for the things of itself. He who feeds you today, is the same to whom you will look for food tomorrow. Manna will fall again from heaven in the midst of the desert, before the children of God will lack any good thing.[24]

Letter 15
Our knowledge stands in the way of our becoming wise

L ive in peace, my dear young lady, without any thought for the future—perhaps there will be none for you. You do not even have a present of your own; for you must only use it in accordance with the designs of God, to whom it truly belongs.

Continue the good works that occupy you, since you have an attraction that way and can readily accomplish them. Avoid distractions and the consequences of your excessive vivacity. Above all things, be faithful to the present moment; and you will receive all necessary grace.

It is not enough to be detached from the world; we must become lowly also. In detachment, we renounce the things without; in lowliness, we abandon self. Every shadow of perceptible pride must be left behind. The pride of wisdom and virtue is more dangerous than that of worldly fortune; for it has a show of right and is more refined.

We must be lowlyminded in all points and appropriate nothing to ourselves,—our virtue and courage least of all. You rest too much in your own courage, disinterestedness, and uprightness. The babe owns nothing. It treats a diamond and an apple alike. Be a babe. Have nothing of your own, forget yourself, give way on all occasions, and let the smallest be greater than you.

Pray simply from the heart, from pure love. Do not pray from the head, from the intellect alone.

Your true instruction is to be found in deprivation, deep recollection, silence of the whole soul before God, renouncing your own spirit, and in the love of lowliness—obscurity, feebleness, and annihilation. This [state of] ignorance is the accomplished teacher of all [spiritual] truth. Knowledge cannot attain to it, or can only reach it superficially,

Letter 16
Those who endeavor to injure us are to be loved and welcomed as the hand of God

I sympathize, as I should, in all your troubles, but I can do nothing else except pray to God that He would console you. You have great need of the gift of His Spirit to sustain you in your difficulties and to restrain your natural liveliness under the trials that are so fitted to excite it. As to the letter touching your birth, I think you should lay it before God alone and beg His mercy upon him who has sought to injure you.

I have always perceived, or thought that I perceived, that you were sensitive on that point. God always attacks us on our weak side. We do not aim to kill a person by striking a blow at insensible parts, such as the hair or nails, but by endeavoring to reach at once the vital organs, the immediate seats of life.

When God would have us die to self, He always touches the tenderest spot, that which is fullest of life. It is thus that He distributes crosses. Allow yourself to be humbled.

Silence and peace under humiliation are the true good of the soul. We are tempted, under a thousand specious pretexts, to speak humbly. But it is far better to be humbly silent. The humility that can yet talk has need of careful watching. Self-love derives comfort from its outward words.

Do not allow yourself to get excited by what is said about you. Let the world talk. Strive only to do the will of God. As for the will of people, you could never succeed in doing it to their satisfaction, and it is not worth the pains.

A moment of silence, of peace, and of union to God will amply recompense you for every malicious word that will be uttered against you. We must love others without expecting friendship from them. They leave us and return; they go and come. Let them do as they will. Their favor is but a feather, the sport of the wind.

See God only in them. It is He that afflicts or consoles us, by means of them, according to our need.[25]

Letter 17
Quietness in God is our true resource

Warmth of imagination, ardor of feeling, acuteness of reasoning, and fluency of expression can do but little. The true agent is a perfect abandonment before God, in which we do everything by the light that He gives and are content with the success that He bestows.

This continual death is a blessed life known to few. A single word uttered from this rest will do more, even in outward affairs, than all our most eager and unwanted care. It is the Spirit of God that then speaks the word; and it loses none of its force and authority,—but enlightens, persuades, moves, and edifies. We have accomplished everything and have scarcely said anything.

On the other hand, if left to the excitability of our natural temperament, we talk forever, indulging in a thousand subtle and superfluous reflections. We are constantly afraid of not saying or doing enough. We get angry, excited, exhausted, distracted, and finally make no headway.

Your [physical] disposition has an important need of these maxims. They are as necessary for your body as your soul. Your physician and your spiritual adviser should act together.

Let the water flow beneath the bridge. Let people be people—that is to say: weak, vain, inconstant, unjust, false, and presumptuous. Let the world be the world still. You cannot prevent it. Let every one follow their own inclination and habits. You cannot recast them, and the best course is to let them be as they are and bear with them.

Do not think it strange when you witness unreasonableness and injustice. Rest in peace in the bosom of God. He sees it all more clearly than you do, and yet permits it. Be content to do quietly and gently what it becomes you to do, and let everything else be to you as though it were not.

Letter 18
True friendships are founded only in God

We must be content with what God gives, without having any of our own. It is right that His will should be done, not ours, and that His will should become ours without the least reservation, in order that it may be done on earth as it is done in heaven.[26] This is a hundred times more valuable an attainment than to be engaged in the view or consolation of self.

Oh, how near are we to each other when we are all united in God! How well we converse when we have but a single will and a single thought in Him who is all things in us!

Would you find your true friends, then? Seek them only in Him who is the single source of true and eternal friendship.

Would you speak with or hear from them? Sink in silence into the bosom of Him who is the word, the life, and the soul of all those who speak and live the truth? You will find in Him not only every want supplied, but everything perfect, which you find so imperfect in the creatures in whom you confide.

Letter 19
The cross is a source of our pleasure

I sympathize with all your distresses, but we must carry the cross with Christ in this transitory life. We will soon have no time to suffer. We will reign with God our consolation, who will have wiped away our tears with His own hand, and from before whose presence pain and sighing will forever flee away.

While this fleeting moment of trial is permitted us, let us not lose the slightest portion of the worth of the cross. Let us suffer in humility and in peace. Our self-love exaggerates our distresses and magnifies them in our imagination.

When we bear a cross in simplicity, without the interference of self-love to make it seem greater, it is as if we bear only half a cross.

Suffering in this simplicity of love, we are not only happy in spite of the cross, but because of it. For love is pleased in suffering for the Well-Beloved, and the cross that forms us into His image is a consoling bond of love.

Letter 20
Absence of feeling and the revelation of self are not sufficient causes of distress

I pray God that this new year may be full of grace and blessing to you. I am not surprised that you do not enjoy recollection [of your recent circumstances as you did] of your being delivered from a long and painful agitation. Everything is liable to be exhausted. A lively disposition, accustomed to active exertion, soon languishes in solitude and inaction. For a great number of years you have been necessarily much distracted by external activity, and it was this circumstance that made me fear the effect of the life of abandonment upon you.

You were at first in the fervor of your beginnings, when no difficulties appear formidable. You said with Peter, it is good for us to be here—but it is often with us as it was with Him that we know not what we say.[27] In our moments of enjoyment, we feel as if we could do everything. But in the time of temptation and discouragement, we think we can do nothing and believe that all is lost. But we are deceived alike in both.

You should not be disturbed at any distraction that you may experience. The cause of it lays concealed within [you] even when you felt such zeal for inward reflection on spiritual matters.[28] Your temperament and habits all contribute to making you active and eager. It was only weariness and exhaustion that caused you to relish an opposite life. But, by fidelity to grace, you will gradually become permanently introduced into the experience of that which you have had a momentary taste.

God bestowed it so you might see to what place He would lead you. He then takes it away so we may be made to understand that it does not belong to us, that we are neither able to procure nor preserve it, and that it is a gift of grace which must be requested in all humility.

Do not be amazed at finding yourself sensitive, impatient, haughty, and self-willed. You must be made to realize that this is your natural disposition. We must bear the yoke of the daily confusion of our sins, says St. Augustine.[29] We must be made to feel our weakness, our wretchedness, our inability to correct ourselves. We must despair of our own heart and have no hope but in Christ. We must see ourselves as we truly are, without flattering ourselves that we are better,[30] and without neglecting a single effort for our correction.

We must be instructed as to our true character, while waiting for God's time to take it away. Let us become lowly under His all-powerful hand—yielding and manageable as often as we perceive any resistance in our will.

Be silent as much as you can. Be in no haste to judge. Suspend your decisions, your likes, and your dislikes. Stop at once when you become aware that your activity is hurried, and do not be too eager even for good things.

Letter 21
The imperfection of others is to be borne in love

It is a long while since I renewed [with you] the assurance of my attachment to you in our Lord. It is, nevertheless, greater than ever. I desire with all my heart that you may always find in your household the peace and consolation that you enjoyed in the beginning.

To be content with even the best of people, we must be contented with little and bear a great deal. Those who are most perfect have many imperfections. We, on the other hand, have great faults, so that between the two mutual toleration becomes very difficult. We must bear one another's burdens, however, and fulfill the law of Christ.[31] In this way, we set one against the other in love.

Peace and unanimity will be much aided by frequent silence, habitual inward reflection,[32] prayer, self-abandonment, renunciation of all vain criticisms, and a faithful departure from the vain reflections of a jealous and difficult self-love. This simplicity would put an end to a great deal of trouble! Happy is the person who neither listens to self nor to the tales of others!

Be content with leading a simple life, according to your condition. Be obedient, and bear your daily cross. You need it, and it is bestowed by the pure mercy of God. The grand point is to despise self from the heart, and to be willing to be despised, if God permits it.

Feed upon Him alone. St. Augustine says that his mother lived upon prayer. You do the same, and die to everything else. We can only live to God by the continual death of self.

Letter 22
Fear of death is not taken away
by our own courage, but by the grace of God[33]

I am not in the least surprised to learn that your awareness of death becomes more active—to the same degree that age and infirmity bring it nearer, I experience the same thing. There is an age at which death is forced upon our consideration more frequently by more irresistible reflections and by a time of retirement in which we have fewer distractions. God makes use of this rough trial to undeceive us in respect to our courage, to make us feel our weakness, and to keep us in all humility in His own hands.

Nothing is more humiliating than a troubled imagination in which we search in vain for our former confidence in God. This is the crucible of humiliation, in which the heart is purified by a sense of its weakness and unworthiness. In His sight "shall no man living be justified."[34] "Yea, the heavens are not clean in His sight."[35] And "in many things we offend all."[36] [In this state of humiliation,] we perceive our faults and not our virtues. Indeed, our virtues would now be dangerous to perceive,—even if they are real.

We must go straight on through this [spiritual] deprivation without interruption, just as we were endeavoring to walk in the way of God before being disturbed. If we should perceive any fault that needs correction, we must be faithful to the light given us; but do it carefully, lest we be led into false[37] scruples. We must then remain at peace,—not listening to the voice of self-love, mourning over our approaching death; but detaching ourselves from life, offering it in sacrifice to God, and confidently abandoning ourselves to Him.

When dying, St. Ambrose[38] was asked whether he was not afraid of the judgments of God. "We have a good master," he said, and so must we say to ourselves. We need to die in the most impenetrable uncertainty—not only as to God's judgment upon us, but as to our own characters. We must, as St. Augustine has it, be so reduced as to have nothing to present before God but our wretchedness and His mercy.[39]

Our wretchedness is the proper object of His mercy, and His mercy is all our merit. In your hours of sadness, read whatever will strengthen your confidence and establish your heart. "Truly God is good to Israel, even to such as are of a clean heart."[40] Pray for this cleanness of heart,[41] which is so pleasing in His sight, and which renders Him so compassionate to our failings.

Letter 23
Sensitiveness under reproof is the surest sign we needed it

I greatly desire that you may have peace within you. You know that it cannot be found except in lowliness of mind. But lowliness is not real unless it is produced by God on every proper occasion. These occasions are chiefly when we are blamed by someone who disapproves of us, and when we experience inward weakness. We must accustom ourselves to bearing both these trials.

We are truly lowly when we are no longer taken by surprise at finding ourselves corrected from without and incorrigible within. We are then like little children, below everything, and are willing to be so. We feel that our reprovers are right, but that we are unable to overcome ourselves in order to correct our faults.

[In this state] we despair of ourselves, and expect nothing [good] except from God. The reproofs of others, harsh and unfeeling as they may be, seem to us less than we deserve. If we cannot bear them, we condemn our sensitiveness more than all our other imperfections. Correction cannot then make us more humble than it finds us.

Our interior rebellion, far from hindering the profit of the correction, convinces us of its absolute necessity. Indeed, the reproof would not have been felt if it had not cut into some living part [within us]. If only death [of self] had been there, we would not have [rebelled at] the correction. Therefore, the more acutely we feel [the correction], the more certainly we know that it was necessary.

I beg your forgiveness if I have said anything too harsh. But do not doubt my affection for you, and count as nothing everything that comes from me. See only the hand of God, which makes use of my awkwardness to deal you a painful blow. The pain proves that I have touched a sore spot.

Yield to God, submit passively[42] to all His dealings; and you will soon be at rest and in harmony within. You know well enough how to give this advice to others. This occasion is important [to you], even critical.

O what grace will descend upon you, if you will bear, like a little child, all the means God employs to humiliate and dispossess you of your senses and will! I pray that He may so diminish you that you can no longer be found at all.

Letter 24
Imperfection is intolerant of imperfection

It has seemed to me that you have need of more enlargement[43] of heart in relation to the defects of others. I know that you cannot help seeing them when they come before you, nor prevent the opinions you involuntarily form concerning the motives of some of those about you.

You cannot even get rid of a certain degree of trouble that these things cause you. It will be enough if you are willing to bear with those defects that are unmistakable, refrain from condemning those that are doubtful, and not allow[44] yourself to be so afflicted by them as to cause a coolness of feeling between you.

Perfection is easily tolerant of the imperfections of others—it becomes all things to all people. We must not be surprised at the greatest defects in good souls and must quietly let them alone until God gives the signal of gradual removal. Otherwise, we shall pull up the wheat with the tares.[45]

God leaves, in the most advanced souls, certain weaknesses entirely disproportioned to their eminent state. When excavating the soil from a field, workers leave pillars of earth to indicate the original level of the surface and to measure the amount of material removed. In the same way, God leaves pillars of testimony to the extent of His work in the most pious souls.

Such persons must labor to their individual degree for their correction, and you must labor to bear with their weaknesses. You know from experience the bitterness of the work of correction. Strive then to find means to make it less bitter to others. You have not an eager zeal to correct, but a sensitiveness that easily shuts up your heart.

I pray you more than ever not to spare my faults. If you should think you see one, which is not really there, there is no harm done. If I find that your counsel wounds me, my sensitiveness demonstrates that you have discovered a sore spot. But if not, you will have done me an excellent kindness in exercising my humility and accustoming me to reproof.

I should be more lowly than others in proportion as I am higher in position, and God demands of me a more absolute death to everything. I need this simplicity, and I trust it will be the means of cementing rather than of weakening our attachment.

Letter 25
We should listen to God and not to self-love

I beseech you not to listen to self. Self-love whispers in one ear and the love of God in the other. The first is restless, bold, eager, and impetuous. The other is simple, peaceful, and speaks but a few words in a mild and gentle voice.

The moment we attend to the voice of self crying in our ear, we can no longer hear the modest tones of holy love. Each speaks only of its single object.

Self-love entertains us with self, which, according to it, is never sufficiently well attended to. It talks of friendship, regard, esteem; and is in despair at everything but flattery.

The love of God, on the other hand, desires that self should be forgotten; that it should be trodden under foot and broken as an idol; and that God should become the self of espoused souls and occupy them as others are occupied by self.

Let the vain, complaining babbler, self-love, be silenced so that in the stillness of the heart we may listen to that other love ,which only speaks when addressed.

Letter 26
Absolute trust is the shortest road to God

I have no doubt but that God constantly treats you as one of his friends—that is, with crosses, sufferings, and humiliations. The ways and means of God to draw souls to Himself accomplish His design much more rapidly and effectively than all the efforts of the creature. For His ways and means destroy self-love at its very root—where, with all our pains, we could scarce discover it. God knows all its windings and attacks it in its strongest holds.

If we had strength and faith enough to trust ourselves entirely to God and to follow Him simply wherever He should lead us, we would have no need of any great effort of mind to reach perfection. But since we are so weak in faith that we need to know the entire way rather than simply trust in God, our road is lengthened and our spiritual affairs get behind.

Abandon yourself as absolutely as possible to God, and continue to do so to your latest breath; and He will never desert you.

Letter 27
The time of temptation and distress is no time to form resolves

Your excessive distress is like a summer torrent, which must be allowed to run its course. Nothing makes any impression upon you, and you think you have the most substantial evidence for the most imaginary states—this is the ordinary result of great suffering.

God permits you, notwithstanding your excellent faculties, to be blind to what lies immediately before you, and to think you see clearly what does not exist at all. God will be glorified in your heart if you will be faithful in yielding to His designs. But nothing would be more unwise than the forming of resolutions in a state of distress, which is manifestly accompanied by an inability to do anything according to God.

When you have become calm, then do in a spirit of recollection what you perceive to be nearest the will of God concerning you. Return gradually to devotion, simplicity, and the oblivion of self. Commune and listen to God, and be deaf to self.

Then do all that is in your heart; for I have no fear that a spirit of that sort will permit you to take any wrong step. But to suppose that we are sane—when we are in the very agony of distress, and under the influence of a violent temptation of self-love—is to ensure our being led astray.

Ask any experienced advisers, and they will tell you that you are to make no resolutions until you have re-entered into peace and recollection. You will learn from them that the readiest way to self-deception is to trust to ourselves in a state of suffering in which nature is so unreasonable and irritated.

You will say that I desire to prevent you doing as you should, if I forbid your doing it at the only moment when you are capable of it. God forbid! I neither desire to permit nor hinder. My only wish is to advise you that you will not be found lacking toward God.

Now it is as clear as day that you would fall in that respect if you took counsel at the hands of a self-love wounded to the quick and an irritation verging upon despair. Would you change anything in order to gratify your self-love, when God does not desire it? God forbid!

Wait, then, until you shall be in a condition to be advised. To enjoy the true advantages of illumination, we must be equally ready for every alternative and must have nothing that we are not cheerfully disposed at once to sacrifice for His sake.

Letter 28
Who has love, has all

I have thought frequently, since yesterday, on the matters you communicated to me; and I have increasing confidence that God will sustain you. Though you take no great pleasure in spiritual exercises, you must not neglect to be faithful in them, as far as your health will permit. A convalescent has but little appetite, but must still eat to sustain life. It would be very helpful to you, if you could occasionally have a few minutes of Christian conversation with those of your family in whom you can confide and with your topic of conversation being guided in perfect liberty by your impressions at the moment. God does not call you by any lively emotions—and I heartily rejoice at it—if you will but remain faithful.

For a faithfulness unaided by delights is far purer and safer from danger than one accompanied by those tender feelings that may be seated too exclusively in the imagination.

A little [spiritual] reading and recollection every day will give you unemotional light and strength for all the sacrifices God will require of you. Love Him, and I will acquit you of everything else—for everything else will come by love.

I do not ask from you a love tender and emotional, but only that your will should lean towards love; and that, notwithstanding all the corrupt desires of your heart, you should prefer God before self and the whole world.

Letter 29
Weakness is preferable to strength; practice is better than knowledge

I am told, my dear child in our Lord, that you are suffering from sickness. I suffer with you; for I love you dearly. But I cannot but kiss the hand that smites you, and I pray you to kiss it lovingly with me. You have heretofore abused your health and the pleasures derived from it. This weakness and its attendant pains are the natural consequences of such a course.

I pray God only that He may depress your spirit even more than your body; and while He comforts the latter according to your need, that He may entirely vanquish the former.

O how strong we are when we begin to perceive that we are but weakness and infirmity! Then we are ever ready to believe that we are mistaken and to correct ourselves while confessing it. Then our minds are ever open to the illumination of others. Then we are authoritative in nothing, and say the most decided things with simplicity and deference for others. Then we do not object to being judged, and submit without hesitation to the censure of the first comer.

At the same time, we judge no one without absolute necessity. We speak only to those who desire it—mentioning the imperfections we seem to have discovered—without dogmatism and rather to gratify their wishes than from a desire to be believed or create a reputation for wisdom.

I pray God that He may keep you faithful to His grace and that He who "hath begun a good work in you will perform it until the day of Jesus Christ."[46]

We must bear with ourselves with patience and without flattery, and remain in unceasing subjection to every means of overcoming our thoughts and inward repugnancies. We will thus become more pliable to the impressions of grace in the practice of the gospel. But let this work be done quietly and peacefully, and let it not be entered upon too eagerly, as though it could all be accomplished in a single day.

Let us reason little, but do much. If we are not careful, the acquisition of knowledge will so occupy this life that we will need another to reduce our acquirements into practice.

We are in danger of believing ourselves advanced towards perfection in proportion to our knowledge of the way. But all our beautiful theories, far from assisting in the death of self,[47] only serve to nourish the life of Adam in us by a secret delight and confidence in our illumination.

Be quit then of all trust in your own power and in your own knowledge of the way; and you will make a great stride towards perfection. Humility and self-distrust with a frank ingenuousness are fundamental virtues for you.

Letter 30
Beware of the pride of reasoning;
the true guide to knowledge is love

Your mind is too much occupied with exterior things—and still worse, with accumulating knowledge,[48] to be able to act with a frequent thought of God. I am always afraid of your excessive inclination to reason. It is a hindrance to that recollection and silence in which He reveals Himself. Be humble, simple, and sincerely separated from people.[49] Be recollected, calm, and devoid of reasonings before God.

The persons who have heretofore had most influence with you have been infinitely dry, reasoning, critical, and opposed to a true interior life. However little you might listen to them, you would hear only endless reasonings and a dangerous curiosity that would insensibly draw you out of grace and plunge you into the depths of nature. Habits of long standing are easily revived, and the changes that cause us to revert to our original position are less easily perceived—because they are natural to our constitution. So distrust them, and beware of beginnings that in fact include the end.

It is now four months since I have had any leisure for study. But I am very happy to forego study and not to cling to anything when providence would take it away. It may be that during the coming winter I will have leisure for my library, but I will enter it then, keeping one foot on the threshold, ready to leave it at the slightest intimation. The mind must keep fasts as well as the body.

I have no desire to write, or to speak, or to be spoken about, or to reason, or to persuade any. I live every day aridly[50] enough and with certain exterior inconveniences that beset me. But I amuse myself whenever I have an opportunity, if I need recreation.

Those who keep records of me,[51] and are afraid of me are sadly deceived. God bless them! I am far from being so foolish as to inconvenience myself for the sake of annoying them. I would say to them as Abraham said to Lot, "Is not the whole land before thee?"[52] If you go to the east, I will go to the west.

Happy is the one who is indeed free! The Son of God alone can make us free.[53] But He can only do it by snapping every bond. How is this to be done? By that sword that divides husband and wife, father and son, brother and sister.[54] The world is then no longer of any account. But as long as it is anything to us, our freedom is but a word; and we are as easily captured as a bird whose leg is fastened by a thread. It seems to be free because the string is not visible, but it can only fly that length and thus is a prisoner. You see the moral. What I would have you possess is more valuable than all you are fearful of losing.

Be faithful in what you know so that you may be entrusted with more. Distrust your intellect, which has so often misled you. My own has been such a deceiver that I no longer count upon it. Be simple and firm in your simplicity. "The fashion of this world passeth away."[55] We will vanish with it if we make ourselves like it by reason of vanity. But the truth of God remains forever,[56] and we will dwell with it, if it alone occupies our attention.

Again I warn you, beware of philosophers and great reasoners. They will always be a snare to you and will do you more harm than you will know how to do them good. They linger and pine away in discussing exterior trifles—and never reach the knowledge of the truth. Their curiosity is an insatiable spiritual greed. They are like those conquerors who ravage the world without possessing it. Solomon, after a deep experience of it, testifies to the vanity of their researches.[57]

We should never study but on an express intimation of Providence. And we should do it as we go to market—to buy the provision necessary for each day's needs. Then, too, we must study in the spirit of prayer.

God is at the same time the truth and the love. We can only know the truth in proportion as we love—when we love it, we understand it well. If we do not love Love, we do not know Love. Those who love much—and remain humble and lowly in their ignorance—are the well-beloved ones of the Truth. They know of what philosophers not only are ignorant, but do not desire to know.

Would that you might obtain that knowledge that is reserved for babes and the simple-minded, while it is hid from the wise and prudent.[58]

Letter 31
The gifts of God are not to be rejected on account of the channel that brings them

I am glad you find in the person of whom you speak, the qualities you were seeking. God puts what He pleases where He pleases. Naaman could not be healed by all the waters of Syria, but must apply to those of Palestine.[59]

What does it matter from what quarter our light and help come? The source is the important point, not the conduit. The best channel is the one that most exercises our faith, puts to shame our human wisdom, makes us simple and humble, and undeceives us in respect to our own power.

Receive, then, whatever God bestows in dependence upon the Spirit that "bloweth where it listeth." We know not "whence it cometh and whither it goeth."[60] But we need not seek to know the secrets of God—let us only be obedient to what He reveals.

Too much reasoning is a great distraction. Those who reason—the undevout wise—quench the inward spirit as the wind extinguishes a candle. After being with them for a while, we perceive our hearts dry and our mind off its center. Shun conversations with such people—they are full of danger to you.

There are some who appear spiritually alive, but whose appearance deceives us. It is easy to mistake a certain warmth of the imagination for true spiritual life. Such persons are eager in the pursuit of some outward good to which they are attached. But they are distracted by this anxious desire, are perpetually occupied in discussions and reasonings, and know nothing of that inward peace and silence, which listens to God. They are more dangerous than others because their distraction is more disguised.

Search their depths; and you will find them restless, fault-finding, eager, constantly occupied without, harsh and crude in all their desires, sensitive [to themselves], full of their own thoughts, and impatient of the slightest contradiction. In a word, spiritual busy-bodies, annoyed at everything, and almost always annoying.

Letter 32
Poverty and despoilment are the ways of Christ

Everything contributes to prove you. But God who loves you, will not suffer your temptations to exceed your strength.[61] He will make use of the trial for your advancement. But we must not look inward with curiosity to behold our progress, our strength, or the hand of God, which is not less efficient because it is invisible. Its principal operations are conducted in secrecy—for we would never die to self if He always visibly stretched out His hand to save us. God would then sanctify us in light, life, and the possession of every spiritual grace. But it would not be upon the cross—in darkness, privation, nakedness, and death.

The directions of Christ are not: "If any will come after Me, let them enjoy themselves; let them be gorgeously clothed; let them be intoxicated with delight—as Peter was on the mount[62]—let them be glad in their perfection in Me and in themselves; let them behold themselves; and be assured that they are perfect."

On the contrary, His words are: "If any will come after me, I will show them the road they must take. Let them deny themselves, take up their cross and follow Me in a path beside precipices, where they will see nothing but death on every hand."[63] St. Paul declares that we desire to be clothed upon, but that, on the contrary, it is necessary to be stripped [of ourselves] to very nakedness, so we may then put on [life, which is] Christ.[64]

Allow Him, then, to despoil self-love of every adornment, even to the inmost covering under which it lurks, so you may receive the robe whitened by the blood of the Lamb,[65] and

41

having no other purity than His.[66] O how happy is the soul that no longer possesses anything of its own, not even anything borrowed; that abandons itself to the Well-Beloved and is jealous of every beauty but His!

O spouse, how beautiful art thou, when thou hast no longer anything of thine own! Thou shall be altogether the delight of the bridegroom, when He shall be all thy comeliness! Then He will love thee without measure, because it will be Himself that He loves in thee.

Hear these things and believe them. This pure truth will be bitter in your mouth and belly, but it will feed your heart upon that death which is the only true life. Give faith to this, and do not listen to self. It is the grand seducer, more powerful than the serpent that deceived our mother.[67] Happy is the soul that hearkens in all simplicity to the voice that forbids it to hear its sympathetic self!

Letter 33
The will of God is our only treasure

I desire that you may have that absolute simplicity of abandonment that never measures itself or excludes anything in the present life, no matter how dear to our self-love. Illusions do not come from such an abandonment as this, but from one that has secret reservations.

Be as lowly and simple in the midst of the most exacting society as in your own closet. Do nothing from the reasonings of wisdom or from natural pleasure, but do all from submission to the Spirit of life and death—death to self and life in God.

Let there be no enthusiasm, no search after certainty within, no looking forward for better things. Let it not be as if the present, bitter as it is, were not sufficient to those whose sole treasure is the will of God. Do not act as if you would compensate self-love for the sadness of the present with the prospects of the future!

We deserve to meet with disappointment when we seek such vain consolation. Let us receive everything in lowliness of spirit, seeking nothing from curiosity and withholding nothing from a disguised selfishness.

Let God work, and think only of dying to the present moment without reservation, as though it were the whole of eternity.

Letter 34
Abandonment is not a heroic sacrifice, but a simple sinking into the will of God

Your sole task, my dear daughter, is to bear your infirmities both of body and mind. "When I am weak," says the Apostle, "then am I strong"[68] and "strength is made perfect in weakness."[69] We are only strong in God in proportion to our weakness in ourselves. Your feebleness will be your strength if you accept it in all lowliness.

We are tempted to believe that weakness and lowliness are incompatible with abandonment because abandonment is represented [by some] as a generous act of the soul by which it testifies its great love and makes the most heroic sacrifices. But a true abandonment does not at all correspond to this flattering description. It is a simple resting in the love of God, as an infant lies in its mother's arms.

A perfect abandonment must even go so far as to abandon its abandonment. We renounce ourselves without knowing it. If we knew it, it would no longer be complete; for there can be no greater support than a consciousness that we are wholly given up.

Abandonment does not consist in doing great things for self to take delight; but in simply suffering our weakness and infirmity, in letting everything alone. It is peaceful; for it would no longer be sincere if we were still restless about anything we had renounced.

43

It is thus that abandonment is the source of true peace. If we have not peace, it is because our abandonment is exceedingly imperfect.

Letter 35
Daily dying takes the place of final death

We must bear our crosses. Self is the greatest of them. We are not entirely rid of self until we can tolerate ourselves as simply and patiently as we do our neighbor.

If we die in part every day of our lives, we will have but little to do on the last [day].

What we so much dread in the future will cause us no fear when it comes—if we do not suffer its terrors to be exaggerated by the restless anxieties of self-love.

Bear with yourself, and consent in all lowliness to be supported by your neighbor.

O how utterly will these little daily deaths destroy the power of the final dying!

Letter 36
Suffering belongs to the living, not the dead

Many are deceived when they suppose that the death of self is the cause of all the agony they feel. The truth is their suffering is only caused by the remains of life.

Pain is seated in the living, not the dead parts. The more suddenly and completely we die, the less pain we experience.

Death is only painful to the one who resists it. The imagination exaggerates its terrors. The soul argues endlessly to show the propriety of the life of self.

Self-love fights against death, like a sick person in the last struggle.

But we must die inwardly as well as outwardly. The sentence of death has gone forth against self as well as against the body.

Our great care should be that self die first, and then our bodily death will be but a falling asleep.

Happy are they who sleep this sleep of peace!

Letter 37
The limits of our grace are those of our temptation

I sympathize sincerely with the sufferings of your dear sick one and with the pain of those whom God has placed about her to help her bear the cross. Let her not distrust God, and He will proportion her suffering in accordance to the patience that He will bestow. No one can do this but He who made all hearts and whose office it is to renew them by His grace.

Those in whom He operates know nothing of the proper proportions. Not seeing the magnitude of future trials, nor the grace prepared by God to meet the trials, they are tempted to be discouraged and depressed.

Like those who have never seen the ocean, they stand at the coming in of the tide between the water and an impassable wall of rock, and think they perceive the terrible certainty that the approaching waves will surely engulf them. They do not see that they stand within the point at which God with unerring finger has drawn the boundary beyond which the waves cannot pass.

God proves the righteous as with the ocean. He stirs it up and makes its great billows seem to threaten our destruction. But He is always at hand to say, "thus far shall thou go and no further." "God is faithful, who will not suffer you to be tempted above that ye are able."[70]

Letter 38
Resisting God is an effective bar to grace

By the light of God, you perceive in the depth of your conscience what grace demands of you, but you resist Him. Hence your distress.

You begin to say within [yourself], "It is impossible for me to undertake to do what is required of me. This is a temptation to despair. Despair as much as you please of self, but never of God. He is all good and all powerful, and will grant you according to your faith.

If you will believe all things, all things shall be yours, and you shall remove mountains. If you believe nothing, you shall have nothing, but you alone will be to blame.

Look at Mary. When the most incredible thing in the world was proposed to her, she did not hesitate but exclaimed, "be it unto me according to Thy word."[71]

Open your heart. It is now so shut up that you not only have not the power to do what is required of you, but you do not even desire to have it. You have no wish that your heart should be enlarged, and you fear that it will be.

How can grace find room in so narrowed a heart? All that I ask of you is that you will rest in a teachable spirit of faith and that you will not listen to self.

Simply comply passively in everything with lowliness of mind, and receive peace through [inner reflection on Christ]; and everything will be gradually accomplished for you. Those things that seemed the greatest difficulties in your hour of temptation will be insensibly smoothed away.

Letter 39
God speaks more effectively in the soul than to it

Nothing gives me more satisfaction than to see you simple and peaceful. Simplicity brings back the state of Paradise. We have no great pleasures and suffer some pain. But we have no desire for the former and receive the latter with thanksgiving.

This interior harmony and this exemption from the fears and tormenting desires of self-love create a satisfaction in the will that is above all the joys of intoxicating delights. Dwell, then, in your terrestrial paradise; and take good care not to leave it from a vain desire of knowing good and evil.[72]

We are never less alone than when we are in the society of a single faithful friend and never less deserted than when we are carried in the arms of the All-Powerful.

Nothing is more affecting than the instant help of God. What He sends by means of His creatures contracts no virtue from that foul and barren channel—it owes everything to the source. And so, when the fountain breaks forth within the heart itself, we have no need of the creature.

God, who at sundry times and in divers manners spake in time past unto the fathers by the prophets, hath in these last days spoken unto us by His Son.[73]

Shall we then feel any regret that the feeble voices of the prophets have ceased?

O how pure and powerful is the immediate voice of God in the soul! It is certain [and clear] whenever Providence cuts off all the [other] channels.

Letter 40
The circumcision of the heart

Our eagerness to serve others frequently arises from mere natural generosity and a refined self-love. It may soon turn into dislike and despair. But true charity is simple and ever the same toward the neighbor, because it is humble, and never thinks of self. Whatever is not included in this pure charity, must be cut off.

It is by the circumcision of the heart that we are made children and inheritors of the faith of Abraham,[74] in order that we may, like him, quit our native country without knowing whither we go.[75] Blessed lot!—to leave all and deliver ourselves up to the jealousy of God, the knife of circumcision!

Our own hand can effect nothing but superficial reforms. We do not know ourselves and cannot tell where to strike. We would never light upon the spot that the hand of God so readily finds. Self-love arrests our hand and spares itself. It has not the courage to wound itself to the quick. And besides, the choice of the spot and the preparation for the blow deaden its force.

But the hand of God strikes in unexpected places; it finds the very joint of the harness and leaves nothing unscathed. Self-love then becomes the patient. Let it cry out, but see to it that it does not stir under the hand of God lest it interfere with the success of the operation. It must remain motionless beneath the knife. All that is required is faithfulness in not refusing a single stroke.

I am greatly attached to John the Baptist, who wholly forgot himself that he might think only of Christ. He pointed to Him,[76] he was but the voice of one crying in the wilderness to prepare the way,[77] he sent Him all his disciples,[78] and it was this conduct, far more than his solitary and austere life, that entitled him to be called the greatest among them that are born of women.[79]

Endnotes

1 See the Pure Gold Classic book, *Mme. Jeanne Guyon*, published by Bridge-Logos Publishers. In it is a lengthy letter that Fénelon wrote to Mme. Guyon in response to a letter she had written to him concerning her doctrines on the deeper inner spiritual life.

2 Colossians 3:3

3 2 Corinthians 9:7

4 Known as "Theresa of Ávila." (1515-1582). Spanish nun and mystical writer who founded the reformed order of Carmelites (1562). Her works include *The Way of Perfection*, published posthumously.

5 James 1:17

6 Hebrews 12:10

7 Hebrews 4:12

8 Acts 10:42

9 Matthew 8:26

10 Exodus 34:14, Deuteronomy 4:24

11 2 Corinthians 11:14

12 Original text: "God requires it."

13 Matthew 5:3

14 1 Corinthians 2:2

15 1 Corinthians 8:1

16 A position of difficulty, perplexity, distress, or need.

17 Job 3:25

18 1 Kings 19:11

19 1 Corinthians 10:13

20 Luke 7:47

21 Saint Francois de Sales, (1567-1622), French churchman, and bishop of Geneva, his book *Introduction to the Devout Life* has been translated into almost every language.

22 Matthew 3:9

23 Matthew 6:34

24 Psalm 34:10

25 Hebrews 12:10

26 Matthew 6:10

27 Mark 9:5-6

28 Original text:" . . . you felt such zeal for recollection."

29 Saint Augustine, (354-430). Early church (Roman Catholic) father and philosopher who served (396-430) as the bishop of Hippo (in present-day Algeria). He wrote the autobiographical *Confessions* (397) and the voluminous *City of God* (413-426).

30 Original text: "We must bear with ourselves, without flattering, and . . ."

31 Galatians 6:2

32 Original text: "habitual recollection"

33 Hebrews 2:14-15

34 Psalm 143:2

35 Job 15:15

36 James 3:2

37 Scruples, as used by Fénelon, undoubtedly refers to any uneasy feelings arising from conscience or principle about the decency, propriety, or appropriateness of a course of action

38 Saint Ambrose, (Ca, 340?-397). Writer, composer, and bishop of Milan (374-397) who imposed orthodoxy on the early Christian Church.

39 In the certainty of His mercy upon us because of the sacrifice of our Lord Jesus Christ on our behalf.

40 Psalm 73:1, Romans 5:1-2, 8-11; 10:9-11

41 1 Corinthians 6:11, Hebrews 10:22, Revelation 1:5

42 Original word: acquiesce

43 Original word: enlargedness

44 Original word: suffer

45 Matthew 13:28-29

46 Philippians 1:6

47 Romans 6:6, Ephesians 4:22, Colossians 3:9

48 Original word: augmentation

49 Original text: "abstracted with men." Abstracted implies being so deep in thought as to be mentally elsewhere, so it is uncertain exactly what Fénelon meant. If writing to a woman, he might have meant being emotionally uninvolved with men.

50 Probably meaning dull and without interest

51 Original text: "make almanacs upon me"

52 Genesis 13:9

53 John 8:36

54 Luke 12:51-53

55 1 Corinthians 7:31

56 Mark 13:31

57 Ecclesiastes 12:8-14

58 Matthew 11:25

59 2 Kings 5:10-12

60 John 3:8

61 1 Corinthians 10:13

62 Matthew 17:4
63 Matthew 16:24
64 2 Corinthians 5:2-4
65 Revelation 7:14
66 Revelation 22:1
67 Genesis 3:1-7
68 2 Corinthians 12:10
69 2 Corinthians 12:9
70 1 Corinthians 10:13
71 Luke 1:38
72 Genesis 3:5
73 Hebrews 1:1-2
74 Romans 4:6
75 Hebrews 11:8
76 John 1:29
77 John 1:23
78 John 1:35-37
79 Matthew 11:11

Maxims of the Saints[1]

Article One

There are various kinds of love of God. At least, there are various feelings that go under that name. First, there is what may be called mercenary or selfish love. This is the love of God that originates in a sole regard for our own happiness. Those who love God with no other love than this love Him just as the miser loves money and the voluptuous person loves pleasures. They attach no value to God, except as a means to an end and that end is the gratification of themselves.

Such love, if it can be called by that name, is unworthy of God. He does not ask for it. He will not receive it. In the language of Francis de Sales, "it is sacrilegious and impious."

Second, there is the kind of love that does not exclude a regard to our own happiness as a motive of love, but that requires this motive to be subordinate to a much higher one— namely, that of a regard to God's glory. It is a mixed state in which we regard ourselves and God at the same time. This love is not necessarily selfish and wrong.

On the contrary, when the two objects of it—God and ourselves—are relatively in the right position, it is unselfish and right. By the right position, we mean when we love God as He should be loved and love ourselves no more than we should be loved. Which is to further say; when love for ourselves is clearly and definitely subordinated to love for God.

Article Two

All of the subjects of this mixed love are not equally advanced.

Mixed love becomes pure love when the love of self is relatively, though not absolutely, lost in a regard to the will of God. This is always the case when the two objects are loved in their proper proportions. So this pure love is mixed love that is combined properly.

Pure love is not inconsistent with mixed love, but is mixed love carried to its true result. When this result is attained, the motive of God's glory so expands itself and so fills the mind that the other motive—that of our own happiness—becomes so small and so recedes from our inward notice as to be practically annihilated. It is then that God becomes what He always should be: the center of our soul toward which all its affections move and the great moral sun of the soul from which all its light and all its warmth proceed. It is then that we think no more of ourselves. We have become the people of a "single eye." Everything of ourselves and our own happiness is entirely lost sight of in our simple and fixed look to God's will and God's glory.

We lay ourselves at His feet. Self is known no more. Not because it is wrong to regard and to desire our own good, but because the good of self is withdrawn from our notice. When the sun shines, the stars disappear. When God is in our soul, how can we think of ourselves? So we love God and God alone. And we love all other things only as they are in and for God.

Article Three

In the early stages of Christian experience, our motives that have a regard to our personal happiness are more prominent and effective than at later stages. There is nothing wrong with this. [When speaking to others about the condition of their soul,] it is proper even when addressing religious people to appeal to their fear of death, to the impending judgments of God, to the terrors of hell, and to the joys of heaven.

Such appeals are recognized in the Holy Scriptures, and are in accordance with the views and feelings of good people in all ages of the world. The motives involved in them are powerful aids to beginners in religion. They are very helpful in suppressing the passions and strengthening the practical virtues.

We should not think lightly, therefore, of the grace of God that is manifested in that inferior form of religion which stops short of the more glorious and perfected form of pure love. We are to follow God's grace, and not to go before it.

We are to advance step by step to the higher state of pure love, while watching carefully God's inward and outward providence. As we do, we receive increased grace by improving the grace we have, until the dawning light becomes the perfect day.

Article Four

Those who are in the state of pure or perfect love have all the moral and Christian virtues in themselves. If temperance, forbearance, chastity, truth, kindness, forgiveness, and justice may be regarded as virtues, there can be no doubt that they are all included in holy love. That is to say, the principle of love will not fail to develop itself in each of these forms. St. Augustine says that love is the foundation, source, or principle of all the virtues. This view is sustained also by St. Francis de Sales and by St. Thomas Aquinas.[2]

The state of pure love does not exclude the mental state that is called Christian hope. When we analyze it into its elements, hope in the Christian may be described as the desire of being united with God in heaven, accompanied with the expectation or belief of being so [because of the work of Christ].[3]

Article Five

Souls who are perfected in love are truly the subjects of sanctification; yet they do not cease to grow in grace. It may not be easy to specify and describe the degrees of sanctification, but there seem to be at least two conditions or states of experience after persons have reached this stage.

The first may be described as the state of holy resignation. In this state, a soul thinks more frequently of its own happiness than it will at a subsequent state.

The second state is that of holy indifference. In this state, a soul absolutely ceases either to desire or to will except in cooperation with the Divine leading. Its desires for itself, as it has greater light, are more completely and permanently merged in the one higher and more absorbing desire of God's glory and the fulfillment of His will.

In this state of experience, we cease to do what we will be likely to do, and may very properly do, in a lower state. We no longer desire our own salvation merely as an eternal deliverance, or merely as involving the greatest amount of personal happiness. Instead, we desire it chiefly as the fulfillment of God's pleasure and as resulting in His glory, and because He Himself desires and wills that we should so desire and will.

Holy indifference is not inactivity. It is as far as possible from it. It is indifference to anything and everything out of God's will, but it is the highest life and activity to anything and everything in His will.

Article Six

One of the clearest and best established maxims of holiness is that when the holy soul arrives at the second state mentioned, it ceases to have desires for anything out of the will of God.

Nevertheless, when the holy soul is really in the state called the state of non-desire, it may properly desire everything in relation to the correction of its imperfections and weaknesses, its perseverance in its religious state, and its ultimate salvation, which it has reason to know from the Scriptures or in any other way that God desires.

It may also desire all temporal good—houses and lands, food and clothing, friends and books, and exemption from physical suffering. In essence, it may desire anything to the degree and only to the degree that it has reason to believe such desire is coincident with God's desire [for it]. The holy soul not only desires specific things that are sanctioned by the known will of God, but also the fulfillment of His will in all respects, unknown as well as known. Being in faith, it commits itself to God in darkness as well as in light. Its nondesire is simply its not desiring anything that is outside of God—[that is, God's will and God himself].

Article Seven

In the history of inward experience, we often find accounts of individuals whose inward life may properly be characterized as extraordinary. They represent themselves as having extraordinary communications—such as dreams, visions, and revelations. Without stopping to inquire whether these inward results arise from an excited and disordered state of the physical system or from God, the important remark to be made here is that these things o whatever extent they may exist—do not constitute holiness.

The principle that is the life of common Christians in their common mixed state is the same principle that originates and sustains the life of those who are truly "the pure in heart." It is the principle of faith working by love.[4] The difference is that in the truly pure in heart it exists to a greatly increased degree.

This is obviously the doctrine of St. John of the Cross, who teaches us that we must walk in the night of faith. That is to say, we must walk in the night that surrounds us because of our complete ignorance of what is before us. And we walk with faith alone for our soul's guide—faith in God, in His Word, and in His providences.

Again, the persons who have (or are supposed to have) the visions and other remarkable states to which we have referred are sometimes disposed to make their own experience (imperfect as it obviously is) the guide of their life, considered as separate from and as above the written law. Great care should be taken against such an error like this. God's Word is our true rule.

Nevertheless, there is no interpreter of the divine Word like that of a holy heart; or (what is the same thing) of the Holy Ghost dwelling in the heart. If we give ourselves wholly to God, the Comforter will take up His abode with us and guide us into all the truth that will be necessary for us.

Truly holy souls, therefore—continually looking to God for a proper understanding of His Word—may confidently trust that He will guide them aright. A holy soul, in the exercise of its legitimate powers of interpretation, may deduce important views from the Word of God that would not otherwise be known—but it cannot add anything to it.

Again, God is the regulator of the affections, as well as of the outward actions. Sometimes the state that He inspires within us is that of holy love. Sometimes He inspires affections that have love and faith for their basis, but have a specific character and appear under other names, such as humility, forgiveness, or gratitude. But in all cases there is nothing holy except what is based upon the antecedent or prevenient[5] grace of God.

In all the universe, there is but one legitimate Originator. [Because of that,] humanity's business is that of concurrence. And this view is applicable to all the stages of Christian experience, from the lowest to the highest.

Article Eight

Writers often speak of abandonment. The term has a meaning somewhat specific. The soul in this state does not renounce everything—and thus become brutish in its indifference—but it renounces everything except God's will.

Souls in the state of abandonment not only forsake outward things, but, what is still more important, forsake themselves.

Abandonment, or self-renunciation, is not the renunciation of faith or of love or of anything else—except selfishness.

The state of abandonment, or entire self-renunciation, is generally accompanied—and perhaps we may say, carried out and perfected—by temptations that are more or less severe. We cannot really know whether we have renounced ourselves, except by being tried on those very points to which our self-renunciation, either real or supposed, relates.

One of the severest inward trials is that by which we are taken off from all inward sensible[6] supports and are made to live and walk by faith alone. Pious and holy people who have been the subjects of inward crucifixion often refer to the trials that have been experienced by them.

They sometimes speak of them as a sort of inward and terrible purgatory. "Only mad and wicked people," says Cardinal Bona, "will deny the existence of these remarkable experiences, attested as they are by people of the most venerable virtue, who speak only of what they have known in themselves."

Trials are not always of the same duration. The more cheerfully and faithfully we give ourselves to God, to be smitten in any and all of our idols, whenever and wherever He chooses; the shorter will be the work. God makes us to suffer no longer than He sees to be necessary for us.

We should not be premature in concluding that inward crucifixion is complete, and our abandonment to God is without any reservation whatever. The act of consecration, which is a sort of incipient step, may be sincere. But the reality of the consecration can be known only when God has applied the appropriate tests.

The trial will show whether we are wholly the Lord's. Those who prematurely draw the conclusion that they are expose themselves to great illusion and injury.

Article Nine

The state of abandonment, or of entire self-renunciation, does not take from the soul the moral power that is essential to its moral agency. Nor that antecedent or prevenient grace without which even abandonment itself would be a state of moral death. Nor the principle of faith, which prevenient grace originated and through which it now operates. Nor the desire and hope of final salvation, although it takes away all uneasiness and unbelief connected with such a desire. Nor the fountains of love that spring up deeply and freshly within it. And it takes away neither the hatred of sin nor the testimony of a good conscience.

But it takes away that uneasy hankering of the soul after pleasure either inward or outward, and the selfish vivacity and eagerness of nature, which is too impatient to wait calmly and submissively for God's time of action. By fixing the mind wholly upon God, it takes away the disposition of the soul to occupy itself with reflex acts—that is, with the undue examination and analysis of its own feelings.

It does not take away the pain and sorrow naturally incident to our physical state and natural sensibilities. But it takes away all uneasiness, all murmuring—leaving the soul in its inner nature and in every part of its nature where the power of faith reaches, calm and peaceable as the God that dwells there.

Article Ten

God has promised life and happiness to His people. What He has promised can never fail to take place. Nevertheless, it is the disposition of those who love God with a perfect heart to leave themselves entirely in His hands—irrespective, in some degree of the promise. By the aid of the promise (without which they must have remained in their original weakness) they rise, as it were, above the promise, and rest in God's essential and eternal will in which the promise originated.

This is so much the case, that some individuals—across whose path God had spread the darkness of His providences and who seemed to themselves for a time to be thrown out of His favor and to be hopelessly lost—have submitted without protest to the terrible fate that now seemed to await them.

Such was the state of mind of St. Francis de Sales,[7] as he prostrated himself in the church of St. Stephen des Grez. The language of such persons, uttered without complaint, is, "My God, my God, why hast Thou forsaken me?"[8] They claim God as their God and will not abandon their love of Him, although they believe at the time that they are forsaken of Him.

They choose to leave themselves, under all possible circumstances, entirely in the hands of God. Their language is—even if it should be His pleasure to separate them forever from the enjoyments of His presence—"Not my will, but Thine, be done."[9]

It is perhaps difficult to perceive how souls whose life, as it were, is the principle of faith can be in this situation. Take the case of the Savior. It is certainly difficult to conceive how the Savior, whose faith never failed, could yet believe Himself forsaken. And yet it was so.

We know that it is impossible for God to forsake those who put their trust in Him. He could just as soon forsake His own Word—and, what is more, He could just as soon forsake His own nature.

Nevertheless, holy souls may sometimes, in a way and under circumstances that we may not fully understand, believe themselves to be forsaken and beyond all possibility of hope. Yet such is their faith in God and their love for Him, that the will of God, even under such circumstances, is dearer to them than anything and everything else.

Article Eleven

One great point of difference between the First Covenant (or the covenant of works) that says to people, "Do this and live," and the Second Covenant (or the covenant of grace) that says, "Believe and live," is this—the first covenant did not lead people to anything that was perfect. It showed people what was right and good, but it failed in giving them the power to fulfill what the covenant required.

People not only understood what was right and good, they also knew what was evil. But in their love and practice of depravity, they no longer had power themselves to flee from it.

The new or Christian covenant of grace not only prescribes and commands, but gives also the power to fulfill.

In the practical dispensations of divine grace, there are a number of principles that it is important to remember.

God being love, it is a part of His nature to desire to communicate Himself to all moral beings and to make Himself one with them in a perfect harmony of relations and feelings. The position of God is that of giver. The position of human beings is that of recipient. Humanity was harmonized with God by the blood and power of the cross; and God once more became [for them] the infinite fullness, the original and overflowing fountain, giving and ever ready to give.

The relationship between God and people in the fact of their moral agency is such that their only part of that relationship is to receive. Souls true to the grace given them will never suffer any diminishing of it. On the contrary, the great and unchangeable condition of continuance and of growth in grace is cooperation with what we now have.

This is the law of growth, not only deducible from God's nature, but expressly revealed and declared in the Scriptures: "For whosoever hath, to him shall be given, and he shall have more abundance; but whosoever hath not, from him shall be taken away even that he hath."[10]

A faithful cooperation with grace is the most effective preparation for attracting, receiving, and increasing grace. This is the great secret of advancement to those high degrees that are permitted—namely, a strict, unwavering, faithful cooperation, moment by moment.

It is important to understand correctly the doctrine of cooperation. A disposition to cooperate is opposed to the sinful indolence that falls behind and to the hasty and unrighteous zeal that runs before. It is in the excess of zeal—which has a good appearance but in reality has unbelief and self at the bottom—that we run before God.

Cooperation, by being calm and peaceable, does not cease to be effective. Souls in this purified but tranquil state are souls of power—watchful and triumphant against self, resisting temptation, and fighting even to the shedding of blood against sin.[11] But it is, nevertheless, a combat free from the turbulence and inconsistencies of human passion.

For such souls contend [fight their battles] in the presence of God, who is their strength.[12] [And they fight their battles] in the spirit of the highest faith and love; and under the guidance of the Holy Ghost, who is always tranquil in His operations.

Article Twelve

Those in the highest state of Christian experience desire nothing except that God may be glorified in them by the accomplishment of His holy will. But it is not inconsistent with this that holy souls possess that natural love that exists in the form of love for themselves.

Their natural love, however—which within its proper degree is innocent love—is so absorbed in the love of God that it ceases, for the most part, to be a distinct object of consciousness. So much so, that practically and truly they may be said to love themselves IN and FOR God.

In his state of innocence, Adam loved himself both as the reflected image of God and for God's sake. So we may either say that he loved God in himself or that he loved himself IN and FOR God. And it is because holy souls (extending their affections beyond their own limit) love their neighbor on the same principle of loving—namely, IN and FOR God—that they may be said to love their neighbors as themselves.

It does not follow—because the love of ourselves is lost in the love of God—that we are to take no care and to exercise no watch over ourselves. None will be so seriously and constantly watchful over themselves as those who love themselves IN and

FOR God alone. Having the image of God in themselves, they have a strong motive to guard and protect it, perhaps as strong a motive as that which controls the actions of angels.

It may be thought, perhaps, that this is inconsistent with the main principle in the doctrines of holy living. That principle requires in the highest stages of inward experience to avoid those reflective acts that consist in self-inspection because such acts have a tendency to turn the mind away from God. The apparent difficulty is reconciled in this way: The holy soul is a soul with God—moving as God moves, doing as God does, looking as God looks.

If, therefore, God is looking within us (as we may generally learn from the intimations of His providences) then it is a sign that we are to look within ourselves. Our little eye, our small and almost imperceptible ray, must look in, in the midst of the light of His great and burning eye. It is thus that we may inspect ourselves without a separation from God.

On the same principle, we may be watchful and careful over our neighbors—watching them not in our own time but in God's time. Not in the censoriousness of nature, but in the kindness and forbearance of grace. Not as separate from God, but in concurrence with Him.

Article Thirteen

The soul in the state of pure love acts in simplicity. Its inward rule of action is found in the decisions of a sanctified conscience. These decisions, based upon judgments that are free from self-interest, may not always be absolutely right because our views and judgments are limited and can extend only to things in part. But they may be said to be relatively right, in that they conform to things so far as we are permitted to see them and understand them. And when we act in accordance with them, they convey to the soul a moral assurance that we are doing as God would have us do.

Such a conscience is enlightened by the Spirit of God. When we act under His divine guidance—looking at what now is and not at what may be, looking at the right of things and not at their relations to our personal and selfish interests—we are said to act in simplicity. This is the true mode of action.

In this singleness of spirit, therefore, we do things, as some experimental writers express it, without knowing what we do. We are so absorbed in the thing to be done, and in the importance of doing it rightly, that we forget ourselves.

Perfect love has nothing to spare from its object for itself, and those who pray perfectly are never thinking about how well they pray. [In the same way, those who act perfectly are never thinking about how well they act, and those who love perfectly are never thinking about how well they love.][13]

Article Fourteen

Holy souls are without impatience, but not without trouble. They are above murmuring, but not above affliction. The souls of those who are thus wholly in Christ may be regarded in two points of view, or rather in two parts. The natural appetites, propensities, and affections, on the one hand, which may be called the inferior part. And the judgment, the moral sense, and the will, on the other, which may be described as the superior part.

As things are in the present life, those who are wholly devoted to God may suffer in the inferior part, and may be at rest in the superior. Their wills may be in harmony with God's will. They may be approved in their judgments and conscience, and at the same time may suffer greatly in their physical relations, and in their natural sensibilities.

In this manner, Christ suffered much through His physical being upon the Cross, while His will remained firm in its union with the will of His heavenly Father. He felt the painful longings of thirst, the pressure of the thorns, and the agony of the spear. He was deeply afflicted also for the friends He left behind Him, and for a dying world. But in His inner and higher nature—where He felt Himself sustained by the secret voice uttered in His sanctified conscience and in His unchangeable faith—He was peaceful and happy.

Article Fifteen

A suitable repression of the natural appetites is profitable and necessary. We are told that the body should be brought into subjection. Those physical mortifications, therefore, that are for this purpose are not to be disapproved. When practiced within proper limits, they tend to correct evil habits, to preserve us against temptation, and to give self-control.

The practice of austerities, with the views and on the principles indicated, should be accompanied with the spirit of recollection, love, and prayer. Christ himself, whose retirement to solitary places, whose prayers and fastings are not to be forgotten, has given us the pattern that it is proper for us to follow. We must sometimes use force against our stubborn nature. "And from the days of John the Baptist until now the kingdom of heaven suffereth violence, and the violent take it by force. "[14]

Article Sixteen

The simple desire of our own happiness, kept in due subordination, is innocent. This desire is natural to us, and is properly called the principle of SELF-LOVE. When the principle of self-love passes its appropriate limit, however, it becomes selfishness. Self-love is innocent; selfishness is wrong. Selfishness was the sin of the first angel, "who rested in himself," as St. Augustine expresses it, instead of referring himself to God.

In many Christians a prominent principle of action is the desire of happiness. They love God and they love heaven; they love holiness and they love the pleasures of holiness; they love to do good and they love the rewards of doing good. This is well, but there is something better. Such Christians are inferior to those who forget the nothingness of the creature in the infinitude of the Creator, and love God for His own glory alone.

Article Seventeen

No period of the Christian life is exempt from temptation. The temptations in the earlier stages are different from those in a later period, and are to be resisted in a different manner.

Sometimes the temptations in the transition state from mixed love to pure love are somewhat peculiar, being intended to test whether we love God for Himself alone.

In the lower or mixed state the methods of resisting temptations are various. Sometimes the subject of these trials boldly faces them, and endeavors to overcome them by a direct resistance. Sometimes the subject turns and flees.

But in the state of pure love, when the soul has become strong in the divine contemplation, it is the common rule laid down by religious writers that the soul should keep itself fixed upon God in the exercise of its holy love, just as at other times. This is the most effective way of resisting the temptation, which would naturally increase its efforts in vain upon a soul in that state.

Article Eighteen

The will of God is the ultimate and only rule of action. God manifests His will in various ways. The will of God may in some cases be determined by the [intellectual and reasoning] operations of the human mind, especially when under a religious or gracious guidance; [such as that of a spiritual director or counselor].[15]

But God reveals His will chiefly in His written Word. And nothing that is at variance [at odds] with His written or revealed will can be declared to be the will of God, which may also be called His positive will [His sure and certain will].

If we sin, it is because God permits us to sin.[16] But it is also true that He disapproves and condemns sin as being contrary to His immutable holiness.

It is the business of sinners to repent. The state of penitence has temptations peculiar to itself. Sinners are sometimes tempted to murmuring and rebellious feelings, as if God had unjustly left them. When penitence is true, and in the highest state, it is free from the variations of human passion.

Article Nineteen

Among other distinctions of prayer, whether vocal or silent, are found in the prayer of the lips and the prayer of the affections. Vocal prayer that does not have the heart in it is superstitious and wholly unprofitable. To pray without reflecting upon God and without love, is to pray like the heathens who thought to be heard for the multitude of their words.[17]

Nevertheless, when attended by right affections, vocal prayer should be recognized and encouraged as being calculated to strengthen the thoughts and feelings it expresses, and to awaken new ones. Also, because it was taught by the Son of God to His Apostles,[18] and it has been practiced by the whole Church in all ages. To make light of this sacrifice of praise, the fruit of our lips,[19] would be an impiety.

In its common form, silent prayer is also profitable. Each has its peculiar advantages, just as each has its place.

There is also a prayer that may be called the [contemplative] prayer of silence. This is a prayer too deep for words. The common form of silent prayer is voluntary. In the prayer of contemplative silence, the lips seem to be closed almost against the will.

Article Twenty

The principles of holy living extend to everything. For instance, in the matter of reading, those who have given themselves wholly to God can read only what God permits them to read. They cannot read books, however characterized by wit or power, merely to indulge an idle curiosity or to please themselves alone.

In reading, this may be a suitable way: namely, to read only a little at a time, and to interrupt the reading with intervals of religious reflection, so that the Holy Spirit can imprint Christian truths more deeply into us.

God, in the person of the Holy Ghost, is the great inward teacher to the fully renovated mind. This is a great truth. At the same time, we are not to suppose that the presence of the inward teacher exempts us from the necessity of the outward lesson. The Holy Ghost, operating through the medium of a purified judgment, teaches us also by the means of books, especially by the Word of God, which is never to be laid aside.

Article Twenty-One

One characteristic of the lower states of religious experience is that they are sustained to a considerable degree by meditative and reflective acts. Because faith is comparatively weak and temptations are strong in souls in these lower states, it is necessary for them to gain strength by meditating and reflecting upon various truths that apply to their situations, and to consider the motives resulting from such truths [that is, to think carefully of the reasons why these applied truths cause or motivate them to think and act the way they do.]

Accordingly, such souls lay before themselves all the various motives resulting from sorrows in their lives and all the motives resulting from happiness—that is, all the motives of fear and hope. [Those fears and hopes that motivate them to think and act the way they do.]

It is different, however, with those who have given themselves wholly to God in the exercise of pure or perfect love. The soul does not find it necessary to delay and to meditate in order to discover motives of action. It finds its motive of action—a motive simple, uniform, peaceable, and still powerful beyond any other power—in its own principle of life.

Meditation, inquiry, and reasoning are exceedingly necessary to the great body of Christians, and absolutely indispensable to those in the beginnings of the Christian life. To take away these helps would be to take away the child from the breast before it can digest solid food. Still, they are only the props and not the life itself.

Article Twenty-Two

The holy soul delights in acts of contemplation—to think of God and of God only. But the contemplative state without any interruption is hardly consistent with the condition of the present life. It may sometimes occur spontaneously, however, and should not be resisted. It is those times when the attraction towards God is so strong that we find ourselves incapable of profitably employing our minds in meditative and discursive acts of our own.

Article Twenty-Three

There are two states. One is the meditative and discursive state, which deliberately reflects, compares, reasons, and supports itself by aids and methods of that nature. The other is the contemplative state, which rests in God without such aids.

Of the two, the contemplative state is the higher. God will teach [or determine] the times of both. Neither state is entirely exclusive of the other, nor should it be.

Article Twenty-Four

In some cases, God gives such eminent grace that the contemplative prayer, which is essentially the same as the prayer of silence, becomes the habitual state. We do not mean that the mind is always in this state. But whenever the season of reflection and prayer returns, the mind habitually assumes the contemplative state, in distinction from the meditative and discursive.

It does not follow that this eminent state is invariable. Souls may fall from this state by some act of infidelity in themselves, or God may place them temporarily in a different state.

Article Twenty-Five

The Apostle Paul says, "Whether therefore ye eat, or drink, or whatsoever ye do, do all to the glory of God."[20] And in another passage, he says, "Let all your things be done with charity."[21] And again, "By love, serve one another."[22] These passages, along with many others, imply two things. First, that everything that is done by the Christian should be done from a holy principle. Second, that this principle is love.

Article Twenty-Six

Our acceptance with God, when our hearts are wholly given to Him, does not depend upon our being in a particular state, but simply upon our being in that state in which God in His providence requires us to be.

The doctrine of holiness, therefore—while it recognizes and requires, on its appropriate occasions, the prayer of contemplation or of contemplative silence—is not only not inconsistent with other forms of prayer, but is not at all inconsistent with the practice of the ordinary acts, duties, and virtues of life.

It would be a great mistake to suppose that a person who bears the Savior's image is any the less a good neighbor or a good citizen because of it. Or that such a person can think less or work less when called to it. Or is not characterized by the various virtues appropriate to our present situation. Those virtues are temperance, truth, forbearance, forgiveness, kindness, chastity, and justice. There is a law involved in the very nature of holiness that requires it to adapt itself to every variety of situation.

Article Twenty-Seven

It is in accordance with the views of Dionysius the Areopagite[23] to say that the holy soul in its contemplative state is occupied with the pure or spiritual divinity. That is to say, it is occupied with God in distinction from any mere image of God, such as could be addressed to the touch, the sight, or any of the senses.

This is not all. It does not satisfy the desires of the soul in its contemplative state to occupy itself merely with the attributes of God—with His power, wisdom, goodness, and the like. Rather, it seeks and unites itself with the God of the attributes. The attributes of God are not God himself. The power of God is not an identical expression with the God of power. Nor is the wisdom of God identical with the God of wisdom.

The holy soul, in its contemplative state, loves to unite itself with God, considered as the subject of His attributes. It is not infinite wisdom, infinite power, or infinite goodness that it loves and adores, but the God of infinite wisdom, power, and goodness.

Article Twenty-Eight

Christ is "the way, the truth, and the life."[24] The grace that sanctifies and the grace that justifies are by Him and through Him.[25] He is the true and living way.[26]

No one can gain the victory over sin and be brought into union with God without Christ.[27] And when we may be said to have arrived at the end of the way, by being brought home to the divine fold and reinstated in the divine image, it would be sad indeed if we forgot that the way itself was Christ, as He is sometimes called.

At every period of our progress, however advanced it may be, our life is derived from God through Christ and for Christ. The most advanced souls are those who are most possessed with the thoughts and the presence of Christ.

Any other view would be extremely harmful. It would be to snatch from the Christians life eternal, which consists in knowing the only true God and Jesus Christ, His Son whom He has sent.[28]

Article Twenty-Nine

The way of holiness is wonderful, but it is not miraculous. Those in it walk by simple faith alone. And perhaps the most remarkable and wonderful part of it is that so great a result is produced by so simple a principle.

When persons have arrived at the state of divine union in accordance with the prayer of the Savior and are made one with Christ in God,[29] they no longer seem to put forth distinct inward acts. Their state appears to be characterized by a deep and divine repose.

Rather than distinct acts, there is one continuous act of faith, which brings them into moral and religious union with the divine nature. This faith is kept firm and unbroken through an abundance of divine grace.

The appearance of absolute continuity and unity in this blessed state is increased perhaps by the entire freedom of the mind from all eager, anxious, unquiet acts. The soul is not only at unity with itself in the specific areas that have been mentioned, but it has also a unity of rest.

This state of continuous faith and of consequent repose in God is sometimes called the passive state. At such times, the soul ceases to originate acts that precede the grace of God. The decisions of its consecrated judgment are the voice of the Holy Ghost in the soul. But if the soul first listens passively, it is subsequently its business to yield an active and effective cooperation in the line of duty that those decisions indicate.

The more pliant and supple the soul is to the divine suggestions, the more real and effective is its own action, though without any excited and troubled movement. The more a soul receives from God, the more it should return to Him what it has received from Him. This ebbing and flowing, if one may so call it, this communication on the part of God and the correspondent action on the part of the soul, constitute the order of grace on the one hand, and the action and faithfulness of the creature on the other.

Article Thirty

It would be a mistake to suppose that the highest state of inward experience is characterized by great excitements— raptures and ecstasies. Or by any movements of feeling that would be regarded as particularly extraordinary.

One of the remarkable results in a soul in which faith is the sole governing principle is that it is entirely peaceful. Nothing disturbs it. And being peaceful, it reflects distinctly and clearly the image of Christ. It is like the quiet lake that shows in its own clear and beautiful heart the exact forms of the objects around and above it.

Another result is that having full faith in God and being divested of all selfishness and resistance in itself, the soul is perfectly accessible and pliable to all the impressions of grace.

Article Thirty-One

It does not follow that those who possess the graces of a truly sanctified heart are at liberty to reject the ordinary methods and rules of perception and judgment. They exercise and value wisdom, while they reject the selfishness of wisdom. The rules of holy living would require them to constantly make a faithful use of all the natural light of reason, as well as the higher and spiritual light of grace.

A holy soul values and seeks wisdom, but does not seek it in an unholy and worldly spirit. And when it is made wise by the Spirit of wisdom, who dwells in all hearts that are wholly devoted to God, it does not turn back from the giver to the gift and rejoice in its wisdom as its own.

The wisdom of the truly holy soul is a wisdom that considers things in the present moment. It judges duty from the facts that now are—including, however, those things that have a relation to the present.

It is important to understand that the present moment necessarily possesses a moral extension. So that in judging the things that are in it, we are to include all those things that have a natural and near relation to the thing actually at hand.

It is in this manner that the holy soul lives in the present, committing the past to God, and leaving the future with that approaching hour that will transform it into the present. "Sufficient unto the day is the evil thereof."[30] Tomorrow will take care of itself. When it comes, it will bring its appropriate grace and light. When we live that way, God will not fail to give us our daily bread.[31]

Such souls draw on themselves the special protection of providence, under whose care they live. They are like little children resting in the bosom of their mother, without a far extended and unquiet forecast. Conscious of their own limited views, and keeping in mind the instructions of the Savior, "Judge not, that you be not judged,"[32] they are slow to pass judgment upon others. They are willing to receive reproof and correction. Apart from the will of God, they have no choice or will of their own in anything.

These are the children whom Christ permits to come near Him. They combine the wisdom of the serpent with the simplicity of the dove. But they do not appropriate their wisdom to themselves as their own wisdom, any more than they appropriate to themselves the beams of the natural sun when they walk in its light.

These are the poor in spirit, whom Christ Jesus has declared blessed.[33] They are as much removed from any contented self-satisfaction in what others might call their merits, as all Christians should be from their temporal possessions. They are the "little ones," to whom God is well pleased to reveal His mysteries, while He hides them from the wise and prudent.[34]

Article Thirty-Two

The children of God, as distinguished from the mere servants of God, have the liberty of children. They have a peace and joy that is full of innocence. They take with simplicity and without hesitation the refreshments of both mind and body. They do not speak of themselves, except when called to do it in providence and in order to do good. Their simplicity and truth of spirit are of such a nature that they speak of things just as they appear to them at the moment.

When the conversation turns upon their own works or characters, they express themselves favorably or unfavorably, much as they would if they were speaking of others. If, however, they have occasion to speak of any good of which they have been the instrument, they always acknowledge with humble joy that it comes from God alone.

There is a liberty that might more properly be called license. There are persons who insist that purity of heart renders pure—in those of this purity—whatever they are prompted to do, however irregular [or wrong] it may be in others. This is a great error.

Article Thirty-Three

It is the doctrine of both Augustine and Thomas Aquinas that the principle of holy love existing in the heart necessarily includes in itself—or implies the existence—of all other Christian virtues.

Those who love God with all their heart will not violate the laws of purity because it would be a disregard for the will of God, whom they love above all things. Under such circumstances, their love becomes the virtue of chastity. They have too much love and reverence for the will of God to murmur or complain under the dispensations of His providence. Under such circumstances, their love becomes the virtue of patience. On the appropriate occasions, therefore, this love becomes by turns all the virtues. As their love is perfect, so the virtues that flow out of it and are modified from it will not be less so.

It is a maxim in the doctrines of holiness that the holy soul is crucified to its own virtues, although it possesses them in the highest degree. The meaning of this saying is this: The holy soul is so crucified to self in all its forms that it practices the virtues without contented self-satisfaction in its virtues as its own and even without thinking how virtuous it is.

Article Thirty-Four

The Apostle Paul speaks of Christians as dead. "Ye are dead," he says, "and your life is hid with Christ in God."[35] In their full meaning, these expressions will apply only to those Christians who are in the state of unselfish or pure love. Their death is a death to selfishness. They are dead to pride and jealousy, self-seeking and envy, to malice, inordinate love of their own reputation—anything and everything that constitutes the fallen and debased life of nature. They have a new life, which is "hid with Christ in God."

Article Thirty-Five

Some persons of great piety, in describing the highest religious state, have called it the state of transformation. But this can be regarded as only a synonymous expression for the state of pure love.

In the transformed state of the soul, as in the state of pure love, love is its life. In this principle of love, all the various affections of the soul have their constituting or their controlling element. There can be no love without an object of love.

As the principle of love, therefore, allies the soul with another, so from the other, who is God, proceeds all of love's power of movement—or direction. In itself love remains without preference for anything. Consequently, it is accessible and yielding to all the touches and guidance of grace, however slight they may be. It is like a spherical body that is placed upon a level and even surface and is moved with equal ease in any direction.

Having no preferences of itself in this state, the soul has but one principle of movement—that which God gives it. In this state the soul can say with the Apostle Paul, "I live; yet not I, but Christ liveth in me."[36]

Article Thirty-Six

Souls who have experienced the grace of sanctification in its higher degrees do not have as much need of set times and places for worship as others do. The purity and the strength of their love are such that it is very easy for them to unite with God in acts of inward worship at all times and places. They have an interior closet. The soul is their temple—and God dwells in it.

This, however, does not exempt them from those outward methods and observances that God has prescribed. Besides, they owe something to others, and a disregard of the ordinances and duties of the Church could not fail to be harmful to beginners in the Christian life.

Article Thirty-Seven

The practice of confession is not inconsistent with the state of pure love. The truly renovated soul can still say, "Forgive us our trespasses."[37] Though it does not sin deliberately and knowingly now, its former state of sin can never be forgotten.

Article Thirty-Eight

In the transformed or pure love state, there should be not only the confession [to God][38] of those transgressions properly called sins, but also the confession of those more smaller transgressions called faults. We should sincerely disapprove such faults in our confession, and should condemn them and desire their removal [from us]: Not merely with a view to our own cleansing and deliverance, but also because God wills it and because He would have us to do it for His glory.

Article Thirty-Nine

It is sometimes the case that people misjudge the holiness of individuals by considering it from the person's outward appearance. Holiness is consistent with the existence of various infirmities in the same person (such as an unpleasing form, physical weakness, ineffective judgment, imperfect speech, defective manners, a lack of knowledge, and the like).

Article Forty

There are three particular ways in which the holy soul may be said to be united with God without anything intervening or producing a separation.

First. The holy soul is united to God intellectually. The soul is not united to God by any idea that is based upon the senses, and that could give only a material image of God. Rather it is united by an idea that is internal and spiritual in its origin, and that makes God known to the soul as a true being, but without form.

Second. The holy soul is united to God affectionately. The soul is united to God when its affections are not given to Him indirectly through a self-interested motive, but are given simply because He is what He is. When the soul loves God for His own sake, it is united to Him in love without anything intervening.

Third. The holy soul is united to God practically. This is the case when the soul does the will of God from the constantly operative impulse of holy love, and not by simply following a prescribed form.

Article Forty-One

Some devout writers on inward experience use the phrase spiritual nuptials. It is a favorite method with some of these writers to represent the union of the soul with God by the figure of the bride and the bridegroom. Similar expressions are found in the Scriptures.

We are not to suppose that such expressions mean anything more, in reality, than that intimate union that exists between God and the soul when the soul is in the state of pure love.

Article Forty-Two

We find again other forms of expression, which it is proper to notice. The union between God and the soul is sometimes described by devout writers as an essential union and sometimes as a substantial union—as if there were a union of essence, substance, or being, in the literal or physical sense. They mean to express nothing more than the fact of the union of pure love, with the additional idea that the union is firm and established. Thus it is not subject to those breaks and inequalities, to that lack of continuity and uniformity, that characterize inferior degrees of love.

Article Forty-Three

When St. Paul said, "As many as are led by the Spirit of God, they are the sons of God,"[39] it may be understood that he was speaking especially of the holy soul.

Those who are in a state of simple faith, which can always be said of those who are in the state of pure love, are the "little ones" of the Scriptures. We are told that they are the ones whom God teaches. "I thank Thee", says the Savior, "O Father, Lord of Heaven and Earth, that Thou hast hid these things from the wise and prudent, and hast revealed them unto babes."[40]

Taught as they are by the Spirit of God who dwells in them, these souls possess a knowledge that the wisdom of the world could never impart. But such knowledge never renders them otherwise than respectful to spiritual teachers, docile to the instructions of the Church, and conformable in all things to the precepts of the Scriptures.

Article Forty-Four

The doctrine of pure love has been known and recognized as a true doctrine among the truly contemplative and devout in all ages of the Church. The doctrine, however, has been so far above the common experience that the pastors and saints of all ages have exercised discretion and care in making it known, except to those to whom God had already given both the attraction and light to receive it.

Acting on the principle of giving milk to infants and strong meat to those that were more advanced, they addressed in the great body of Christians only the motives of fear and of hope, founded on the consideration of personal happiness or misery. It seemed to them that the motive of God's glory, which is a motive that requires us to love God for Himself alone without a distinct regard and reference to our own happiness, could, as a general rule, only be profitably addressed to those who are somewhat advanced in inward experience.

Article Forty-Five

Among the various forms of expression indicative of the highest experience, we sometimes find that of divine union, or union with God.

Union with God,[41] not a physical but a moral or spiritual union, necessarily exists in souls who are in the state of pure love. The state of divine union is not a higher state than that of pure love, but may rather be described as the same state.

Strive after it—but do not too readily or easily believe that you have attained to it.

After much fatigue and many dangers, travelers arrive at the top of a mountain. As they look abroad from that high position, and in that clear atmosphere, they see their native city—and it seems to them to be very near. Overjoyed at the sight, and perhaps deceived by their position, they proclaim themselves as already at the end of their journey.

But they soon find that the distance was greater than they supposed. They are obliged to descend into deep valleys, climb over high mountains, conquer rugged rocks, ford raging streams, and force their tired feet over many miles of weary roads before they reach their city that they once thought was so near.

It is the same in relation to the sanctification of the heart. True holiness of heart is the object at which all true Christians aim. They see it before them as an object of transcendent beauty, and as perhaps near at hand. But as they advance toward it, they find the way longer and more difficult than they had imagined.

But if on the one hand we should be careful not to mistake an intermediate stopping place for the end of the trip, we should be equally careful on the other not to be discouraged by the difficulties we meet. We must remember always that the obligation to be holy is always binding upon us, and that God will help those who put their trust in Him.

For whatsoever is born of God overcometh the world; and this is the victory that overcometh the world—EVEN OUR FAITH.[42]

Endnotes

1 Maxim: A clear and precise statement in a few words of a fundamental principle, general truth, or rule of conduct. Fénelon wrote *The Maxims of the Saints* in defense of the doctrines of pure love taught by Mme. Jeanne Guyon, though he did not mention her name in his book.

2 St. Thomas Aquinas (1225-1274). Italian Dominican monk, theologian, and philosopher. The outstanding representative of Scholasticism, he applied Aristotelian methods to Christian theology. His masterwork is *Summa Theologica* (1266-1273).

3 Romans 8:24; 1 Corinthians 15:19; Galatians 5:5; Colossians 1:5, 23, 27; Titus 1:2, 3:7; Hebrews 6:18-19

4 Galatians 5:6

5 Prevenient: coming before, preceding.

6 Sensible: Perceptible by the senses or the mind—readily perceived.

7 St. Francis of Sales, (1567-1622). French ecclesiastic who maintained in his many writings, such as *Introduction to a Devout Life* (1609), that spiritual perfection is possible not just for religious contemplatives but also for people involved in secular pursuits.

8 Mark 15:34

9 Luke 22:42

10 Matthew 13:12

11 Hebrews 12:4

12 For more on the presence of God, see *The Practice of the Presence of God* by Brother Lawrence. A Pure Gold Classic published by Bridge-Logos Publishers.

13 For further study on the subject of love, see *The Greatest Thing in the World—LOVE* by Henry Drummond and revised and expanded by Harold J. Chadwick—a Pure Gold Classic published by Bridge-Logos Publishers.

14 Matthew 11:12

15 At that time in the Roman Catholic Church, many Catholics were assigned a confessor and a director. The confessor was a priest or bishop who heard their confessions, and the director was a priest or bishop who directed or guided their religious life. Sometimes both offices were combined in the same person. See the Pure Gold Classic, *Mme. Jeanne Guyon*, published by Bridge-Logos Publishers for additional references to this.

16 Although this sounds strange with only a shallow reading, it is scriptural that God could prevent us from sinning if it served His purpose to do so, or allow us to sin if it served His purpose to do so. "And God said to him in a dream, 'Yes, I know that you did this in

the integrity of your heart. For I also withheld you from sinning against Me; therefore I did not let you touch her.'" (Genesis 20:6, NKJV).

17 Matthew 6:7

18 Luke 11:2

19 Hebrews 13:15

20 1 Corinthians 10:31

21 1 Corinthians 16:14

22 Galatians 5:13b

23 Areopagite: A member of the council of the Areopagus. The Areopagus was the highest judicial and legislative council of ancient Athens.

24 John 14:6

25 Colossians 1:16

26 Hebrews 10:20

27 John 15:5

28 John 17:3

29 John 17:22-23

30 Matthew 6:34

31 Matthew 6:11

32 Matthew 7:1

33 Matthews 5:3

34 Luke 10:21

35 Colossians 3:3

36 Galatians 2:20

37 Luke 11:4

38 1 John 1:9

39 Romans 8:14

40 Luke 10:21

41 For further study on union with God, see the Pure Gold Classics: *Madame Jeanne Guyon, Experiencing Union with God through Inner Prayer,* & *The Way and Results of Union with God.* Published by Bridge-Logos Publishers.

42 1 John 5:4

Christian Counsel
on Various Matters
Pertaining to the Inner Life

I counsel thee to buy of me gold tried in the fire,
that thou mayest be rich; and white raiment, that
thou mayest be clothed, and that the shame of
thy nakedness do not appear; and anoint thine
eyes with eyesalve, that thou mayest see.[1]

1
There is little knowledge of God in the world

What people need most is the knowledge of God. Many
people know for certain because of their reading that the
Bible gives a historical account of a series of miracles and
observable providences of God. They have reflected seriously
on the corruption and instability of worldly things, and may
even be convinced that the reformation of their lives on certain
principles of morality is desirable for their salvation. But the

whole structure is lacking a foundation—it is a pious and Christian exterior that possesses no soul.

In them, the living principle that animates every true believer, God—the all and in all, the author and the sovereign of all—is lacking. He is infinite in all things—in wisdom, power, and love. Why should it be a wonder, therefore, if everything that comes from His hand has the same infinite character and brings to nothing the efforts of human reason?

When God works, His ways and His thoughts are declared by the prophet to be as far above our ways and our thoughts as the heavens are above the earth.[2] He experiences no effort when He executes what He has decreed; for to Him all things are equally easy. He speaks and causes the heavens and the earth to be created out of nothing,[3] and does it with as little difficulty as He causes water to descend or a stone to fall to the ground. His power is co-extensive with His will—when He wills a thing, the thing is already accomplished.

When the Scriptures represent Him as speaking forth the creation of the world, it should not be thought that it was necessary that He speak the word of command so that the universe He was about to create would hear and obey His will. That word was simple and internal, neither more nor less than the thought in which He conceived what He was about to do and the will to do it. The thought was fertile,[4] and without being rendered external,[5] produced from Him as the fountain of all life, the sum[6] of the things that exist.

His mercy, too, is but His pure will. He loved us before the creation of the world. He saw and knew us,[7] and prepared His blessings for us. He loved and chose us from all eternity. Every new blessing we receive is derived from this eternal origin; He forms no new will concerning us. It is not He that changes, but we.

When we are righteous and good, we are conformed to His will and pleasing to Him. When we depart from well doing and cease to be good, we cease to be conformed to Him and to please Him. This is the immutable [unchangeable] standard that the changeable creature is continually approaching and leaving.

God's justice against the wicked and His love toward the righteous are the same thing. It is the same quality that unites Him to everything that is good, and is incompatible with everything that is evil. Mercy is the goodness of God seeing our wickedness and striving to make us good. Perceived[8] by us in time,[9] grace has its source in the eternal love of God for His creature. From Him alone proceeds true goodness. Alas, for that presumptuous soul that seeks it in itself!

It is God's love toward us that gives us everything. But the richest of His gifts is that we may love Him with that love that is His right. When He is able by His love to produce that love in us, He reigns within. There He establishes our life, our peace, our happiness. When that is done, we already begin to taste that blissful existence that He enjoys. His love toward us is stamped with His own character of infinity. It is not like ours, limited and constrained. When He loves, all the measures of His love are infinite.

He comes down from Heaven to earth to seek the creature of clay whom He loves. He becomes creature and clay with them. He gives them the Bread of Life to eat[10]. These are the miracles of divine love in which the Infinite [love—or God] outstrips all the affection we can manifest. We then love like God, with a love utterly incomprehensible.

It is the height of folly to seek to measure infinite love by human wisdom. Far from losing any element of its greatness in these excesses [toward us], God impresses upon His love the stamp of His own grandeur, while He manifests a delight in us limited only by [His] infinity. O how great and lovely is He in His mysteries! But, [foolishly], we want eyes to see them and have no desire to see God in everything.

2

The necessity of knowing and loving God

It is not astonishing that people do so little for God and that the little they do costs them so much. They do not know Him and scarcely believe that He exists. The impression they have is rather a blind yielding to general opinion than a lively and distinct conviction of God. They suppose the general opinion is right because they do not dare to examine the evidence for themselves and because they are indifferent in the matter—their souls being distracted by their affections and passions for other objects.

But their only idea of God is of something wonderful, far off, and unconnected with us. They think of Him as a stern and powerful being, ever making demands upon us, opposing our desires and passions, and threatening us with great evils. They further think that it behooves everyone to be on guard against His terrible judgment.

Those are the inward thoughts of the small number who think seriously about religion. They say they fear God, and in truth they may, but they fear Him only and do not love Him. It is like a child in fear of the tutor who punishes, or like the servant in dread of the blows of one who is served in fear and whose interests are totally disregarded. Would they like to be treated by a son or a servant in the same way that they treat God?

It is because they do not know God. If they did know Him, they would love Him. God is love, says the Apostle John.[11] Those who do not love Him do not know Him, for how could we know love without loving it? It is plain, then, that all those who have until now only feared God have not known Him.

But who will know You, O my God? Those who seek with their whole heart to know You, who will not think of themselves with approval any longer, and to whom all that is not You will be as though it did not exist!

90

The world cannot receive this saying because it is full of self, vanity, and lies—and is empty of God. But I trust that there will always be souls hungering for God, who will relish the truth that I am about to set forth.

O my God, before You made the heavens and the earth, there was no one [and nothing] but You. You existed, and because of the infinity of your years there was no beginning. You were alone. Outside of You there was nothing, and You rejoiced in this blessed solitude. You are all-sufficient in Yourself, and You have no need of anything outside of Yourself. No one can give anything to You, and it is You who gives to all by Your all-powerful Word—that is, by Your simple will. Nothing is difficult for Your will, and it does whatever it wishes from its own strength.

You caused this world—which was not as yet—to begin to exist. But You did not do it like the workers of the world who find the materials for their work ready made for them, and whose art consists in bringing them together, and arranging them by slow degrees in the proper order. You found nothing ready made, but created all the materials for Your work. It was to nothing that You said, "Let the world be,"[12] and it was. You only spoke and it was done.

But why did You create all these things? They were all made for humanity and humanity was made for You. This is the order that You appointed, and woe to those who invert it—those who desire that everything be for them and make themselves the center of their own universe! They break the fundamental law of creation.

No! Lord, You cannot yield the essential and exclusive rights of a creator—it would degrade You. You can pardon the guilty soul that has warred against You, because You can fill it with Your pure love. But You cannot cease to be in conflict with the soul that directs all Your gifts to itself, and refuses to embrace You as its Creator with a sincere and disinterested[13] affection. To have no feeling but fear is not to think of itself with concern for You, but is to think of You solely with concern for itself.

To love You with an eye only for the good You can bestow is not to lose oneself in You, but to lose You in self! What then must we do in order that we may be lost in You? We must renounce, forget, and forever lose sight of self. We must no longer have any will, glory, or peace—but You only. In a word, we must love You without loving self except in and for You.

God who made us out of nothing, recreates us, as it were, every moment. It does not follow that because we were yesterday, we will of course be today. If it was not for God's all-powerful hand preventing it, we would cease to exist and return into the nothingness out of which He formed us. Of ourselves we are nothing. We are but what God has made us, and exist only for so long as He pleases. He has but to withdraw the hand that sustains us and we plunge into the abyss of annihilation—just as a stone held in the air falls by its own weight when its support is removed. Existence and life, then, are only ours because they are continuously given to us by God.

There are blessings, however, of a purer and higher order than these. A well-ordered life is better than life. Virtue is of higher price than health. Uprightness of heart and the love of God are as far above temporal goods as the heavens are above the earth. If then these lower and baser gifts are held only through the mercy and at the pleasure of God, how much more reason must it be true of the sublime gift of His love!

They know You not, then, O my God, who regard You as an all-powerful being, separate from themselves, giving laws to all nature, and creator of everything that we behold. They know You only in part! They do not know that which is most marvelous and which most nearly concerns Your rational creatures! To know that You are the God of my heart,[14] that there You do what pleases You, is what elevates and affects me! When I am good, it is because You make me so. Not only do You turn my heart as pleases You, but You give me one like

Your own! It is Yourself that You love in me. You are the life of my soul, just as my soul is the life of my body. You are more intimately present to me than I am to myself. This I [this self]—to which I am so attached and which I have so ardently loved—should be strange to me in comparison with You. You are the giver of it. Without You it never would have been. Therefore, You require that I love You better than it.

O incomprehensible power of my Creator! O rights of the Creator over the creature that the creature will never sufficiently understand! O miracle of love that God alone could perform! God interposes Himself, as it were, between me and myself. He separates me from myself. He desires to be nearer to me by His pure love than I am to myself. He would have me look upon this me as a stranger. He would have me escape from its walls, wholly sacrifice it to Him, returning it absolutely and unconditionally to Him from whom I received it.

What I am should certainly be less precious to me than He by whom I am. He made me for Himself and not to be my own. That is, He made me to love Him and to will what He wills, and not to seek my own will.

Do you feel your heart revolt at this total sacrifice of self to Him who has created you? I weep for your blindness. I am sympathetic to your bondage to self and pray God to deliver you from it by teaching you to love Him above every other object.

O my God, in the souls that are offended at Your pure love I see the darkness and rebellion resulting from the fall! You did not make our hearts for this monstrous passion of appropriation. The Scriptures teach us that Adam's original uprightness when he was created consisted in his having no claim upon himself but acknowledging that he belonged to his Creator.

O Father, Your children are sadly changed, and no longer bear Your image![15] They are enraged and discouraged when they are told they should belong to You just as You belong to

Yourself! They desire to reverse this holy order and would madly raise themselves into Gods.[16] They desire to be their own, to do everything for self—or, at the very least, to surrender themselves with certain reservations and conditions, and for their own advantage.

O monstrous usurpation! O unknown rights of God! O the ingratitude and insolence of the creature! Miserable nothing! What have you to keep for yourself? What have you that belongs to you? What have you that did not come from on high, and should not return there? Everything—yes, even this that I would divide with God—is a gift of God, and was only made for Him. Everything within you cries out against you and for your Creator. Be still, then, you created being who would deny your Creator, and surrender yourself wholly to Him.

My God, what a consolation it is to know that everything within me as well as outside me is the work of Your hand! You are always with me.[17] When I do wrong, You are within me, reproaching me with the evil that I do, raising within me regrets for the good that I abandon, and opening to me Your arms of mercy. When I do good, You inspire the desire, and do it in me and with me. It is You who loves good and hates evil in my heart, who suffers and prays, who does good to the neighbor and gives alms to the poor.

I do all these things but by Your means: You cause me to do them. It is You who puts them in me. These good works, which are Your gifts, become my works. But they do not cease to be Your gifts. They cease, however, to be good works if I look at them for a moment as emanating from myself, or if I forget that they are good only because they come from You.

You, then, (it is my delight to believe it!) are continually working within me.[18] There You labor invisibly like a miner in the bowels of the earth. You do everything and yet the world doesn't see You, and attributes nothing to You. Even I myself wandered everywhere vainly searching for You outside of myself. I ran over all the wonders of nature that I might form some concept of Your greatness. I asked Your creatures about You and not once thought of finding You in the depths of my heart where You had never ceased to dwell. No, O my God, it is not necessary to descend into the depths, pass beyond the seas, or ascend into the heavens to find You.[19] You are nearer to us than we are to ourselves.

O my God, You who are at once so great and so condescending, so high above the heavens and so accommodating to the misery of the creature, so infinite and so intimately enclosed in the depths of my heart, so terrible and so lovely, so jealous and so easy to be entreated of those who converse with You with the familiarity of pure love, when will Your children cease to be ignorant of You? Where will I find a voice loud enough to reproach the whole world with its blindness, and to tell it with authority all that You are?

When we tell people to look for You in their own hearts, it is as though we directed them to search for You in the remotest and most unknown lands! What territory is more distant or more unknown to the greater part of them, vain and dissipated as they are, than the ground of their own hearts? Do they ever know what it is to enter within themselves? Have they ever endeavored to find the way? Can they even form the most distant concept of the nature of that interior sanctuary, that impenetrable depth of the soul where You desire to be worshipped in spirit and in truth?[20] They are always outside themselves, busy with the external objects of their ambition or their pleasure.

Alas, my God, how can they understand heavenly truths, since, as our Lord says, they cannot even understand [and believe] those that are earthly?[21] They cannot conceive what it is to enter within themselves by serious meditation. So what would they say if they were told to come out of themselves so that they might be lost in God?

As for me, my Creator, I shut my eyes to all exterior things, which are but vanity and vexation of spirit.[22] I do it so that I may enjoy in the deepest recesses of my heart an intimate companionship with You through Jesus Christ, Your Son, who is Your wisdom and eternal understanding. He became a child so that by His childhood and the folly of His cross, He might put to shame our vain and lying wisdom. Cost what it may, and in spite of my fears and speculations, I desire to become lowly and a fool, still more despicable in my own eyes than in those of the wise in their own conceit. Like the apostles, I would become drunk with the Holy Spirit,[23] and be content with them to become the sport of the world.[24]

I find You everywhere within [me]. It is You who does every good thing that I seem to do. I have a thousand times experienced that I could not of myself control my temper, overcome my [bad] habits, subdue my pride, follow my reason, or will again the good that I had once willed. It is You who must both give the will and keep it pure. Without You, I am but a reed shaken by the wind.[25]

You are the author of all the courage, uprightness, and truth that I possess. You have given me a new heart that longs after Your righteousness, and that is thirsty for Your eternal truth. You have taken away the old man full of filth and corruption— who was jealous, vain, ambitious, restless, unrighteous, and devoted to his own pleasure. In what a state of misery I lived. Ah, could I ever have believed that I would be enabled to turn to You, and shake off the yoke of my tyrannical passions?

But behold a marvel that eclipses all the rest! Who but You could ever have snatched me from myself, and turned all my hatred and contempt against my own heart? I have not done this, for it is not by our own power that we depart from self. No! You, O Lord, shone with Your own light into the depth of my heart which could not be reached by any other, and there revealed the whole of my foulness.

I know that even after seeing it, I have not changed it. That I am still filthy in Your sight, and that my eyes have not been able to discover the extent of my pollution. But I have, at least, seen a part, and I desire to see all of it. I am despised in my own sight, but the hope that I have in You causes me to live in peace—for I will neither flatter my defects nor allow them to discourage me. I take Your side, O God, against myself. It is only by Your strength that I am able to do this.

Behold what God has worked within me! And You continue Your work from day to day in cleansing me from the old Adam and in building up the new.[26] This is the new creation that is gradually going on.[27]

I leave myself, Father, in Your hands. Make and remake this clay, shape it or grind it to atoms—it is Your own, it has nothing to say.[28] Only let it always be subservient to Your ever-blessed designs, and let nothing in me oppose Your good pleasure for which I was created.

Require, command, forbid, what would You have me do, or not do?[29] Exalted or abased, rejoicing or suffering, doing Your work or laid aside, I will always praise You alike, ever yielding up all my own will to Your will! Nothing remains for me but to adopt the language of Mary, "Be it unto me according to Thy word."[30]

Let me, O my God, stifle forever in my heart every thought that would tempt me to doubt Your goodness. I know that You cannot but be good. O merciful Father, let me no longer reason about grace, but silently abandon myself to its operation. Grace performs everything in us, but does it with and through us. It is by it, therefore, that I act, that I forbear, that I suffer, that I wait, that I resist, that I believe, that I hope, and that I love—all in cooperation with grace.

Following its guidance, it will do all things in me, and I will do all things through it. It moves the heart, but the heart must move. There is no salvation without our action.[31] I must work, then, without losing a moment, that I may put no hindrance in the way of the grace that is incessantly working within me.

All the good is of grace; all the evil is of self. When I do right, it is grace that does it. When I do wrong, it is because I resist grace. I pray God that I may not seek to know more than this. All else will but serve to nourish a presumptuous curiosity. O my God, keep me always in the number of those babes to whom You reveal Your mysteries, while You conceal them from the wise and prudent![32]

You enable me to understand clearly that You make use of the evils and imperfections of the creature to do the good that You have determined beforehand. You conceal Yourself in the uninvited visitors who intrude upon the work of Your impatient children, so that they may learn not to be impatient, and that they may die to the gratification of being free to study or work as they please. You avail Yourself of slanderous tongues to destroy the reputation of Your innocent children, so that they may offer to You the sacrifice of both their innocence and their too highly-cherished reputation. Thus You make them nothing in their own eyes, and turn their hearts fully to You.

And this is because You are all Love, and consequently all jealousy. O jealous God—for that You are called,[33] a divided heart displeases You, and a wandering one excites Your pity. You are infinite in all things, in love as well as in wisdom and power. When You love, You love like an infinite God. You move heaven and earth to save Your loved ones. You became man, a babe, the vilest of men, covered with reproaches, dying with infamy and under the pangs of the Cross—all this is not too much for an infinite love.

Our finite love and limited wisdom cannot understand it. How can the finite comprehend the Infinite? It has neither eyes to see it nor a heart to take it in. The debased and narrowed soul of humanity and its vain wisdom are offended, and can perceive no trace of God in this excess of love. But for myself, it is by this very character of infinity that I recognize it—this is the love that does all things. It is the love that brings to pass even the evils we suffer, and so shapes them that they are but the instruments of preparing the good that has not yet arrived.[34]

But when will we return love for His love? When will we seek Him who seeks us and constantly carries us in His arms? When He bears us along in His tender and paternal bosom, it is then that we forget Him. In the sweetness of His gifts, we forget the Giver. His ceaseless blessings, instead of melting us into love, distract our attention and turn it away from Him.

3
Pure Love

"The Lord hath made all things for Himself."[35]

Everything belongs to Him and He will never release His right to anything. Free and intelligent creatures are His as much as those which are otherwise. He attributes every unintelligent thing totally and absolutely to Himself, and He desires that His intelligent creatures should voluntarily make the same disposition of themselves. It is true that He desires our happiness, but that is neither the chief end of His work, nor an end to be compared with that of His glory. It is for His glory only that He wills our happiness, which is a subordinate consideration that He attributes to the final and essential end of His glory.

To enter into His designs in this respect, we must prefer God before ourselves and endeavor to will our own happiness for His glory. If we try to do it any other way, we invert the order of things. And we must not desire His glory on account of our own salvation. Instead, the desire for His glory should impel us to seek our own happiness as a thing that He has been pleased to make a part of His glory.

It is true that all holy souls are not capable of exercising this unreserved preference for God over themselves, but there must at least be an inferred preference. An unreserved preference is more perfect, but is reserved for those whom God has endowed with light and strength to prefer Him to themselves. Prefer Him to such a degree as to desire their own happiness simply because it adds to His glory.

People have a great dislike for this truth, and consider it to be a very hard saying,[36] because they are lovers of self from self-interest. They understand, in a general and superficial way, that they must love God more than all His creatures. But they have no conception of loving God more than themselves, and loving themselves only for Him.

They can utter these great words without difficulty, because they do not enter into their meaning. They shudder, however, when it is explained to them that God and His glory are to be preferred before ourselves and everything else. To such a degree, in fact, that we must love His glory more than our own happiness, and must attribute our happiness to His glory, as a subordinate means to an end. [In other words, it is the full glory to God that will make us happy—nothing else will or can.]

4
Prayer and the principal exercises of piety

True prayer is only another name for the love of God. Its excellence does not consist in the multitude of our words— "for your Father knoweth what things ye have need of, before ye ask him."[37]

The true prayer is that of the heart, and the heart prays only for what it desires. To pray, then is to desire—but to desire what God would have us desire. Those who ask for what is not from the bottom of their heart's desire are mistaken in thinking that they pray. Let them spend days in reciting prayers, in meditation, or in inciting themselves to pious exercises; they do not once pray truly if they do not really desire the things for which they ask.

Oh, how few there are who pray! For there are few who desire what is truly good! Crosses, external and internal humiliation, renouncement of our own wills, the death of self, and the establishment of God's throne upon the ruins of self love, these are [the things that are] indeed good. Not to desire these is not to pray. To desire them seriously, soberly, constantly, and with reference to all the details of life, this is true prayer. Not to desire them, and yet to suppose we pray, is an illusion like that of the wretched who dream themselves happy.

Alas! How many souls full of self, and of an imaginary desire for perfection in the midst of hosts of voluntary imperfections, have never yet uttered this true prayer of the heart! It is in reference to this that St. Augustine says: "He that loveth little, prayeth little. He that loveth much, prayeth much."

On the other hand, that heart in which the true love of God and true desire exist, never ceases to pray. Love, hid in the bottom of the soul, prays without ceasing, even when the mind is drawn another way. God continually beholds the desire that He has himself implanted in the soul, though it may at times be unconscious of its existence. God's heart is touched by it. It continually attracts Hhis mercies. It is that Spirit that, according to St. Paul, "helpeth our infirmities . . . [and] maketh intercession for us with groanings which cannot be uttered."[38]

Love desires that God would give us what we need, and that He would have less regard to our frailty than to the purity of our intentions. It even covers over our trifling defects, and purifies us like a consuming fire: "He maketh intercession for the Saints according to the will of God."[39] For "we know not what we should pray for as we ought,"[40] and, in our ignorance, frequently request what would be harmful [to us]. We would like fervor of devotion, distinct sensible joys and apparent perfections, which would serve to nourish within us the life of self and a confidence in our own strength. But love leads us on, abandons us to all the operations of grace, puts us entirely at the disposal of God's will, and thus prepares us for all His secret designs.

It is then we will all things and yet [we will] nothing. What God gives, is precisely what we would have desired to ask. For we will whatever He wills and only that. This state, therefore, contains all prayer—it is a work of the heart that includes all desire. The Spirit prays within us for those very things that the Spirit Himself wills to give us. Even when we are occupied with outward things, and our thoughts drawn off by the providential engagements of our position, we still carry within us a constantly burning fire. [It is a fire] that not only cannot be extinguished, but that nourishes a secret prayer, and is like a lamp continually lit before the throne of God, "I sleep, but my heart waketh."[41] "Blessed are those servants, whom the Lord when He cometh shall find watching."[42]

There are two principal points of attention necessary for the preservation of this constant spirit of prayer that unites us with God. We must continually seek to cherish it, and we must avoid everything that tends to make us lose it.

In order to cherish it, we should pursue a regulated course of reading, have appointed seasons of secret prayer, and frequent states of meditation during the day. We should greatly fear and be exceedingly cautious to avoid all things that have a tendency to make us lose this state of prayer. Thus we should decline those worldly occupations and associates that dissipate the mind, pleasures that excite the passions, and everything calculated to awaken the love of the world and those old inclinations that have caused us so much trouble.

There is an infinity of detail in these two principles, and only general directions can be given, because each individual case presents features peculiar to itself.

We should choose those books for reading that instruct us in our duty and in our faults. These are books that point out the greatness of God, teach us what is our duty to Him, and show how very far we are from performing it. [We should not waste time on] those barren productions that melt and sentimentalize the heart. The tree must bear fruit,[43] and we can only judge the life of the root by [the productivity of the tree].

The first effect of a sincere love is an earnest desire to know all that we should do to gratify the object of our affection. Any other desire is a proof that we love ourselves under a pretense of loving God. [It is proof] that we are seeking an empty and deceitful consolation in Him, and that we would use God as an instrument for our pleasure, instead of sacrificing that for His glory. God forbid that His children should so love Him! Cost what it may, we must both know and do without reservation what He requires of us.

Seasons of secret prayer must be regulated by the leisure, disposition, condition, and inward impulse of each individual.

Meditation is not prayer, but it is its necessary foundation— it brings to mind the truths that God has revealed. We should be conversant not only with all the mysteries of Jesus Christ, and the truths of His Gospel, but also with everything that they should accomplish in us for our regeneration. We should be penetrated and colored by them as wool is by the dye.

They should become so familiar to us, that, in consequence of seeing them at all times and ever near to us, we may acquire the habit of forming no judgment except in their light. They must be to us our only guide in matters of practice, as the rays of the sun are our only light in matters of perception.

When these truths are once incorporated in us, then it is that our praying begins to be real and fruitful. Up to that point, it was but the shadow [of prayer]. We thought we had penetrated to the inmost recesses of the gospel, when we had barely set foot upon the vestibule. All our most tender and lively feelings, all our firmest resolutions, all our clearest and farthest views, were but the rough and shapeless mass from which God would hew in us His likeness.

When His celestial rays begin to shine within us, then we see in the true light. Then there is no truth to which we do not instantaneously assent, just as we admit, without any process of reasoning, the splendor of the sun the moment we behold its rising beams. Our union with God must be the result of our faithfulness in doing and suffering all His will.

Our meditations should become deeper and more interior every day. I say deeper, because by frequent and humble meditation upon God's truth, we penetrate further and further in search of new treasures. [They also become] more interior, because as we sink more and more to enter into these truths, they also descend to penetrate the very substance of our souls. It is then that a simple word goes further than whole sermons.

The very things that had fruitlessly and coldly been heard a hundred times before, now nourish the soul with a hidden manna, and have an infinite variety of flavors for days in succession. We should also be careful that we do not stop meditating upon truths that have previously been blessed to us. [We should continue] so long as there remains any nourishment in them, and they yield us anything. That is a certain sign that we still need their ministration.

We derive instruction from them without receiving any precise or distinct impression. There is an indescribable something in them that helps us more than all our reasonings. We behold a truth, we love it, and rest upon it. When we do, it strengthens our soul and detaches us from ourselves. Let us dwell upon [that truth] in peace as long as possible.

As to the manner of meditating, it should not be subtle or composed of long reasoning. Simple and natural reflections derived immediately from the subject of our thoughts are all that is required.

We need take a few truths and meditate upon them without hurry, without effort, and without seeking for far-fetched reflections.

Every truth should be considered with reference to its practical bearing. To receive it without employing all means to put it faithfully in practice at whatever cost, is to desire to "hold the truth in unrighteousness."[44] It is a resistance to the truth impressed upon us and, of course, to the Holy Spirit. This is the most terrible of all unfaithfulness.

As to a method in prayer, each of us must be guided by personal experience. Those who profit by using a strict method need not depart from it. Those who cannot so confine themselves, may make use of their own method. [But in so doing, they must not] cease to respect that which has been useful to many, and which so many pious and experienced persons have highly recommended. A method is intended to assist. If it is found to hinder instead of assist, however, the sooner it is discarded the better.

In the beginning, the most natural method is to take a book or Bible, [read a few passages], and stop reading whenever we feel so inclined by the passage that we are reading. Whenever that passage no longer ministers to our interior nourishment, we should continue our reading.

As a general rule, those truths that we highly relish, and which shed a degree of practical light upon the things that we are required to give up for God, are leadings of divine grace, which we should follow without hesitation. "The wind (Spirit) bloweth where it listeth,"[45] (John iii. 8,) and "where the Spirit of the Lord is, there is liberty."[46]

In the progress of time, the proportion of reflections and reasonings will diminish, and those of tender feelings that affect views and desires will increase as we become sufficiently instructed and convinced by the Holy Spirit. The heart is thus satisfied, nourished, warmed, set on fire. Then a word alone will give it employment for a long time.

Finally, increase of prayer is indicated by an increase of simplicity and steadiness in our views. [At that point], a great multitude of objects and considerations are no longer necessary. Our intercourse with God now resembles that with a friend. At first, there are a thousand things to be told, and as many to be asked. But after a time, these diminish, while the pleasure of being together does not. Everything has been said, but the satisfaction of seeing each other, of feeling that one is near the other, or reposing in the enjoyment of a pure and sweet friendship, can be felt without conversation. The silence is eloquent and mutually understood. Each feels that they are in perfect sympathy with each other, and that their two hearts are unceasingly poured one into the other, and constitute but one.

Thus it is that in prayer our communion with God becomes a simple and familiar union, far beyond the need of words. But let it be remembered that God Himself must alone institute this prayer within us. Nothing would be more rash or more dangerous, than to dare to attempt it of ourselves. We must allow ourselves to be led step by step, often by some one experienced in the ways of God, who may lay the immovable foundations of correct teaching, and of the complete death of self in everything.

As precautions against wanderings, we must avoid close and intimate association with those who are not pious, especially when we have been led astray before by their infectious maxims. They will open our wounds afresh. For they have a secret associate deep in our souls. There is in our souls a soft and insinuating counselor who is always ready to blind and deceive us.

Would you judge others? Observe their companions. How can they who love God, and who love nothing except in and for God, enjoy the intimate companionship of those who neither love nor know God, and who look upon love for Him as a weakness? Can a heart full of God and sensible of its own frailty ever rest, and be at ease with those who have no feelings in common with it, but are ever seeking to rob it of its treasure? Their delights, and the pleasures of Him who is the source of all faith, are incompatible.

I am well aware that we cannot and should not break with those friends to whom we are bound by respect for their natural good nature, by their services, by the tie of sincere friendship. Friends whom we have treated with a certain familiarity and confidence, would be wounded to the quick, if we were to separate from them entirely. We must gently and imperceptibly diminish our association with them, without abruptly declaring our alteration of sentiment. We may see them in private, distinguish them from our less intimate friends, and confide to them those matters in which their integrity and friendship enable them to give us good advice. We may also invite them to think with us on certain matters, although the reasons and motives governing our thinking are more pure and elevated than theirs. In short, we may continue to serve them, and to manifest all the attentions of a cordial friendship, without allowing our hearts to be embarrassed by them.

How perilous is our state without this precaution! If from the first, we do not boldly adopt all measures to render our piety entirely free and independent of our unregenerate friends, it is threatened with a speedy downfall. If a person surrounded by such companions be of a yielding disposition and inflammable passions, it is certain that those friends, even the best-intentioned ones, will lead that soul astray. They may be good, honest, faithful, and possessed of all those qualities that render friendship perfect in the eye of the world.

But to those [who are united to God] they are infected, and their amiability only increases the danger. Those who have not this estimable character, would be sacrificed at once. We are blessed when a sacrifice that cost us so little, may serve to give us so precious a security for our eternal salvation!

Not only, then, should we be exceedingly careful whom we see, but we must also reserve the necessary time that we may see God alone in prayer. Those who have positions of importance to fill, have generally so many indispensable duties to perform, that without the greatest care in the management of their time, none will be left to be alone with God. If they have ever so little inclination for dissipation, the hours that belong to God and their neighbor disappear altogether.

We must be firm in observing our rules. This strictness

seems excessive, but without it everything falls into confusion. We become dissipated, relaxed, and lose strength. We insensibly[47] separate from God, surrender ourselves to all our pleasures, and only then begin to perceive that we have wandered. But by then it is almost hopeless to think of trying to return.

Prayer, prayer! This is our only safety. "Blessed be God, which hath not turned away my prayer, nor His mercy from me."[48] To be faithful in prayer, it is essential that we arrange all the activities of our day with a regularity nothing can disturb.

5
Conformity to the life of Jesus Christ

We must imitate Jesus—live as He lived, think as He thought, and be conformed to His image,[49] which is the seal of our sanctification.

What a contrast! Nothingness strives to be something, and the Omnipotent becomes nothing! I will be nothing with You, my Lord! I offer You the pride and vanity that have possessed me in the past. Help my will. Remove from me occasions of my stumbling: "turn away mine eyes from beholding vanity."[50] Let me behold nothing but You and myself in Your presence, that I may understand what I am and what You are.

Jesus Christ was born in a stable. He was obliged to travel into Egypt. Thirty years of His life were spent in a workshop. He suffered hunger, thirst, and weariness. He was poor, despised, and miserable. He taught the doctrines of Heaven, and no one would listen. The great and the wise persecuted, captured, and subjected Him to frightful torments. They treated Him as a slave and put Him to death between two criminals, having preferred to give liberty to a murderer, rather than to allow Him to escape their hatred. This was the life that our Lord chose—while we are horrified at any kind of humiliation [for ourselves], and cannot bear the slightest appearance of contempt.

Let us compare our lives with that of Jesus Christ, reflecting that He was the Master and that we are the servants. That He was all-powerful, and that we are but weakness. That He was abased and that we are exalted. Let us so constantly bear our wretchedness in mind, that we may have nothing but contempt for ourselves. With what justification can we despise others, and dwell upon their faults, when we ourselves are filled with nothing else? Let us begin to walk in the path that our Savior has marked out, for it is the only one that can lead us to Him.

How can we expect to find Christ if we do not seek Him in the states of His earthly life, in loneliness and silence, in poverty and suffering, in persecution and contempt, in annihilation and the cross? The saints find Him in heaven, in the splendors of glory and in unspeakable pleasures. But it is only after having dwelt with Him on earth in reproaches, in pain, and in humiliation.

To be a Christian is to be an imitator of Jesus Christ.[51] In what can we imitate Him if not in His humiliation? Nothing else can bring us near to Him. We may adore Him as Omnipotent, fear Him as just, love Him with all our heart as good and merciful—but we can only imitate Him as humble, submissive, poor, and despised.

Let us not imagine that we can do this by our own efforts. Everything that is written is opposed to it. But we may rejoice in the presence of God. Jesus chose to be made partaker of all our weaknesses. He is a compassionate high-priest who voluntarily submitted to be tempted in all points like as we are. Let us, then, have all our strength in Him who became weak that He might strengthen us. Let us enrich ourselves out of His poverty, confidently exclaiming, "I can do all things through Christ which strengtheneth me."[52]

Let me follow in Your footsteps, O Jesus! I would imitate You, but cannot without the aid of Your grace! O humble and lowly Savior, grant me the knowledge of the true Christian, and [give me the grace] that I may willingly despise myself. Let me learn the lesson, so incomprehensible to the mind of humanity, that I must die to myself by an abandonment that will produce true humility.

Let us earnestly engage in this work, and change this hard heart, so rebellious to the heart of Jesus Christ. Let us make some approaches toward the holy soul of Christ. Let Him animate our souls and destroy all our repugnancies. O lovely Christ, who suffered so many injuries and reproaches for my sake, let me esteem and love them for Your sake,[53] and let me desire to share Your life of humiliation!

6
Humility

What a mercy humiliation is to a soul that receives it with a steadfast faith! There are a thousand blessings in it for ourselves and for others, for our Lord bestows His grace upon the humble.[54] Humility makes us charitable toward our neighbor. Nothing will make us so tender and indulgent to the faults of others as a view of our own.

Two things produce humility when combined. The first is a sight of the abyss of wretchedness from which the all-powerful hand of God has snatched us, and over which He still holds us, as it were, suspended in the air. The other is the presence of that God who is All in all, who is Everything to everything.

Our faults, even those most difficult to bear, will all be of service to us if we make use of them for our humiliation, without relaxing our efforts to correct them. It does no good to be discouraged. Discouragement is the result of a disappointed and despairing self-love. The true method of profiting by the humiliation of our faults, is to see them in all their deformity without losing our hope in God, and without having any confidence in ourselves.

We must bear with ourselves without either flattery or discouragement—a balance seldom attained. For we either expect great things of ourselves and of our good intentions, or wholly despair of either. We must hope nothing for self, but wait for everything from God. Utter despair of ourselves, in consequence of a conviction of our helplessness, and unbounded confidence in God, are the true foundations of a strong spiritual structure.

It is a false humility that acknowledges itself unworthy of the gifts of God, but does not dare to confidently expect them. True humility consists in a deep view of our utter unworthiness and an absolute abandonment to God, without the slightest doubt that He will do the greatest things in us.

Those who are truly humble will be surprised to hear anything exalted of themselves. They are mild and peaceful, of a contrite and humble heart, and merciful and compassionate. They are quiet, cheerful, obedient, watchful, fervent in spirit, and incapable of strife. They always take the lowest place, rejoice when they are despised, and consider every one superior to themselves. They are lenient to the faults of others in view of their own, and are very far from preferring themselves before anyone. We may judge our advancement in humility by the delight we have in humiliations and contempt.

7
Prayer

Many are tempted to believe that they no longer pray when they stop enjoying a certain pleasure in the act of prayer. But, if they will reflect that perfect prayer is only another name for love to God, they will be undeceived.

Prayer, then, does not consist in sweet feelings, or in the charms of an excited imagination, or in that illumination of the intellect that traces with ease the highest truths in God, or in any comfort received from praying. All these things are external gifts from His hand. In their absence, however, love may exist even more purely, for the soul may then attach itself immediately and solely to God, instead of to His gifts.

This is the love by naked faith that is the death of nature, because it leaves it no support. When we are convinced that all is lost, that very conviction is the evidence that all is gained.

Pure love is in the will alone. It is not sentimental love, for the imagination has no part in it. It loves, if we may so express it, without feeling, as faith believes without seeing. We need not fear that this love is an imaginary thing—nothing can be less so with the will separated from all imagination. The more of the operations of our minds are purely intellectual and spiritual, the nearer they are to reality and the perfection that God requires of us. In this state, the operations are more perfect; faith is in full exercise, and humility is preserved.

Such love is pure, for it is the love of God in and for God. We are attached to Him, but not for the pleasure that He bestows on us. We follow Him, but not for the loaves and fishes.[55]

[Some may exclaim and ask] if it can be that a simple will united with God is the whole of piety? [They may question] how we can be assured that this will is not a mere idea, a trick of the imagination, instead of a true willing of the soul?

I would indeed believe that it was a deception, if it were not the parent of faithfulness on all proper occasions. For a "good tree bringeth forth good fruit,[56] and a true will makes us truly earnest and diligent in doing the will of God. A true will, however, is still compatible in this life with those little failings that are permitted by God so that the soul may be humbled. If, then, we experience only these little daily frailties, let us not be discouraged, but extract from them their proper fruit—humility.

True virtue and pure love reside in the will alone. It is a great virtue to always desire God, to keep the mind steadily turned toward Him, and to bring it back whenever it is perceived to wander. In short, to will nothing but what He wills, and in the absence of all sensible[57] enjoyment to remain the same in the spirit of a submissive, irreclaimable, burnt-offering.

Do you think it is nothing to repress all the uneasy reflections of self-love, to press forward continually without knowing where we go, and do it without stopping? Further, to cease from self-satisfied thoughts of self—or at least, to think of ourselves as we would of another, and to fulfill the indications of Providence at the moment and no more? Is this not more likely to be the death of the Old Adam than fine sentiments—sentiments in which we are, in fact, thinking only of self? And even more likely a death than doing external acts and congratulating ourselves on our advancement because we have performed them?

It is a sort of infidelity to simple faith when we desire to be continually assured that we are doing well. It is, in fact, [wrong] to desire to know how we are doing, which we will never know, and which it is the will of God that we be ignorant about. It is being frivolous along the way in order to reason about the way. The safest and shortest course is to renounce, forget, and abandon self, and through faithfulness to God think no more of it. This is the whole of Christianity—to get out of self and self-love in order to get into God.

As to involuntary wanderings, they are no hindrance to love, inasmuch as love is in the will, and the will only wanders when it wills to wander. As soon as we perceive that we have wandered, we stop it instantly and return to God. Thus, while the external senses of the spouse are asleep, the heart is watching—its love knows no intermission.

Tender parents do not always have their child distinctly in mind. They think and imagine a thousand things unconnected with the child, but those things do not interfere with the paternal affection. The moment their thoughts rest again upon their child, they love, and feel in the depths of their souls that though they have ceased to think of their child, they have not for an instant failed to love the child. Such should be our love to our Heavenly Father—a love simple, trustful, confident, and without anxiety.

If our imagination take wing and our thoughts wander, let us not be perplexed. All these things are not that "hidden man of the heart, in that which is not corruptible, even the ornament of a meek and quiet spirit," of which St. Peter speaks.[58] Let us only turn our thoughts, whenever we can, toward the face of the Well-beloved[59] without being troubled at our wanderings. When He shall see fit to enable us to preserve a more constant sense of His presence with us, He will do so.

He sometimes removes [the sense of His presence] for our advancement. It pleases us with too many thoughts that are true distractions, diverting the mind from a simple and direct look toward God, and withdrawing us from the shades of naked faith.

We often seek in these reflective thoughts a resting-place for our self-love, and consolation for self in the testimony we endeavor to extract from them. Thus the warmth of our feelings causes us to wander. But we never pray so purely as when we are tempted to believe that we do not pray at all. We fear that we do not pray rightly, but we should only fear being left to the desolation of a sinful nature, and to a philosophical unfaithfulness that perpetually seeks a demonstration of its own operations in faith. In short, to impatient desires for consolation in sight and feeling.

There is no more bitter penance than this state of pure faith without sensible support. So it seems to me [that this state is] the most effective, the most crucifying, and the least illusive. Strange temptation! We look impatiently for sensible consolation from the fear of not being penitent enough! But why do we not consider the renouncement of that consolation that we are so strongly tempted to seek, as a proof of our penitence?

Remember our Lord [seemingly] abandoned by His Father on the Cross. All feeling, all reflection withdrawn so His God might be hidden from Him. This was indeed the last blow that fell upon the man of sorrows, the consummation of the sacrifice!

[There is never a time when] we should abandon ourselves so [much] to God as when He seems to abandon us. Let us enjoy light and consolation when it is His pleasure to give it to us, but let us not attach ourselves to His gifts, but to Him. And when He plunges us into the darkness of pure faith, let us still press on through the agonizing night.

Moments are worth days in this tribulation. The soul is troubled and yet at peace. Not only is God hidden from it, but it is hidden from itself, that all may be of faith. It is discouraged, but feels nevertheless an immovable will to bear all that God may choose to inflict. It wills all, accepts all, even the troubles that try its faith, and thus in the very height of the tempest, the waters beneath are secretly calm and at peace, because its will is one with God's.

Blessed be the Lord who performs such great things in us, notwithstanding our unworthiness!

8
Meditation

When the solid foundation of a perfect conversion of heart has been laid, along with a definite repentance and a serious meditation of all the Christian virtues, both theoretically and practically, we gradually become so accustomed to the truths we have considered, that we regard them at last with a simple and steady look. We no longer find it necessary to go back continually to examine and convince ourselves of each of them in detail.

They are then all embraced in a certain enjoyment of God, so pure and so intimate, that we find everything in Him. It is no longer our intellect that examines and reasons—it is our will that loves and plunges into the infinite Good.

But this is [may] not [yet be] your state. You [may still have to] walk for a long while in the way of the those who are just beginning to seek God [for Himself alone]. So [though] ordinary meditation [may yet be] your lot, be happy that God condescends to admit you to it.

Walk then in the spirit like Abraham, without knowing whither you go.[60] be content with your daily bread,[61] and remember that in the desert the manna of today could not be preserved until tomorrow without corrupting.[62] The children of God must be shut up to the grace of the present moment, without desiring to foresee the designs of Providence concerning them.[63]

Since you now have the opportunity, meditate upon all the mysteries of Jesus Christ and upon all the Gospel truths that you have ignored and rejected for so long a time. When God will have entirely removed from your mind the impression of all your worldly maxims, and the Spirit will have left there no trace of your old prejudices, it will then be necessary to determine the direction in which you are attracted by grace, and to follow step by step without [trying to] anticipate [where you are going].

In the meantime, dwell in peace in the bosom of God,[64] like a little child on the breast of its mother. Be satisfied with thinking on your chosen subject simply and easily. Allow yourself to be led gently to the truths that affect you, and that nourish your heart. Avoid all exertions that excite the intellect, which often tempt us to believe that there is more piety in a dangerous liveliness of the imagination, than in a pure and upright intention of abandonment to God. Avoid likewise all elaborate speculation. Confine yourself to simple reflections, and return to them frequently. Those who pass too rapidly from one truth to another feed their curiosity and restlessness. They even distract their intellect by considering too many viewpoints.

Give every truth time to send down deep roots into your heart. The main point is to love. Nothing gives rise to such severe fits of indigestion as eating too much and too hastily. [It is the same with truth, so] digest every truth leisurely, if you would extract the essence of it for your nourishment, but let there be no restless self-reflective acts. Know that your exercise will not be acceptable [to God] unless performed without restlessness or agitation.

I am well aware that you will have enough distractions. Bear them without impatience, dismiss them, and return quietly to your subject as soon as you perceive that your imagination has wandered. In this way, these involuntary distractions will produce no injurious effects. [In addition], the patience with which you bear them without being discouraged will advance you further than a more continuous meditation, in which you might take more self-satisfaction. The true method of conquering wandering thoughts is never to attack them directly with harshness, and never to be discouraged by their frequency or duration.

Allow yourself, then, to be quietly occupied by the subject you have chosen. Let the exercise be as holy as you can make it. To this end, consider the following directions:

Do not burden yourself with a great number of thoughts upon a subject. Simply dwell upon each sufficiently long to allow it to provide its proper nourishment to your heart. You will gradually become accustomed to regard each truth steadily by itself, without flitting from one to another. This habit will serve to fix [the truths] deeply in your soul.

[In this way you will also] acquire a habit of dwelling upon your themes with pleasure and peaceful acceptance, instead of considering them rapidly and intellectually as most persons do. Thus the foundation will be firmly laid for all that God intends to do in you. [By this He will] discipline the natural activity of your mind that is always disposed to seek novelties, instead of deeply imprinting the truths that are in some degree already familiar [to you].

You must not, however, forcibly make your mind [dwell upon] a subject that no longer seems to afford any nourishment [to it]. I would advise only that you should not abandon [the subject] so long as it still ministers food [to you].

As to your affections, retain all that the view of your subject naturally and quietly induces. But do not attempt to stir yourself up to great efforts, for they will exhaust and agitate you, and even cause [periods of dryness]. Such efforts will occupy you too much with your own exertions, and implant a dangerous confidence in your own power. In short, they will attach you too firmly to sensible pleasures, and will thus present you great trouble in a time of dryness.

Be content, then, to follow with simplicity, and without too many reflections, the emotions that God excites [within you] in [light of] your subject, or of any other truth. As for higher things, have no thoughts of them. There is a time for everything, and it is of the greatest importance that you cause nothing to happen prematurely.

One of the cardinal rules of the spiritual life is this—we are to live exclusively in the present moment, without casting a look beyond [this moment]. You remember that the Israelites in the desert followed the pillar of fire, or of cloud,[65] without knowing where it was leading them. They had a supply of manna for only one day—anything more than that became useless.

There is no necessity now for moving rapidly. Think only of laying a solid foundation. See that it is deep and broad by an absolute renunciation of self, and by an abandonment without reserve to the requirements of God. Let God, then, raise upon this foundation such a building as He pleases. Shut your eyes and commit yourself to Him. How wonderful is this walking with Abraham in pure faith, not knowing where we go![66] How full of blessings is the path!

God will be your guide. He Himself will travel with you, as we are told He did with the Israelites, to bring them step by step across the desert to the Promised Land. Ah, what will be your blessedness if you will but surrender yourself into the hands of God, permitting Him to do whatever He will, not according to your desires, but according to His own good pleasure!

9
Mortification

God calls us hourly and momentarily to the exercise of self-discipline. But nothing can be more false than the maxim that we should always choose that which denies us the most. Such a plan would soon destroy our health, our reputation, our business, our relationship with our relatives and friends, and the good works that Providence requires of us.

I have no hesitation in saying that we should avoid certain things that experience has shown us will injure our health, such as certain kinds of food, etc. This course will, no doubt, spare us some suffering. But it does not tend to pamper the body or require the employment of expensive or delicious substitutes. On the contrary, it contributes to a sober and, therefore, disciplined life in many areas.

Failures in self-control are due to a lack of self-discipline. They are not due either to courage in enduring pain, or to indifference to life, but to a weak hankering for pleasure, and impatience of anything that annoys.

Submitting to self-control for the purpose of preserving our health is a great constraint. But we would much rather suffer and be sick than be constantly restraining our appetites. We love liberty and pleasure more than health.

But God arranges everything in the heart that is devoted to Him. He causes us to fall in quietly with every regulation, and takes away a certain lack of pliability in our will, and a dangerous confidence in ourselves. He blunts the desires, cools the passions, and detaches the person not only from exterior things but from self. In so doing, He renders the person mild, amiable, simple, lowly, ready to will or not, according to His good pleasure.[67]

Let it be so with us. God desires it, and is ready to work it [in us]. Let us not resist His will. The self-discipline that comes in God's order [and from Him] is more usable [and durable] than any enjoyment in devotion that results from our own desires and choice.

In regard to strict disciplines, each of us must consider our temptations, condition, need, and temperament. A simple self-discipline, consisting in nothing more than an unshaken faithfulness in providential crosses, is often far more valuable than severe self-denials that render the life more noticeable and tempt to a vain self-complacency. Whoever will refuse nothing that comes in God's order, and seek nothing out of that order, need never fear to finish the day's work without partaking of the cross of Jesus Christ.[68]

When a soul is not faithful in providential disciplines, there is reason to fear some illusion in those that are sought through the fervor of devotion. Such fervor is often deceitful, and it seems to me that a soul in this case would do well to examine its faithfulness under the daily crosses allotted by Providence.

10
Self-abandonment

If you want to fully understand the meaning of self-abandonment, think of the interior difficulty that you felt, and that you very naturally witnessed, when I directed you always to count as nothing this self that is so dear to us. To abandon one's self is to count one's self as nothing. Those who have perceived the difficulty of doing it, have already learned what the renunciation is that so revolts our nature. Since you have felt the blow, it is evident that it has fallen upon the sore spot in your heart. Let the all-powerful hand of God work in you, because He well knows how to tear you from yourself.

The origin of our trouble is that we love ourselves with a blind passion that amounts to idolatry. If we love anything beyond [ourselves], it is only for our own sakes. We must be undeceived concerning all those generous friendships in which it appears as though we so far forgot ourselves as to think only of the interests of our friend. If the motive of our friendship is not low and gross, it is nevertheless still selfish. The more delicate, more concealed, and more proper our motive is in the eyes of the world, the more dangerous it becomes, and the more likely to poison us by feeding our self-love.

In those friendships that appear to ourselves and to the world to be so generous and disinterested, we seek, in short, the pleasure of loving without recompense. We do it by indulgencing in the noble sentiment that we have raised ourselves above the weak and sordid of our race. Besides the tribute that we pay to our own pride, we seek from the world the reputation of disinterestedness and generosity.

We desire to be loved by our friends, although we do not desire to be served by them. We hope that they will be charmed with what we do for them without any expectation of return [to us]. In this way we get that very return that we seem to despise. For what is more delicious to a delicate self-love, than to hear itself applauded for not being self-love?

You may have seen some who seem to think of every one but themselves. They were the delight of good people, well disciplined, and seemed entirely forgetful of self. The self-oblivion is so great that self-love even imitates it, and finds no glory equal to that of seeming to seek none at all.

If genuine, this moderation and self-renunciation would be the death of nature. Instead, it becomes the most subtle and imperceptible food of a pride that despises all ordinary forms of glory. A pride that desires only that which is obtained by trampling under foot all the gross objects of ambition that captivate ordinary minds.

But it is not a difficult matter to unmask this modest arrogance—this pride that seems to be no pride at all. So much so, in fact, that it appears to have renounced all the ordinary objects of desire. But condemn it, and it cannot bear to be found fault with. Let those whom it loves fail to repay it with friendship, esteem, and confidence, and it is stung to the quick.

It is easy to see, therefore, that it is not disinterested, though it tries so hard to seem so. It does not indeed accept payment in gross coin as others. It does not desire insipid praise, or money, or that good fortune that consists in office and dignities. Nevertheless, it must be paid. It is greedy for the esteem of good people. It loves that it may be loved again and be admired for its disinterestedness. It seems [to everyone] to forget self, but that is only the means by which it draws the attention of the whole world upon self alone.

It does not, indeed, make all these reflections [to itself] in full detail. It does not say [to itself] in so many words, "I will deceive the whole world with my generosity so that the world will love and admire me. No, it would not dare to speak such gross and unworthy words to itself. It deceives itself with the rest of the world. It admires itself in its generosity, as a woman admires her beauty in a mirror. It is affected by believing that it is more generous and more disinterested than the rest of humanity. The illusion it prepares for others extends to itself. It deludes itself that it is what it deludes others to believe it is—that is, generous, and this is what pleases it more than anything else.

However little we may have looked within to study the occasions of our pleasure and our grief, we will have no difficulty in admitting that pride, as it is more or less subtle, has various tastes. But give it what taste you will, it is still pride. That which appears the most restrained and the most reasonable, is the most devilish. In esteeming itself, it despises others. It pities those who are pleased with foolish vanities. It recognizes the emptiness of greatness and rank. It cannot stand those who are intoxicated with good fortune. It would, by its moderation, be above fortune, and thus raise itself to a new height by putting under foot all the false glory of others. Like Lucifer, it would become like to the Most High.[69] It would be a sort of divinity, above all human passions and interests, and it does not see that it seeks to place itself above everyone by this deceitful pride that blinds it.

We may be sure, then, that it is the love of God only that can make us come out of self. If His powerful hand did not sustain us, we would not know how to take the first step in that direction.

There is no middle course. We must refer everything either to God or to self. If to self, we have no other God than self. If to God, we are then in a proper state. In that state, regarding ourselves only as one among the other creatures of God, without selfish interests, and with a single eye to accomplish His will, we enter into that self-abandonment that you desire so earnestly to understand.

But nothing will so shut your heart against the grace of abandonment as that philosophic pride and self love in the disguise of worldly generosity. You should be especially in fear of it because of your natural disposition towards it. The greater our inherent endowment of frankness, disinterestedness, pleasure in doing good, sensitivity of feeling, love of honor, and generous friendship, the more lively should be our distrust of self. And the greater should be our fear lest we become complacent in these gifts of nature.

The reason why no creature can draw us out of ourselves is that there is none that deserves to be preferred before ourselves. There is none that has the right to so detach us, or the perfection that would be necessary to unite us to them without reference to ourselves, or the power to satisfy the soul in such an attachment.

Thus it is that we love nothing outside of ourselves, except for the reference it has to self. We choose under the direction of our coarse and brutal passions if we are low and boorish, or under the guidance of a refined desire for glory if we are so refined as not to be satisfied with what is gross and vulgar.

But God does two things, which He only has the power to do. He reveals Himself to us, with all His rights over the creature and in all the charms of His goodness. When He does, we feel that since we have not made ourselves, we are not made for ourselves. That we are created for the glory of Him whom it has pleased to form us. That He is too great to make anything except for Himself. And that, therefore, all our perfection and our happiness should be to be lost in Him.

This is what no created thing, dazzling though it may be, can make us realize in respect to itself. Far from finding in them that infinity that so fills and transports us in God, we discover only a void, a powerlessness to fill our hearts, an imperfection that continually drives us into ourselves.

The second miracle that God works is to operate in our hearts that which He pleases, after having enlightened our understanding. He is not satisfied with having displayed His own charms. He makes us love Him by producing by grace His love in our hearts. Thus He Himself performs within us, what He makes us see we owe to Him.

You desire, perhaps, to know more in detail in what this self-abandonment consists. I will endeavor to satisfy you.

There is little difficulty in understanding that we must reject criminal pleasures, unjust gains, and gross vanities, because the renouncement of these things consists in a contempt that repudiates them absolutely, and forbids our deriving any enjoyment from them. But it is not so easy to understand that we must abandon honestly acquired property, the pleasures of a modest and well-spent life, and the honors derivable from a good reputation and a virtue that elevates us above the reach of envy.

The reason why we do not understand that these things must be given up, is that we are not required to discard them in distaste. But, on the contrary, to preserve them to be used according to the station in which Divine Providence places us.

We have need of the consolation of a mild and peaceful life to console us in life's troubles. With respect to honors, we must regard "that which is convenient," and we must keep the property we possess to supply our wants. How then are we to renounce these things at the very time that we are occupied in the care of preserving them?

We are, moderately and without inordinate emotion, to do what is in our power to retain them in order to make a sober use of them, without desiring to enjoy them or placing our hearts upon them.

I say, a sober use of them, because when we are not attached to a thing for the purposes of self-enjoyment and of seeking our happiness in it, we use only so much of it as we are necessarily obliged to. It is the same as a wise and faithful steward appropriating only so much of the master's property as is precisely required to meet the needs of the household.

So, the abandonment of evil things consists in refusing them with horror. The abandonment of good things consists in using them with moderation for our necessities, and continually studying to retrench all those imaginary needs with which greedy nature would flatter itself.

Remember that we must not only renounce evil, but also good things, for Jesus has said, "Whatsoever he be of you that forsaketh not all he hath, he cannot be my disciple."[70]

It follows, then, that Christians must abandon everything that they have, however innocent. For, if we do not renounce it, it ceases to be innocent.

We must abandon those things that it is our duty to guard with the greatest possible care, such as the good of our family, or our own reputation, for we must have our heart on none of these things. We must preserve them for a sober and moderate use. In short, we must be ready to give them all up whenever it is the will of God to deprive us of them.

We must give up those whom we love best, and whom it is our duty to love. Our renouncement of them consists in this, that we are to love them for God only. We are to make use of the consolation of their friendship soberly, and be ready to part with them whenever God wills it, and never to seek in them the true peace of our heart. This is that chastity of true Christian friendship that seeks in the mortal and earthly friend only the heavenly spouse. It is thus that we use the world and the creature as not abusing them, according to Saint Paul.[71]

We do not desire to take pleasure in them. We only use what God gives us, what He wills that we should love. We accept them with the reserve of a heart that receives them only for necessity's sake, and that keeps itself for a more worthy object.

It is in this sense that Christ would have us leave father and mother, brothers and sisters, and friends,[72] and that He is come to bring a sword upon earth.[73]

God is a jealous God.[74] If you are attached to any creature in the recesses of your soul, your heart is not worthy of Him. He must reject it as a spouse that divides her affections between her bridegroom and a stranger. Having abandoned everything exterior (which is not self), it remains to complete the sacrifice by renouncing everything interior including self.

The renouncement of the body is frightful to most delicate and worldly-minded persons. They know nothing, so to speak, that is more themselves than this body, which they flatter and adorn with so much care. Even when deprived of its graces, they often retain a love for its life amounting to a shameful cowardice, so that the very name of death makes them shudder.

Your natural courage raises you above these fears, and I think I hear you say, "I desire neither to flatter my body, nor to hesitate in consenting to its destruction, whenever it will be the will of God to waste and consume it to ashes."

You may thus renounce the body, and yet there may remain great obstacles in the way of your renouncing your interior self. The more we are able, by the aid of our natural courage, to despise the clay tenement, the more apt we are to set a higher value upon that which it contains.

We feel towards our understanding, wisdom, and virtue, as a young and worldly woman feels towards her beauty. We take pleasure in them. It gives us a satisfaction to feel that we are wise, moderate, and preserved from the excitement that we see in others. We are intoxicated with the pleasure of not being intoxicated with pleasure. We renounce with courageous moderation the most flattering temptations of the world, and content ourselves with the satisfaction derived from a conviction of our self-control.

What a dangerous state! What a subtle poison! How unfaithful you are to God if you yield your heart to this refinement of self-love! You must renounce all satisfaction and all natural complacency in your own wisdom and virtue. Remember, the purer and more excellent the gifts of God, the more jealous He is of them.

He showed mercy to the first human rebel, and denied it to the angels. Both sinned by the love of self, but as the angel was perfect, and regarded as a sort of divinity. God punished his unfaithfulness with a fiercer jealousy than He did the man's disobedience. We may infer from this that God is more jealous of His most excellent gifts than He is of the more common ones. He would have us attached to nothing but Himself, and to regard His gifts, however excellent, as only the means of uniting us more easily and intimately to Him. Whoever contemplates the grace of God with a satisfaction and sort of pleasure of ownership, turns it into poison.

Never appropriate exterior things to yourself then, such as favor or talents, nor even things the most interior. Your good will is no less a gift of God's mercy than the life and humanity that you receive directly from His hands. Live, as it were, on trust. All that is in you, and all that you are, is only loaned to you. Make use of it according to the will of Him who lends it, but never regard it for a moment as your own.

Herein consists true self-abandonment. It is this spirit of self-divesting—this use of ourselves and all we have with a single eye to the movements of God, who alone is the true proprietor of His creatures.

You will desire to know, probably, what should be the practice of this renouncement in detail. But I [cannot] answer that, [for] the feeling is no sooner established in the interior of the soul, than God Himself will take you by the hand so that you may be exercised in self-renunciation in every event of every day.

Self-abandonment is not accomplished by means of painful reflections and continual struggles. It is only by refraining from self-contemplation, and from desiring to master ourselves in our own way, that we lose ourselves in God.

11
Temptations

I know of but two resources against temptations. One is to faithfully follow the interior light in sternly and immediately cutting off everything we are at liberty to dismiss, and which may excite or strengthen the temptation. I say everything that we are at liberty to dismiss, because we are not always permitted to avoid the occasions of evil. Those that are unavoidably connected with the particular position in which Providence has placed us are not considered to be within our power.

The other recourse consists in turning toward God in every temptation, without being disturbed or anxious to know if we have already yielded a sort of half consent [to the temptation], and without interrupting our immediate recourse to God. By examining too closely whether we have been guilty of some unfaithfulness, we incur the risk of being again entangled in the temptation. The shortest and surest way is to act like a little child at the breast. When we show the child a frightful monster, it shrinks back and buries its face in its mother's bosom, so that it may no longer see it.

The sovereign [and ultimate] remedy is the habit of dwelling continually in the presence of God.[75] He sustains, consoles, and calms us.

We must never be astonished at temptations, no matter how outrageous they may be. On this earth all is temptation. Crosses tempt us by irritating our pride, and prosperity by flattering it. Our life is a continual combat, but one in which Jesus Christ fights for us. We must pass on unmoved while temptations rage around us—in the same way that travelers who are overtaken by a storm simply wrap their cloaks more closely about themselves, and push on more vigorously toward their destination.

If the thought of former sins and wretchedness are permitted to come upon us, we must quietly remain before God, enduring in His adorable presence all the shame and humiliation of our transgressions. We must not, however, seek to entertain or to call up so dangerous a recollection.

In conclusion, it may be said that in doing what God wills there is very little to be done by us. Yet there is a wonderful work to be accomplished. It is no less than that of reserving nothing, and making no resistance for a moment to that jealous love that searches inexorably into the most secret recesses of the soul for the smallest trace of self, for the slightest intimations of an affection of which it is not the author. So, on the other hand, true progress does not consist in a multitude of views, nor in austerities, trouble, and strife. It is simply willing nothing and everything, without reservation and without choice, cheerfully performing each day's journey as Providence appoints it for us. We are to seek nothing, refuse nothing, find everything in the present moment, and allow God, who does everything, to do His pleasure in and by us without the slightest resistance. Oh, how happy are we who have attained to this state, and how full of good things is our soul when it is emptied of everything of self!

Let us pray the Lord to open to us the whole infinitude of His paternal heart, that our own may be there submerged and lost, so that it may be one with His! Such was the desire of Paul for the faithful, when he longed for them in the bowels of Jesus Christ.[76]

12
Wandering thoughts and dejection

Two things trouble you. One is how you may avoid wandering thoughts. The other is how you may be sustained against dejection. As to the former, you will never cure them by trying to hold your mind fast upon something.

You must not expect to do the work of grace by the resources and activity of nature. Be simply content to yield your will to God without reservation, and whenever any state of suffering is brought before you, accept it as His will in an absolute abandonment to His guidance.

Do not go out in search of these crucifixions, but when God permits them to reach you without your having sought them, they need never pass without your deriving profit from them.

Receive everything that God presents to your mind, notwithstanding the shrinking of nature, as a trial by which He would exercise and strengthen your faith. Never trouble yourself to inquire whether you will have strength to endure what is presented. For if it should actually come upon you, the moment of trial will have its appointed and sufficient grace.[77] What you must do is quietly consider the afflictions presented to you, and be willing to receive them whenever [you are certain] it is the will of God to bestow them.

Go on cheerfully and confidently in this trust. If this state of your will does not change as a result of a voluntary attachment to something [that is] out of the will of God, it will continue forever.

Your imagination will doubtless wander to a thousand matters of vanity. It will be subject to more or less agitation, according to your situation and the character of the objects presented for its consideration. But what matter? The imagination, as St. Theresa declares, is the fool of the household. It is constantly bustling about in some way or other, [trying] to distract the mind that cannot avoid beholding the images that it exhibits. The attention is inevitable, and is a true distraction. But so long as it is involuntary, it does not separate us from God. Nothing can do that but some distraction of our will—[that is, when we are willingly or deliberately distracted].

You will never have wandering thoughts if you never will to have them, and may then say with truth that you have prayed without ceasing. Whenever you perceive that you have involuntarily strayed away, return without effort, and you will peacefully find God again without any disturbance of soul. As long as you are not aware of it, it is no wandering of the heart. When it is made apparent [to you], look to God at once with fidelity, and you will find that this simple faithfulness to Him will be the occasion of blessing you with His more constant and more familiar indwelling.

A frequent and easy recollection is one of the fruits of this faithful readiness to leave all wanderings as soon as they are perceived. But we must not suppose that it can be accomplished by our own labors. Such efforts would produce trouble, scrupulosity, and restlessness in all those matters in which you have most occasion to be free. You will be constantly dreading lest you should lose the presence of God and continually endeavoring to recover it. You will surround yourself with the creations of your own imagination. When this happens, the sweet and illuminating presence of God, which should assist us in everything that comes before us in His providence, will have the effect of keeping us always in a tumult, and render us incapable of performing the exterior duties of our condition.

Do not be troubled, then, at the loss of the sensible presence of God. But, above all, beware of trying to retain Him by a multitude of argumentative and reflective acts. Be satisfied during the day, and while about the details of your daily duties, with a general and interior view of God. Then if asked at any time about the direction of your heart, you may answer with truth that it is toward God, even though the attention of your mind may then be engaged by something else.

Do not be troubled by the wanderings of your imagination that you cannot prevent. Often we wander through the fear of wandering and the regret that we have done so! What would you say of travelers who instead of constantly advancing in their journey employed their time in anticipating the falls that they might suffer, or in weeping over the place where one had happened? On! on! you would say to them, on! without looking behind or stopping. We must proceed, as the Apostle bids us, that we may abound more and more.[78] The abundance of the love of God will be of more service in correcting us than all our restlessness and selfish reflections.

This rule is simple enough. But nature is accustomed to the intricacies of reasoning and reflection, and so considers it as altogether too simple. We want to help ourselves, and to communicate more movement to our progress. But it is the very excellence of the precept that it confines us to a state of naked faith, sustained by God alone in our absolute abandonment to Him, and leads us to the death of self by stifling all remains of it whatever. In this way, we will not feel we must increase our external devotional acts even if we are exceedingly busy or are feeble in body, but will be contented with turning them all into simple love. Thus we will only act as compelled by love, and will never be overburdened, for we will only do what we love to do.

Dejection often arises from the fact that in seeking God we have not found Him in a way to satisfy us. The desire to find Him is not the desire to possess Him. It is simply a selfish anxiety to be assured for our own comfort that we do possess Him.

Depressed and discouraged, our poor nature is impatient with the restrictions of naked faith, where every support is withdrawn. It is grieved to be traveling, as it were, in the air, where it cannot behold its own progress toward perfection. Its pride is irritated by a view of its defects, and this sentiment is mistaken for humility. Its self-love longs to behold itself perfect. It is annoyed that it is not perfect already, and so is impatient, haughty, and out of temper with itself and everybody else. Sad state! As though the work of God could be accomplished by our ill-humor! As though the peace of God could be attained by means of such interior restlessness!

Martha, Martha! why are you troubled and anxious about many things? One thing is needful, to love Him and to sit attentively at His feet![79]

When we are truly abandoned to God, all things are accomplished without the performance of useless labor. We allow ourselves to be guided in perfect trust. For the future, we will whatever God wills, and shut our eyes to everything else. For the present, we give ourselves up to the fulfillment of His designs.

Sufficient for every day is the good and the evil thereof[80] This daily doing of the will of God is the coming of His kingdom within us,[81] and at the same time our daily bread.[82] If we desire to penetrate the future, which God has hidden from us, we are faithless indeed and guilty of heathen distrust. Leave it to Him. Let Him make it short or long, bitter or sweet. Let Him do with it even as it will please Him.

The most perfect preparation for this future, whatever it may be, is to die to every will of our own, and yield ourselves wholly up to His. In this frame of mind, we will be ready to receive all the grace suitable to whatever state it is the will of God to develop in and around us.

When we are thus prepared for every event, we begin to feel the Rock under our feet at the very bottom of the abyss. We are ready to suppose every imaginable evil of ourselves, but we throw ourselves blindly into the arms of God, forgetting and losing everything else. This forgetfulness of self is the most perfect renouncement of self and acceptance of God. It is the sacrifice of self-love. [Now] it would be a thousand times more agreeable to accuse and condemn ourselves, to torment body and mind, rather than to forget [self].

Such an abandonment is an annihilation of self-love, in which it no longer finds any nourishment. Then the heart begins to expand. We begin to feel lighter for having thrown off the burden of self, which we formerly carried. We are astounded to behold the simplicity and straightness of the way. We thought there was a need of strife and constant exertion, but we now see that there is little to do. [We see] that it is sufficient to look to God with confidence, without reasoning either upon the past or the future, regarding Him as a loving Father, who leads us every moment by the hand.

If some distraction or other should hide Him for a moment, without stopping to look at it, we simply turn again to Him from whom we departed. If we commit faults, we repent with a repentance wholly of love, and when we return to God He makes us feel whatever we should feel. Sin seems hideous, but we love the humiliation of which it is the cause, and for which God permitted it.

As the reflections of our pride upon our defects are bitter, disheartening, and distressing, so the return of the soul toward God is renewing, peaceful, and sustained by confidence. You will find by experience how much more your progress will be aided by this simple, peaceful, turning to God, than by all your chagrin and spite at the faults that exist in you. Only be faithful in turning quietly toward God alone the moment you perceive what you have done. Do not stop to argue with yourself; you can gain nothing from that quarter. When you accuse yourself of your misery, I see but you and yourself in consultation. [Nothing but] poor wisdom ,ill issue from where God is not!

Whose hand is it that must pluck you out of the mire? Your own? Alas! you are buried deeper than thought, and cannot help yourself. Further, this very slough is nothing but self. The whole of your trouble consists in your inability to leave yourself. So how do you expect to increase your chances by dwelling constantly upon your defects, and feeding your sensitiveness by a view of your folly? That way you will only increase your difficulties, while the gentlest look toward God would calm your heart.

It is His presence that causes us to go forth from self, and when He has accomplished that, we are in peace. But how are we to go forth? Simply by turning gently toward God, and gradually forming the habit of so doing, by a faithful persistence in it, whenever we perceive that we have wandered from Him.[83]

The question is not, what is the state of our feelings, but what is the condition of our will. Let us will to have what is the condition of our will. Let us will to have whatever we have, and not to have whatever we have not. We would not even be delivered from our sufferings, for it is God's place to allot to us our crosses and our joys. In the midst of affliction we rejoice, as did the Apostle.[84] But it is not joy of the feelings, but of the will.

The wicked are wretched in the midst of their pleasures, because they are never content with their state. They are always desiring to remove some thorn, or to add some flower to their present condition. The faithful soul, on the other hand, has a will that is perfectly free. It accepts without questioning whatever bitter blessings God develops, and wills and embraces them. It would not be freed from them, if it could be accomplished by a simple wish. For such a wish would be an act originating in self, and contrary to its abandonment to Providence. [Above all things], it desires that this abandonment be absolutely perfect.

If there be anything capable of setting a soul in a large place, it is this absolute abandonment to God. It diffuses in the soul a peace that flows as a river, and a righteousness that is as the waves of the sea.[85]

If there is anything that can render the soul calm, dissipate its doubts and dispel its fears, sweeten its sufferings by the anointing of love, impart strength to it in all its actions, and spread abroad the joy of the Holy Spirit in its countenance and words, it is this simple, free, and child-like repose in the arms of God.

13
Confidence in God

The best rule we can ever adopt, is to receive equally, and with the same submission, everything that God sends us during the day, both internally and externally. Externally, there are disagreeable things that must be met with courage, and pleasant things that must not be allowed to capture our affections. We resist the temptations of the former by accepting them at once, and of the latter by refusing to admit them into our hearts.

The same course is necessary in regard to the internal life. Whatever is bitter serves to crucify us, and works all its benefit in the soul if we receive it simply, with a willingness that knows no bounds, and a readiness that seeks no alleviation.

Pleasant gifts, which are intended to support our weakness by giving us a sensible[86] consolation in our external acts, must be accepted with equal satisfaction, but in a different way. They must be received because God sends them, and not because they are agreeable to our own feelings. Like any medicine, they are to be used without self-complacency, without attachment to them, and without appropriation. We must accept them, but not hold on to them. That way, when God sees fit to withdraw them, we will be neither dejected nor discouraged.

The basic problem lies in our attachment to these transitory and sensible gifts. We imagine we have no regard for anything but the gift of God, while we are really looking to self, appropriating His mercy, and mistaking it for Him. Thus we become discouraged whenever we find that we have been deceived in ourselves. The soul that is sustained by God [alone], however, is not surprised at its own misery. It is delighted to find new proof that it can do nothing of itself, and that God must do everything.

I am never in the least troubled at being poor, when I know that my Father has infinite treasures that He will give me. We will soon become independent of trust in ourselves, if we suffer our hearts to feed upon absolute confidence in God.

We must count less upon sensible delights and the measures of wisdom that plan [or arrange or design] for our own perfection, than upon simplicity, lowliness, renunciation of our own efforts, and perfect pliability to all the designs of grace. Everything else tends to credit our virtues, and thus inspire a secret reliance upon our own resources.

Let us pray God that He would root out of our hearts everything of our own planting, and with His own hands plant there the tree of life, bearing all manner of fruits.[87]

14
How we are to watch ourselves

The following seem to me to be useful practical directions as to the manner in which we should watch ourselves, without being too much occupied with the duty.

Wise and diligent travelers watch all their steps, and keep their eyes always directed to that part of the road that is immediately before them. But they do not continually look behind them to count their steps and examine their footmarks— they would lose time and hinder their progress by so doing.

The soul that God truly leads by the hand (for I do not now speak of those who are learning to walk, and who are yet looking for the road), should watch its path. But [should do so] with a simple, tranquil, vigilance confined to the present moment, and without restlessness from love of self. Its attention should be continually directed to the will of God in order to fulfill it every instant, and not be engaged in reflective acts upon itself in order to be assured of its state—especially when God prefers it should be uncertain. Thus the Psalmist exclaims, "Mine eyes are ever toward the Lord; for He shall pluck my feet out of the net."[88]

In order to keep his feet in safety in a way sown with snares, the Psalmist raises his eyes to the Lord instead of fixing them upon the ground to scrutinize every step. We never watch so diligently over ourselves as when we walk in the presence of God, just as He commanded Abraham.[89] What, in fact, should be the goal of all our vigilance? To follow the will of God step by step. If we who conform to that in all things, we watch over ourselves and sanctify ourselves in everything.

If, then, we never lost sight of the presence of God, we would never cease to watch. [And we would always do so] with a simple, lovely, quiet, and disinterested[90] vigilance. But if we watched with a desire to be assured of our state, our watch would be harsh, restless, and full of self. We must walk not by our own light, but by that of God. We cannot behold the holiness of God without feeling horror at the smallest of our transgressions.

In addition to the presence of God and a state of watchfulness, we may add the examination of [our] conscience according to our need. Conducted, however, in a way that grows more and more simple, easy, and destitute of restless self-contemplations. We examine ourselves not for our own satisfaction, but to conform to the advice we receive [from spiritual guides], and to accomplish the will of God.

In short, we abandon ourselves into the hands of God, and are just as happy in knowing we are there as we would be miserable if we were in our own [hands]. We desire to see nothing of what it pleases Him to conceal. Because we love Him infinitely more than we do ourselves, we make an unconditional sacrifice of ourselves to His good pleasure. We desire only to love Him and to forget ourselves. By thus literally losing our soul in God, we find it again with eternal life.

15

The inward teaching of the Spirit of God

It is certain from the holy Scriptures[91] that the Spirit of God dwells within us, acts there, prays without ceasing, groans, desires, asks for us what we know not how to ask for ourselves, urges us on, animates us, speaks to us when we are silent, suggests to us all truth, and so unites us to Him that we become one spirit.[92]

This is the teaching of faith, and even those instructors who are farthest removed from the interior life cannot avoid acknowledging this much. Still, notwithstanding these theoretical principles, they always strive to maintain that in practice the external law, or at least a certain light of learning and reason, illuminates us within, and that then our understanding [meaning intellect or reasoning power] acts by itself [or on its own] from that instruction. [That is, understanding the external law brings internal illumination, which in turn creates external conformity to the law. We understand the external law, it enlightens our heart, and we then automatically obey the law.]

These instructors do not rely sufficiently upon the interior teacher, the Holy Spirit, who does everything in us. He is the soul of our soul—we could not form a thought or a desire without Him. Alas, what blindness is ours! We reckon ourselves alone in our internal sanctuary, when God is much more intimately present there than we are ourselves.

What, then, you will say, are we all inspired? Yes, doubtless—but not as were the prophets and apostles. Without the actual inspiration of the Spirit of grace, we could not do, will, or believe any good thing. We are, then, always inspired, but we continually stifle the inspiration. God does not cease to speak, but the external noise of the creatures, and of our internal passions, confines us and prevents our hearing. We must silence every creature, including self, so that in the deep stillness of the soul we may perceive the ineffable voice of the Bridegroom. We must lend an attentive ear, for His voice is soft and still,[93] and is only heard by those who hear nothing else!

Ah, how rare is it to find a soul quiet enough to hear God speak! The slightest murmur of our vain desires, or of a love fixed upon self, confounds all the words of the Spirit of God. We hear well enough that He is speaking, and that He is asking for something, but we cannot distinguish what is said, and are often glad enough that we cannot. The least reserve, the slightest self-reflective act, the most imperceptible fear of hearing too clearly what God demands, interferes with the interior voice.

Need we be astonished, then, if so many people who are pious but full of amusements, vain desires, false wisdom, and confidence in their own virtues, cannot hear it—[God's interior voice], and consider its existence to be a dream of fanatics? Alas, what else would they think with their proud reasonings? How effective would be the exterior word of pastors, or even of the Scriptures themselves, if we did not have within the word of the Holy Spirit, giving to the others all their vitality? The outward Word—even the Gospel—without the impregnating, animating, inner word would be but an empty sound. It is the letter that alone kills and the Spirit alone can give us life.[94]

Oh, eternal and omnipotent Word of the Father, it is You who speaks in the depth of our souls! The word that proceeded from the mouth of the Savior, during the days of His mortal life, has only had energy to produce such wondrous fruits, because it has been animated by that Spirit of life that is the Word itself. Thus it is that St. Peter said, "Lord, to whom shall we go? Thou hast the words of eternal life."[95]

It is not, then, the outward law of the Gospel alone that God shows us internally, by the light of reason and faith. It is His Spirit that speaks, touches, operates in [us] and animates us. So it is the Spirit that does in us and with us whatever we do that is good, as it is our soul that gives life to our body, and regulates all its movements.

It is, then, true, that we are continually inspired, and that we do not lead a gracious life, except so far as we act under this interior inspiration. But, Oh God, how few Christians feel it! How few there are who do not annihilate it by their voluntary distractions, or by their resistance!

Let us recognize, then, the fact that God is incessantly speaking in us. He speaks in the unrepentant also. But they are stunned by the noise of the world and their passions and cannot hear Him. The interior voice is to them a fable.

He speaks in awakened sinners, and they feel remorse in their conscience, which is the voice of God reproaching them inwardly for their sins. When they are deeply moved, they have no difficulty in understanding about this interior voice, for it pierces them so sharply. It is in them that two-edged sword of which [the writer of Hebrews] speaks as piercing even to the dividing asunder of soul and spirit.[96]

God causes Himself to be perceived, enjoyed, followed. They hear that sweet voice that buries a reproach in the bottom of the heart, and causes it to be torn in pieces. Such is true and pure contrition.

God speaks, too, in wise and enlightened persons, whose outward life is correct and seems adorned with many virtues. But such are often too full of themselves and their lights to listen to God. Everything is turned into reasoning. They substitute the principles of natural wisdom and the plans of human prudence, for what would come infinitely better through the channel of simplicity and docility to the Word of God.

They seem good, sometimes better than others. They are so, perhaps, up to a certain point, but it is a mixed goodness. They are still in possession of themselves, and desire always to be so, according to the measure of their reason. They love to be in the hands of their own counsel, and to be strong and great in their own eyes.

I thank You, O my God with Jesus Christ, that You have hid Your ineffable secrets from these great and wise ones, while You take pleasure in revealing them to feeble and humble souls![97] It is with babes alone that You are wholly unreserved. The others You treat in their own way. They desire knowledge and great virtues, and You give them dazzling illuminations, and convert them into heroes. But this is not the better part. There is something more hidden for Your dearest children. They lie with John on Your breast.[98]As for these great ones who are constantly afraid of stooping and becoming lowly, You leave them in all their greatness. They will never share Your caresses and Your familiarity—to deserve these, they must become as little children and play upon Your knees.

I have often observed that a rude, ignorant, sinner, just beginning to be touched by a lively sense of the love of God, is much more disposed to listen to this inward language of the Spirit of Grace, than those enlightened and learned persons who have grown old in their own wisdom. God, whose sole desire is to communicate Himself, cannot, so to speak, find where to set His foot in souls so full of themselves, and so fat with their own wisdom and virtues. But, as says the Scripture, "His secret is with the simple."[99]

But where are the simple? I do not find them. God sees them and loves to dwell in them; "My Father and I," says Jesus Christ, "will come unto him and make Our abode with him."[100] A soul delivered from self, abandoned to grace, counting itself as nothing, and walking without thought at the will of that pure love that is its perfect guide, has an experience that the wise can neither receive nor understand!

I was once as wise as any. Thinking I saw everything, I saw nothing. I crept along feeling my way by a succession of reasoning, but there was no ray to enlighten my darkness. I was content to reason. But when we have silenced everything within so we may listen to God, we know all things without knowing anything. We then understand that until that moment we were utterly ignorant of all that we thought we understood [before]. We lose all that we once had, and do not care. We then have nothing more that belongs to self. All things are lost, and we with them.

There is something within that joins with the spouse in the Canticles in saying; "Let me see Thy countenance, let me hear Thy voice; for sweet is Thy voice and Thy countenance is comely."[101] Ah, how sweet is that voice, it makes me tremble within!

"Speak, O beloved, and let none other dare to speak but You! Be still, my soul. Speak, Love!"

It is then that we know all things without knowing anything. Not that we have the presumption to suppose that we possess in ourselves all truth. On the contrary, we feel that we see nothing, can do nothing, and are nothing—we feel it and are delighted at it. But in this unreserved abandonment, we find everything we need from moment to moment in the infinity of God. There we find the daily bread of knowledge, as of everything else, without storing up. Then the unction from above teaches us all truth, while it takes away our own wisdom, glory, interest, even our own will. It makes us content with our powerlessness, and with a position below every creature. We are ready to yield to the merest worms of the dust, and to confess our most secret miseries before the whole world, fearing unfaithfulness more than punishment and confusion of face.

Here it is, I say, that the Spirit teaches us all truth. For all truth is eminently contained in this sacrifice of love, where the soul strips itself of everything to present it to God.

16
Daily faults and the toleration of ourselves

You understand that many of our faults are voluntary in different degrees, though they may not be committed with a deliberate purpose of failing in our allegiance to God. One friend sometimes reproaches another for a fault not expressly intended to be offensive, and yet committed with the knowledge that it would be so. In the same way, God lays this sort of fault to our charge. They are voluntary, for although not done with an express intention, they are still committed freely and against a certain internal light of conscience, which should have caused us to hesitate and wait.

Pious souls are often guilty of these offences. But as for sins committed deliberately, it would be strange indeed if a soul consecrated to God should fall into such.

Little faults become great, and even monstrous in our eyes, in proportion to increase of God's pure light in us. [In the same way that] the rising sun reveals the true dimensions of objects that were dimly and confusedly seen during the night. You can be sure that with the increase of the inward light, the imperfections that you have hitherto seen will be now be revealed as far greater and more deadly in their foundations than you now conceive them. [You will also] witness the development of a crowd of others, whose existence you do not yet have the slightest suspicion.

You will there find the weaknesses necessary to deprive you of all confidence in your own strength. But far from discouraging, this discovery will serve to destroy your self-reliance, and to raze to the ground the edifice of pride. Nothing marks so decidedly the solid progress of a soul as when it is enabled to view its own depravity without being disturbed or discouraged.

It is an important precept to refrain from doing a wrong thing whenever we perceive it in time, and when we do not, to bear the humiliation of the fault courageously.

If a fault is perceived before it is committed, we must see to it that we do not resist and quench the Spirit of God who is advising us of it inwardly. The Spirit is easily offended, and very jealous. He desires to be listened to and obeyed. He retires if He is displeased. The slightest resistance to Him is a wrong, for everything must yield to Him the moment He is perceived. Faults of haste and frailty are nothing in comparison with those where we shut our ears to the voice of the Holy Spirit beginning to speak in the depths of the heart.

Restlessness and an injured self-love will never mend those faults that are not perceived until after they are committed. On the contrary, such feelings are simply the impatience of wounded pride at seeing what confounds it. We must quietly humble ourselves in peace. I say in peace, for it is no humiliation to do it in a irritated and spiteful way. We must condemn our faults, mourn over them, repent of them, and not seek the slightest shadow of consolation in any excuse. [We must do] all this without being bitter against ourselves or discouraged. We peacefully reap the profit of our humiliation. Thus from the serpent itself we draw the antidote to his venom.

It often happens that what we offer to God is not what He most desires to have from us. [He will most often] ask for what we are frequently the most unwilling to give, and the most fearful [of having to give]. He desires the sacrifice of the Isaac, the well-beloved son.[102] All the rest is as nothing in His eyes, and He permits it to be offered in a painful unprofitable manner, because He has no blessings for a divided soul. He will have everything, and until then there is no rest. "Who hath hardened himself against Him, and hath prospered?"[103]

Would you prosper and secure the blessing of God upon your labors? Reserve nothing, cut to the quick and burn, spare nothing, and the God of peace will be with you. What consolation, what liberty, what strength, what enlargement of heart, what increase of grace, will follow when there remains nothing between God and the soul, and when the last sacrifices have been offered up without hesitation!

We must neither be astonished nor disheartened. We are not more wicked than we were. We are really less so. But while our evil diminishes, our light increases, and we are struck with horror at evil's extent. But for our consolation, let us remember that the perception of our disease is the first step to a cure. When we have no sense of our need, we have no healing principle within. It is a state of blindness, presumption, and insensibility, in which we are delivered over to our own counsel and commit ourselves to the current, which has a fatal rapidity that we do not realize until we are called to struggle against it.

We must not be discouraged either by experience of our weakness, or by dislike of the constant activity that may be inseparable from our condition in life. Discouragement is not a fruit of humility, but of pride. Nothing can be worse. Suppose we have stumbled, or even fallen, let us rise and run again. All our falls are useful if they strip us of a disastrous confidence in ourselves, while not taking away a humble and salutary trust in God.

The repugnance that we feel toward our duties, comes no doubt from [our] imperfections. If we were perfect, we would love everything in God's order. But since we are born corrupt, and with a nature revolting against His laws, let us praise Him that He knows how to evolve good from evil, and can make use even of our repugnance as a source of virtue. The work of grace does not always advance as regularly as that of nature, says St. Theresa.

Carefully purify your conscience from daily faults. Allow no sin to dwell in your heart. As small as it may seem, it obscures the light of grace, weighs down the soul, and hinders that constant communion with Jesus Christ that it should be your pleasure to cultivate. You will become lukewarm, forget God, and find yourself growing in attachment to the creature. A pure soul that is humiliated, however, and rises promptly after its smallest faults, is always fervent and always upright.

God never makes us sensible (aware) of our weakness except to give us of His strength[104] We must not be disturbed by what is involuntary. The great point is, never to act in opposition to the inward light, and to be willing to go as far as God would have us.

17
Faithfulness in small matters

St. Francis of Sales says that great virtues and faithfulness in small things are like sugar and salt. Sugar is more delicious, but of less frequent use, while salt enters into every article of our food. Great virtues are rare—they are seldom needed.

When a large occasion[105] comes, we are prepared for it by everything that has preceded, excited by the greatness of the sacrifice, and sustained either by the brilliancy of our action in the eyes of others, or by self-complacency in our ability to do such wonderful things.

Small occasions, however, are unforeseen. They show up repeatedly, and place us continually in conflict with our pride, our laziness, our self-esteem, and our passions. They are calculated to thoroughly subdue our wills, and leave us no retreat. If we are faithful in them, nature will have no time to breathe, and must die to all its inclinations.

It would please us much better to make some great sacrifices, however painful and violent, on condition of obtaining liberty to follow our own pleasure, and retain our old habits in little things. But it is only by this faithfulness in small matters that the grace of true love is sustained and distinguished from the passing excitements of nature.

It is the same with piety[106] as it is with our temporal goods. There is more danger from little expenses than from larger disbursements, and those who understand how to take care of what is insignificant, will soon accumulate a large fortune. Everything great owes its greatness to the small elements of which it is composed. The one who loses nothing will soon be rich.

Consider, on the other hand, that God does not so much regard our actions, as the motive of love from which they spring, and the pliability of our wills to His. People judge our deeds by their outward appearance. But what is most dazzling in the eyes of people, is of no account to God. What He desires is a pure intention, a will ready for anything and ever pliable in His hands, and an honest abandonment of self.

All this can be much more frequently manifested on small than on large occasions. There will also be much less danger from pride, and the trial will be far more searching. Indeed, it sometimes happens that we find it harder to part with a trifle than with an important interest. It may be more of a cross to abandon a vain amusement than to bestow a gift in charity.

We are the more easily deceived about these small matters, in proportion as we imagine them to be innocent, and ourselves indifferent to them. Nevertheless, when God takes them away, the pain of the loss may help us to more easily recognize how excessive and inexcusable were both the use and the attachment. If we are in the habit of neglecting little things, we will be constantly offending our families, our friends, and the public.

No one can well believe that our piety is sincere, when our behavior is loose and irregular in its little details. What ground have we for believing that we are ready to make the greatest sacrifices, when we daily fail in offering the least?

But the greatest danger of all consists in this: by neglecting small matters the soul becomes accustomed to unfaithfulness— [unfaithfulness becomes a habit]. We grieve the Holy Spirit, we return to ourselves, we think it a little thing to be lacking [in our love] toward God. On the other hand, true love can see nothing small. Everything that can either please or displease God seems to be great. Not that true love disturbs the soul with misgivings, but it puts no limits to its faithfulness. It acts simply with God. Since it does not concern itself about those things that God does not require from it, it never hesitates an instant about those that He does [require], whether they are great or small.

Thus it is not by incessant care that we become faithful and exact in the smallest things, but simply by a love that is free from the reflections and fears of restless and doubting souls. We are, as it were, drawn along by the love of God. We have no desire to do anything but what we do, and no will in respect to anything that we do not do. At the very moment when God is following the soul, relentlessly pursuing it into the smallest details, and seemingly depriving it of all its liberty, it finds itself in a large place, and enjoys a perfect peace in Him. Happy soul!

Those persons who are by nature less strict in small matters, should lay down and preserve intact the most rigid laws in respect to them. They are tempted to despise them, they habitually think little of them, and do not sufficiently estimate their importance. They do not consider the imperceptible progress of our passions, and even forget their own sad experience on the subject. They prefer to be deluded by the promise of an imaginary firmness, and to trust to their own courage that has so often deceived them, rather than subject themselves to a never-ceasing faithfulness.

They say it is a small matter, [hardly noticeable]. True, but it is of amazing consequence to you. It is a matter that you love well enough to refuse to give it up to God. It is matter that you sneer at in words so that you may have a pretence to retain it. It is a small matter, but one that you withhold from your Maker, and which will prove your ruin.

It is no nobility of soul that despises small things.[107] On the contrary, it is a shriveled spirit that regards as unimportant what it cannot trace to its necessary and overwhelming results. The more trouble small matters cause us, the more we need to fear negligence, distrust our strength, and put impenetrable barriers between ourselves and the least carelessness.

Finally, judge by your own feelings. What would you think of a friend who owed everything to you, and who was willing from a sense of duty to serve you on those rare occasions that are called great, but who shows neither affection nor the least regard for your wishes in the common things of life?

Do not be frightened at this microscopic attention to small matters. It needs courage at first. But this is a chastisement that you deserve, that you need, and that will work out peace and security for you.[108] Without it, all is trouble and relapse. God will gradually make it pleasant and easy for you, for true love is obedient without compulsion, and without strife or effort.

18
Transitory emotions, faithfulness, and simplicity

We must not be surprised if we frequently perceive in ourselves emotions of pride, self-complacency, confidence in ourselves, desire to follow our own inclination contrary to right, impatience at the weakness of others, or annoyance with our own state. In such cases we must instantly let them drop like a stone to the bottom of the sea, recollect[109] ourselves in God, and wait before acting until our recollection has created the right state in us. If the distraction of business, or of liveliness of imagination, hinders us from calmly and easily entering into such a state, we must at least endeavor to be quiet by the control of the will, and by the desire for recollection. In such a case, the will [and desire] to be recollected deprives the soul of its own will and renders it docile in the hands of God.

If perhaps in your excitement some emotion too nearly allied to a depraved nature escaped you, do not be discouraged. Go straight on. Quietly bear the humiliation of your fault before God, without being delayed by the hurt of self-love at the betrayal of its weakness. Proceed confidently, without being troubled by the anguish of a wounded pride that cannot bear to see itself imperfect. Your fault will be of benefit in causing you to die to self, and to become nothing before Him.

The true method of curing this defect is to become dead to the sensitiveness of self-love, without hindering the course of grace, which had been a little interrupted by this temporary unfaithfulness.

The great point is to renounce your own wisdom by a simplicity of walk, and to be ready to give up the favor, esteem, and praise of every one, whenever the path in which God leads you passes that way. We are not to meddle with things that God does not lay upon us, or uselessly utter hard sayings that those about us are not able to bear.

We must follow after God, never precede Him.[110] When He gives the signal, we must leave all and follow Him.[111] If after an absolute consecration to Him, and a conviction in conscience that He requires something of us, we hesitate, delay, lose courage, dilute what He would have us do, indulge fears for our own comfort or safety, desire to shield ourselves from suffering and disgrace, or seek to find some excuse for not performing a difficult and painful duty, we are truly guilty in His sight. God keep you from such unfaithfulness! Nothing is more dreadful than this inward resistance to Him. It is that sin against the Holy Ghost of which our Lord tells us that ". . . it shall not be forgiven, neither in this world, neither in the world to come."[112]

Other faults committed in the simplicity of your good intentions will be of benefit [to you] if they produce humility, and render you of less account in your own eyes. But resistance to the Spirit of God through pride and a cowardly worldly wisdom, sensitive of its own comfort in performing the work of God, is a fault that will imperceptibly quench the Spirit of Grace in your heart. God, jealous and rejected after so much mercy, will remove [the manifestation of His presence] and leave you to your own resources. You will then turn around in a kind of circle instead of advancing with rapid strides along the King's highway. Your inward life will grow dim and dimmer, without your being able to detect the sure and deep-seated source of your disease.

God would behold in you a simplicity that will contain more of His wisdom as it contains less of your own. He desires to see you lowly in your own eyes, and as docile in His hands as a babe. He desires to create in your heart that childlike disposition so distasteful to the spirit of humanity, but so agreeable to the spirit of the Gospel, in spite of the infection of a scornful and contemptuous world.

By this very simplicity and lowliness, He will heal all the remains of haughty and self-confident wisdom in you, and you will say with David, "And I will yet be more vile than this, and will be base in mine own sight,"[113] from the moment that you give yourself to the Lord.

19
The advantage of silence and reflection

You must endeavor to be as silent as the courtesies of human relationships will permit. The grace [of silence] cherishes the presence of God, saves us many proud and rude expressions, and suppresses a great multitude of idle words and dangerous judgments of our neighbor. Silence humbles our spirit, and gradually detaches it from the world. It constitutes in the heart the sort of solitude that you so much long for, and will supply all your needs in the many uncertainties that surround you. If we never unnecessarily open our mouths, we may enjoy many moments of communion [with God] even when unavoidably detained in society.

You desire to be at liberty so that you may pray to God. But God, who knows much better than we do what we really need, sends uncertainties and restrictions so that you may be confounded. This trial from the hand of God will be far more beneficial to you than the self-sought sweetness of prayer. You know very well that constant retirement is not necessary in order to love God. When He gives you the time, take it and profit by it, but until then wait in faith, well persuaded that what He orders is best.

Frequently raise your heart to Him in separation from the world. Speak only when obliged to. Bear with patience whatever happens to cross you. You are already acquainted with religion, and God treats you according to your necessity. You have more need of humiliation than of illumination. The only thing I fear for you in this state is wanderings, and you may avoid those by silence. Only be faithful in keeping silent when it is not necessary to speak, and God will send grace to preserve you from dissipation when it is.

When you are not permitted to enjoy long seasons of leisure, economize the short ones. Ten minutes faithfully employed before God in the midst of your distractions, will be as valuable to you as whole hours devoted to Him in your more unoccupied moments. Further, these little odds and ends of time will amount to quite a sum in the course of the day, and have the advantage that God will very likely have been more in mind than if you had given it to Him all at once. Love, silence, suffering, yielding our own pleasure to the will of God and to the love of our neighbor, such is our portion.

The crosses that originate with ourselves, are not near as efficient in eradicating self-love as those that come in the daily allotments of God. These latter contribute no ailment for the nourishment of our own wills. Since they proceed immediately from a merciful Providence, they are accompanied by grace sufficient for all our needs. We have nothing to do, then, but to surrender ourselves to God each day, without looking further. He will carry us in His arms as a tender mother bears her child.

Let us believe, hope, and love with all the simplicity of babes.

In every necessity [let us] turn a loving and trusting look toward our heavenly Father. For what says the Scripture, "Can a woman forget her sucking child, that she should not have compassion on the son of her womb? yea, they may forget, yet will I not forget thee."[114]

20
Privation and annihilation is a terror even to the spiritually minded

There is scarcely any one who desires to serve God, but does so for selfish reasons. We expect gain and not loss, consolation and not suffering, riches and not poverty, increase and not decrease. But the work of God in us is for an opposite purpose.[115] [That purpose is for us] to be lost, sacrificed, made less than nothing, and stripped of any excessive delight, even in the gifts of God, so we will be forced to cling to Him alone.

The moment we find ourselves deprived of the delights of grace, that milk for babes,[116] we are at once in despair. This is obvious proof that we were looking to the means instead of to the end, and solely for selfish gratification.

Privations[117] are meat for the mature Christians. By [the privations] the soul is made strong,[118] is separated from self, and offered in a pure sacrifice to God. But we give up everything the moment the privations start. We cannot help thinking that everything is going to ruin, when, in fact, the foundations are just beginning to be solidly laid. Nothing would give us more delight than that God would do all His pleasure with us, provided it should always be to magnify and perfect us in our own eyes. But if we are not willing to be destroyed and annihilated, we will never become that whole burnt offering,[119] which is entirely consumed in the blaze of God's love.

We desire to enter into a state of pure faith, and retain our own wisdom! To be a babe, and great in our own eyes! Ah, what a sad delusion!

21
The proper use of crosses

We can hardly be persuaded of the goodness of God when He loads those whom He loves with crosses. We ask, "Why would He take pleasure in causing us to suffer? Could He not do us good without making us miserable?"

Yes He could, for all things are possible with God.[120] He holds in His omnipotent hands the hearts of people, and turns them as He will, even as the skill of the driver can turn the cart in whatever direction is desired. But able as God is to save us without crosses, He has not chosen to do it. Just as He has not seen fit to create us at once in the full vigor of adulthood, but has allowed us to grow up by degrees amid all the perils and weaknesses of infancy and youth.

In this matter, He is the Master; we have only to adore in silence the depths of His wisdom, without understanding it. Nevertheless, we see clearly that we could never become completely good without becoming humble, unselfish, and inclined to attribute everything to God, without any restless self-reflective acts.

The work of grace, in detaching us from self and destroying our self-love, could not be anything other than painful, without a miracle. But God deos not work a miracle lightly in either His gracious or providential dealings. It would be as great a wonder to see a person full of self become in a moment dead to all self-interest and all sensitiveness, as it would be to see a slumbering infant wake in the morning a fully-developed adult. God works in a mysterious way in grace as well as in nature, concealing His operations under an imperceptible succession of events. [In so doing, He] keeps us in the darkness of faith.[121]

This state of faith is necessary to not only stimulate those who are good, causing them to sacrifice their reason in a life so full of darkness, but also to blind those who by their presumption deserve such a sentence. They behold the works of God but do not understand them. They can see nothing in them but the effects of material laws. They are destitute of true knowledge, for that is only open to those who distrust their own abilities. Proud human wisdom is unworthy to be taken into the counsels of God.

God renders, therefore, the working of grace slow and obscure so He may keep us in the darkness of faith. He makes use of the fickleness and ingratitude of the creature, and of the disappointments and excesses that accompany prosperity, to detach us from them both. He frees us from self by revealing to us our weaknesses and corruptions in a multitude of backslidings. All this dealing appears perfectly natural, and it is by this succession of natural means that we are burnt as by a slow fire. We would like to be consumed at once by the flames of pure love, but such an end would scarcely cost us anything. It is only an excessive self-love that desires in this way to become perfect in a moment and at so little a price.

Why do we rebel against the length of the way?[122] Because we are wrapped up in self; and God must destroy an infatuation [with ourselves] that is a constant hindrance to His work. Of what, then, can we complain? Our trouble is that we are attached to creatures, and still more to self. God prepares a series of events that gradually detaches us from creatures, and separates us from self. The operation is painful, but is made necessary by our corruption, which also makes it distressing. If our flesh were sound, the surgeon would not use a knife. He only cuts in proportion to the depth of the wound, and the diseased condition of the parts. If we suffer greatly, it is because the evil is great. Is the surgeon cruel[123] because he cuts into the [diseased and sensitive flesh]? No, on the contrary, it is both love and skill. He would treat his only and well-beloved son in the same way.

It is the same with God. He never afflicts us, if we may so say, except against His own inclination. His paternal heart is not gratified by the sight of our misery, but He cuts into [that which is diseased and sensitive] so that He may heal the sickness in our souls. He must snatch away from us whatever we cling to too fondly, and all that we love irregularly and to the prejudice of His rights.

He acts in this as we do with children. They cry because we take away the knife they had found for their amusement, but which might have been their death. We weep, we become discouraged, we cry aloud. We are even ready to murmur against God, just as children get angry with their mothers. But God lets us weep, and secures our salvation. He afflicts only to heal, even when He seems to overwhelm, He means nothing but good. It is only to spare us the evils we were preparing for ourselves.

The things we now grieve about for a little while would have caused us to mourn forever. What we think we lost was indeed lost when we seemed to have it. But now God has laid it aside for us so that we may inherit it in the eternity so near at hand. He only deprives us of what we cherish to teach us how to love it purely, solidly, and moderately, and to secure to us its eternal enjoyment in His own bosom. [In doing this, He does] us a thousand times more good than we could ask or think of ourselves.

With the exception of sin, nothing happens in this world out of the will of God. It is He who is the author, ruler, and giver of all. He has numbered the hairs of our head,[124] the leaves of every tree, the sand upon the seashore, and the drops of the ocean. When He made the universe, His wisdom weighed and measured every atom. It is He who breathes into us the breath of life, and renews it every moment. It is He who knows the number of our days, and who holds in HIs all-powerful hand the keys of the tomb to open or to shut.[125]

What we admire is as nothing in the eyes of God. A little more or less of life is a difference that disappears in the light of eternity. What matter whether this fragile vessel, this clay tabernacle, is broken and reduced to ashes a little sooner or later?

Ah, what shortsighted and deceitful views are ours! We are thrown into dismay at the death of a [Christian] man or woman in the prime of life. "What a dreadful loss," exclaims the world. Who has lost anything? The dead man?

He has lost some years of vanity, illusion, and danger to his immortal soul. God has snatched him from the midst of his iniquities, and separated him from a corrupt world and his own weakness. The friends whom he has left?

[By their loss,] they are deprived of the poison of worldly joy. They lose a perpetual intoxication. They get rid of the forgetfulness of God and themselves into which they had sunk. In short, they gain the bliss of detachment from the world through the virtue of the cross [of suffering].

The same blow that saves the dying, prepares the survivors by their suffering to labor courageously for their own salvation. Oh, is it not true that God is good, tender, compassionate toward our misery, even when He seems to launch His thunders at us and we are open-mouthed in our complaints of His severity!

What difference can we discover between two persons who lived a century ago? The one died twenty years before the other, but now they are both gone. The separation that then seemed so abrupt and so long appears as nothing to us, and was, in fact, but short. Those things that are severed will soon be reunited, and no trace of the separation will be visible. We look upon ourselves as immortal, or at least as having a [long life before us].

Oh foolishness and madness, those who die from day to day tread upon the heels of those that are already dead. Life flows like a torrent. That which is gone is but a dream, and even while we contemplate that which now is, it vanishes and is lost in the abyss of the past. So will it be with the future—days, months, and years glide like the billows of a raging river, each hurrying along the other. A few moments more and all is over! Alas, how short our life will someday seem, though it now [often] wearies us with its sad and tedious length!

The disgust of life is the result of the weakness of our self-love. The sick think the night will never end because they cannot sleep, but it is no longer than other nights. We exaggerate all our sufferings by our cowardice. Our sufferings are great, it is true, but they are magnified by timidity. The way to lessen them is to abandon ourselves courageously into the hands of God. We must suffer, but the [purpose] of our pain is to purify our souls and make us worthy of Him.

22
God works internally
to bring us to the true purpose of our creation

In the beginning, God attacked us in externals. Little by little He withdrew those of His creatures whom we loved too much, and contrary to His law. But this outward work, though essential in laying the foundation of the building, goes but a little way towards the completion of the whole edifice. The internal operation, although invisible, is beyond comparison—greater, more difficult, and more wonderful!

There comes a time, when God, having completely stripped us, having mortified the flesh as to the creatures to which it clung, begins an internal work for the purpose of tearing from us our hold upon Self. External objects are now no longer the subjects of His [sanctifying work]. He would now tear from us the I that is the center of our self-love. It was only for the sake of this I that we loved all the rest, and He now pursues it relentlessly and without stopping.

To deprive us of our clothing, would be harsh treatment enough. But that is nothing in comparison with the discipline that should strip off our skin and muscles, and reduce us to a skeleton of bones. Trim up the branches of a tree, and far from killing it, you even add to its vigor, and it shoots out again on every side. But attack the trunk, wither the root, and it fades, languishes and dies. It is the good will of God toward us to use this way make us die to self.

As to the external discipline of the senses, He makes us accomplish it by certain courageous efforts against ourselves. The more the senses are destroyed by the courage of the soul, the more highly does the soul estimate its own virtue, and live by its own labor. But in process of time, God reserves for His own hand the work of attacking the soul in its depths, and depriving it finally of the last vestige of the life of Self.

It is no longer the strength of the soul that is then employed against external things, but its weakness that is turned against itself. It looks at self. It is shocked at what it sees. It remains faithful, but it no longer sees its own faithfulness. Every defect in its previous history rises up in view, and often new faults that it had never before even suspected existed. It no longer finds those supports of fire and courage that formerly nourished it. It faints, and like Jesus it is heavy even unto death.[126] Everything is taken away but the will to keep nothing, and to let God work without reservation.

The soul has not even the consolation of perceiving that it has such a will. It is no longer a perceptible, designed, will. It is now a simple will without reflex acts, and so much the more hidden as it is deeper and more intimate in the soul. In such a state, God sees to everything that is necessary to detach the soul from self. He strips it little by little, removing one after another all the layers [of self] in which [the soul] was wrapped.

Though last operations are not always the greatest, they are, nevertheless, the most severe. Though the outside garments may be more costly than those within, yet the removal of the latter is more painful than that of the former. During the first, we are consoled by reflecting upon what is left us. During the last, nothing is left but bitterness, nakedness, and confusion.

I will perhaps be asked in what these deprivations consist. But I cannot say. They are as various as the characters of people. We each suffer according to our necessity and the designs of God. How is it possible to know what will be taken off from us, when we do not know what we have on? We cling to an infinity of things that we would never suspect. We only feel that they are a part of us when they are snatched away, just as I am only conscious that I have hairs when they are pulled from my head.

Little by little God reveals to us what is within us. Until then, we are entirely ignorant [of them], and we are astonished at discovering in our very virtues defects that we would never have believed ourselves capable of. It is like a cave that appears perfectly dry, but in which the water suddenly springs out from every point, even from those that were the least suspected.

These failings are not commonly the kind that could have been anticipated. That which we expect finds us prepared, and is scarcely suitable to hurry the death of self. God surprises us in the most unlooked-for quarters. They are nothings, but nothings that desolate us and crucify self-love.

Great and striking virtues are no longer appropriate [for us]. They would nourish pride, and communicate a certain degree of strength and internal assurance contrary to the design of God— which is, to make us lose ground. It is then a simple, single, way. Everything is commonplace, [normal, usual].

Others see nothing great, and we ourselves discover within only what seems natural, weak, and feeble. But now we would rather a hundred times fast all our life on bread and water, and practice the greatest austerities, than allow what is going on within us [to continue]. Not because we enjoy a certain taste of pleasure in austerities. Not at all, that delight is gone. But we find in the pliability that God requires in an infinity of little things, more of self-abandonment and death than there would be in great sacrifices.

Nevertheless, God never leaves your soul until He has rendered it supple and pliable by twisting it all manner of ways. At one time you must speak frankly, at another be still. First praised, then blamed, then forgotten, and then examined anew. Brought low, then taken high. Suffering condemnation without uttering a word in self-defense, and yet again speaking well of yourself.

You must be willing to find yourself weak, restless, and irresolute in the merest trifles. Manifesting the waywardness of a little child. Shocking your friends by your coldness. Becoming jealous and suspicious without reason, and relating your most foolish jealousies to those in regard to whom you feel them. Speaking with patience and labor to persons contrary to their desire and your own, and without fruit. Appearing artificial and faithless.

In short, to find yourself dry, feeble, weary of God, tired in mind, and so far separated from every gracious thought as to be tempted to despair. These are examples of some of God's workings that now desolate me. But there is an infinity of others that God assigns to each one according to His own wise purposes.

Let no one tell me that these are only empty imaginations. Can we doubt that God acts immediately in the soul? That He so acts as to make it die to self? that, after having subdued the grosser passions, He attacks all the subtle resources of self-love within, especially in those souls who have generously and without reserve delivered themselves up to the operations of His grace?

The more He would purify them, the more He exercises them internally. The world has neither eyes to see nor ears to hear these trials. But the world is blind. Its wisdom is dead. It cannot coexist with the Spirit of truth. "The things of God," says the Apostle, "knoweth no man but the Spirit of God. . . . the Spirit searcheth . . . the deep things of God."[127]

At first, we dare not yet risk listening to the internal voice calling us to the sacrifices that God is preparing. [We are fearful of what He might say to us, of what He might tell us to do, and so we make His voice uncertain to us, and not hear Him clearly.]

We are like the child Samuel who did not yet know the Lord. When the Lord called, he thought it was Eli. But he was told that he had been dreaming, and that no one spoke to him. Just so, we are uncertain whether it may not be an imagination that would carry us too far. Often the high-priest Eli—[in the form of] our spiritual advisers—tells us that we have been dreaming and to lie down again. But God does not leave us, and continues to wake us until we lend an ear to what He has to say.

If it were a matter of visions, apparitions, revelations, extraordinary illuminations, miracles, things contrary to true teaching, we would be right in not being detained by them. But when God has led us to a certain point of abandonment, and we subsequently have an internal conviction that He still desires us to give up certain innocent things that would tend to make us more simple and more profoundly dead to self, can it be an illusion to yield to such convictions? Yet probably no one follows them without good counsel.

The repugnance that our wisdom and self-love manifest to them is a sufficient evidence that they are of grace. For we see that we are only hindered from following them by selfish considerations.

The more we fear to do these things, the more we have need to do them. For it is a fear that arises only from weakness, lack of pliability, and attachment either to our pleasures or our views. We must die to all the sentiments of the natural life. Thus every pretext for retreat is cut off by the conviction in the depths of the soul that the sacrifices required will assist in causing us to die.

Ease and promptness in yielding to these movements are the means by which souls make the greatest advances. Those who are courageous enough never to hesitate soon make incredible progress. Others argue, and never fail to find a sufficient reason for not following the internal monitor. They are willing and not willing. They want to wait for certainties. They search about for advisers who will tell them not do what they are afraid of doing. They stop at every step, and look back; then weaken in irresolution, and insensibly alienate the Spirit of God. At first they grieve Him by their hesitation, then they irritate Him by formal resistance, and finally quench His operations by repeated opposition.

Further, while they resist they find excuses to conceal and justify their resistance, but they slowly grow dry. They lose their simplicity, and no matter how much effort they make to deceive themselves, they are not at peace. There is always at the bottom of their conscience, a feeling of reproach that they have been lacking toward God.

But as they continue to depart from God and He thereby becomes more distant, their soul becomes hardened by degrees. It is no longer peaceful, but it also no longer seeks true peace. On the contrary, it wanders further and further from it by seeking peace where it is not. It is like a dislocated bone that is a continual source of pain and out of its natural position. Yet it demonstrates no tendency to resume its place but, on the contrary, binds itself fast in its false relations.

Ah, how pitiful is the soul that is just beginning to reject the secret invitations of God, when He demands that it shall die to everything! At first, [rejection] is but an atom. But the atom [quickly] becomes a mountain, and soon forms a sort of chaos between it and God. We play deaf when God demands a lowly simplicity. We are afraid to listen. We are happy when we have been able to convince ourselves that we had not heard. We say that, but are not persuaded.

We get into a tumult. We doubt all our past experience. The graces that had been the most effective in making us humble and simple before God, begin to look like illusions. We look everywhere for spiritual advisers who can calm the trouble within us. We easily find them, for there are so many. [But though many are] gifted with much knowledge and piety, many have yet but little experience.

In this condition, the more we strive to recover, the sicker we get. We are like the wounded deer, bearing in its side the fatal arrow; the more it struggles through the woods to be delivered of its enemy, the deeper it buries the instrument of death into its body. Alas, "who hath hardened himself against Him, and hath prospered?"[128] Can God, who is Himself the true peace, leave the heart peaceful that fights against His designs? Such a person is like someone who has an unknown disorder.

Physicians employ their art in vain to give that person relief. But though that soul is sad, depressed, weakening, no food or medicine can do it any good. It dies [spiritually] day by day. Can we wonder that if we wander from the true way, we would continually stray further and further from the right course?

But some may say that the beginning of these things is a small matter. True, but the end is deplorable. In the sacrifice that we made when we devoted ourselves wholly to God, we reserved nothing and felt happy in so doing. Happy, that is, while we were looking at things with a general view and at a distance. But when God takes us at our word and accepts our offer in detail, we are made aware of a thousand faults that we never before suspected even existed.

Our courage fails, and frivolous excuses are suggested to flatter our feeble and tempted souls. Then we hesitate and doubt whether it is our duty to obey. We do only the half of what God requires of us, and we mix a good quantity of self with the divine influence. We do so in an effort to still obtain some nourishment for that corrupt interior that is determined not to die. A jealous God withdraws. The soul begins to shut its eyes so it will not see that it has no longer the courage to act. And so God withdraws the manifestation of His presence and leaves it to its weakness and corruption, because it desires to be left. But think of the magnitude of its error!

The more we have received from God, the more we should give to God. We have received prevenient[129] love and unique grace. We have received the gift of pure and unselfish love, which so many pious souls have never tasted. God has spared nothing to possess us completely. He has become our interior bridegroom. He has taken pains to do everything for His bride—but He is infinitely jealous.

Do not wonder at the severe nature of His jealousy! What is its object? Is it talents, understanding, the regular practice of external virtues? Not at all. He is easy and condescending in such matters. Love is only jealous about love. The whole of His scrutiny falls upon the state of our will. He cannot share our heart with any other. He tolerates even less the excuses by which we would convince ourselves that our heart is justly divided. [It is such excuses that inflames] the devouring fires of His jealousy.

As long, dear spouse, as pure and disinterested love guides you, so long does the Bridegroom bear with inexhaustible patience all your wrong doing through weakness or carelessness, without prejudice concerning the purity of your love. But from the moment that you refuse anything that God asks, and begin to deceive yourself in the refusal, from that moment He will regard you as a faithless spouse who is trying to conceal the infidelity!

Many souls fall into these ways after having made great sacrifices! False wisdom is the source of the whole difficulty. It is not so much through lack of courage as through excess of reason that we are stopped at this point. It is true that when God has called souls to this state of absolute sacrifice, He treats them in accordance with the gifts He has lavished upon them. He is insatiable for deaths, losses, renunciation.

He is even jealous of His own gifts, because the excellence of the blessings secretly breeds within us a sort of self-confidence. Everything must be destroyed, every vestige must perish! We have abandoned everything—and He comes now to take everything, leaving us absolutely nothing. If there is the smallest thing to which we cling, however good it may appear, there He comes sword in hand and cuts into the remotest corner of the soul.[130]

If we are still fearful anywhere, to that spot He comes, for He always attacks us in our weakest points. He pushes hard, without giving us time to breathe. Do you wonder? Can we be dead while we yet breathe?

We want God to give us the death-stroke, but we long to die without pain. We prefer to die to our own will by the power of the will itself. We want to lose everything and still keep everything. Ah, what agony, what distress, when God has brought us to the end of our strength! We faint like a patient under a painful surgical operation.[131] But the comparison is nothing, for the object of the surgeon is to give us life, while the object of God to make us die.[132]

Poor souls, weak in spirit—how these last blows overwhelm you! The very anticipation of them makes you tremble and fall back! How few there are who determine to cross the frightful desert! Barely two or three see [and enter] the promised land![133]

Woe to those from whom God had reason to expect everything, and who do not accept the grace! Woe to those who resist the interior guidance, and thus sin against the Holy Spirit!

Those who resist the Spirit, striving for their conversion [by their own power] will be punished in this world by affliction, and in the next by the pains of hell.

Happy are those who never hesitate, who fear only that they follow with too little readiness, who would rather do too much against self than too little! Blessed are those who, when asked for a sample, boldly present their entire stock and allow God to cut from the whole cloth! Happy are those who, esteeming themselves as nothing, do not make it necessary for God to spare them! Three-times happy are those whom all this does not frighten!

It is thought that this state is a painful one. That it is a mistake. Here is peace and liberty. Here the heart, detached from everything, is immeasurably enlarged—so much so, it literally becomes unlimited. Nothing constricts it, and in accordance with the promise, it becomes, in a certain sense, one with God Himself. "You only, Oh my God, can give the peace that is then enjoyed!"

The less timid the soul is in the sacrifice of itself, the greater liberty it acquires! At length, when it no longer hesitates to lose everything and forget self, it possesses everything. It is true that it is not a conscious possession, so that the soul says to itself that it is happy, for that would be to return to self after having quit it forever. But it is an image of the condition of the blessed, who will be always ravished by the contemplation of God—without having a moment, during the whole of eternity, to think of themselves and their blessedness. They are so satisfied in these raptures, that they will be eternally rejoicing without once saying to themselves that they are happy.

You grant to those souls who never resist You, O bridegroom of souls, a foretaste of this rapture even in this life. They will all things and nothing. Since it is created things that bind up the heart, these souls who are not restrained by attachment to the creature and do not reflect on self, enter as it were into Your immensity!

Nothing stops them. They become continually more and more lost. But though their capacity should increase to an infinite extent, You would fill it—so they are always satisfied. They do not say that they are happy, but feel that they are so. They do not posses happiness, but their happiness possesses them.

Let any one ask them at any moment, "Do you will to suffer what you suffer? Do you desire to have what you do not have?"

They will answer without hesitation and without reflection, "I will to suffer what I suffer, and do not desire what I do not have. I will everything that God wills. I will nothing else.

This, my God, is true and pure worship in spirit and in truth. You seek such as these to worship You, but seldom find them![134] There are few who do not seek self in Your gifts, instead of seeking You alone in the cross and death to self. Most seek to guide You instead of being guided by You. They give themselves up to You so they may become great, but withdraw when they are required to become little. They say they are attached to nothing, and are overwhelmed by the smallest losses. They desire to possess You, but are not willing to lose self, that they may be possessed by You.

This is not loving You, it is desiring to be loved by You. Oh God, we creatures do not understand for what purpose You have made us.[135] Teach us, and write in the depths of our souls that the clay must allow itself to be shaped at the will of the Potter[136].

23
Christian perfection

Christian perfection is not that rigorous, tedious, cramping thing that many imagine. It demands only an entire surrender of everything to God from the depths of the soul. The moment this takes place, whatever is done for Him becomes easy. Those who are God's without reserve are content in every condition, for they will only what He wills, and desire to do for Him whatever He desires them to do. They strip themselves of everything, and in this nakedness find all things restored a hundredfold. Peace of conscience, liberty of spirit, the sweet abandonment of themselves and theirs into the hand of God, the joy of perceiving the light always increasing in their hearts, and finally the freedom of their souls from the bondage of the fears and desires of this world. These things constitute that return of happiness that the true children of God receive a hundredfold in the midst of their crosses, while they remain faithful.[137]

They are sacrificed, it is true, but it is to that which they love best. They suffer, but they will to endure all that they receive, and prefer that anguish to all the false joys of the world. Their bodies are subject to excruciating pain, their imaginations are troubled, their minds become listless and weak, but the will is firm and peacefully quiet in the interior of the soul. So much so that it responds a joyful Amen! to every stroke from the Hand that would perfect the sacrifice.

What God requires of us is a will that is no longer divided between Him and any creature. It must be a simple, pliable, state of will that desires what He desires, rejects nothing but what He rejects, wills without reserve what He wills, and under no pretext wills what He does not. In this state of mind, all things are proper for us—even our amusements are acceptable in His sight.

Blessed are those who give themselves to God in this way! They are delivered from their passions, and from the opinions of people—their malice, the tyranny of their maxims, and their cold and miserable ridicule. [They are also delivered] from the misfortunes that the world attributes to chance, from the unfaithfulness and fickleness of friends, from the deceptions and snares of enemies, from the wretchedness and shortness of life, from the horrors of an ungodly death, from the cruel remorse that follows sinful pleasures, and finally from the everlasting condemnation of God!

True Christians are delivered from this innumerable multitude of evils. For putting their will into the hands of God, they will only what He wills, and thereby find comfort in the midst of all their suffering by the way of faith and its attending hope.[138]

[Do you see], therefore, what weakness it is to be fearful of consecrating ourselves to God, and of getting too far into so desirable a state!

How happy are those who throw themselves headlong and with their eyes shut into the arms of "the Father of mercies, and the God of all comfort!"[139] Their whole desire then becomes to know what the will of God is concerning them, and they dread nothing so much as not sensing the whole of His requirements. As soon as they see a new light in His Word, they are transported with joy, like a person dying of thirst who finds a spring.

No matter what cross may overwhelm the true children of God, they will everything that happens, and would not have anything removed that their Father appoints [for them]. The more they love God, the more they are filled with contentment. Far from being a burden, the highest requirements of perfection only make His yoke lighter.

What foolishness to fear to be too devoted to God! To fear to be happy! To fear to love the will of God in all things! To fear to have too much courage under inevitable crosses, too much consolation in the love of God, and too great a detachment from the passions that make us miserable!

Let us refuse, then, to set our affections upon things of the earth so we may set them exclusively upon God. I do not say that we must abandon them entirely. For if our lives are already moral and well ordered [in Christ], we have only to change the secret motive of our actions into Love, and we may continue almost the same course of life.

God does not overturn our conditions or the duties attached to them. We may now go on doing for the service of God what we formerly did to satisfy the world and to please ourselves. There will only be this difference. Instead of being harassed by pride, by overbearing passion, and by the malicious censures of the world, we will act with liberty, with courage, and with hope in God. We will be animated with confidence. The expectation [and hope] of things eternal, which advance as things temporal recede from us, will support us in the midst of suffering. God will make us see how great His love is toward us, and the love of God will lend us wings to fly in His ways, and raise us above all our miseries. Is this hard to believe? Experience will convince us. "O taste and see that the Lord is good!" says the Psalmist.[140]

The Son of God says to every Christian, male and female, without exception, "If any man will come after Me, let him deny himself, and take up his cross and follow me."[141] The broad way leads to destruction. We must walk in the strait way, though there be few that travel therein.[142] It is only the violent who take the Kingdom by force.[143] We must be born again,[144] renounce our worldly ways,[145] become children,[146] be poor in spirit,[147] mourn that we may be comforted,[148] and not be of this world,[149] which is cursed because of offences.[150]

Many are frightened at these truths, and their fear arises from this—while they know the exacting nature of Christianity, they are ignorant of its gifts, and of the spirit of love that renders everything easy. They are not aware that Christianity leads to the highest perfection, while bestowing peace through a principle of love that smoothes every rough place.

Those who are completely concentrated to God in truth and in deed are always happy. They prove that the yoke of our Redeemer is easy and His burden light, that in Him is the peace of the soul, and that He gives rest to them that are weary and heavy laden, according to His own blessed promise.[151]

But how unhappy are those poor, weak, souls who are divided between God and the world! They will [to follow Christ completely], and [yet] they do not will [to follow Him completely]. They are torn and distressed at once by their passions and their remorse. They are afraid of the judgments of God and of the opinions of people. They dislike the evil, but are ashamed of the good. They suffer the pains of virtue, without enjoying its consolations. Ah, if they could just have a little courage—just enough to despise the vain conversation, the cold sneers, and the rash judgments of people—what peace they would enjoy in the bosom of God![152]

It is dangerous to our salvation, unworthy of God and of ourselves, and destructive even of our peace of mind, to desire to remain always in our present position. Our whole life is only given to us so that we may advance with rapid strides toward our heavenly country. The world recedes like a deceptive shadow, and eternity already approaches to receive us. Why do we linger and look behind while the light of the Father of Mercies is shining upon us from ahead? Let us hurry to reach the Kingdom of God.

All the vain excuses that are used to cover our reservations toward God are instantly dissipated by the first commandment of the law: "Thou shalt love the Lord thy God with all thy heart, and with all thy soul, and with all thy strength, and with all thy mind."[153] Notice how many expressions are brought together by the Holy Spirit to forestall all the reservations the soul might make to [argue against] this jealous Love—not only with the whole extent and strength of the soul, but with all the intensity of the intellect. How then can we conclude that we love Him if we cannot make up our minds to receive His Word, and to apply ourselves at once to fulfill all His blessed will?

Those who fear that they will discover too clearly what this love demands, are very far indeed from possessing the active and incessant affection required by this commandment.

There is but one way in which God should be loved, and

that is to take no step except with Him and for Him, and to follow, with a generous self-abandonment, everything that He requires.

Those who live in some self-denial, but have still a wish to enjoy a little of the world, think that this is a small matter. But they run the risk of being included in the number of those lukewarm ones whom Christ will spew out of His mouth.[154]

God is not pleased with the souls that say, "I will go this far and no further." Should the creature decree laws to the Creator? What would a king say of his subjects who are willing to serve him but only in their own way? Subjects who are afraid of becoming too interested in his service and his interests, and who are ashamed to publicly acknowledge that they are attached to him? Or rather, what will the King of kings say to us if we serve Him in this wicked manner?

The time [when we will meet our King] is not far distant. It is near, even at hand. Let us act swiftly to prepare for it. Let us love that eternal beauty that never grows old, and that preserves in endless youth those who love nothing but it. Let us despise this miserable world that is already falling to pieces on every side![155]

Have we not seen for years that those who today are high in honor and in the esteem of people, are tomorrow surprised by death and laid side by side in the tomb? Each day some of us will leave this poor world that is the object of so much insane attachment. It is a world filled with misery, vanity, and foolishness—a phantom, whose very form "is passing away!"[156]

24

The way of naked faith and pure love
is better and more certain
than that of enlightenments
and sensible delights

Those who are attached to God only so far as they enjoy pleasure and consolation, resemble those who followed the Lord not to hear His teaching but because they ate of the loaves and were filled.[157] They are ready to say with Peter, "Master, it is good for us to be here: and let us make three tabernacles,"[158] but they do not know what they are saying. After being intoxicated with the joys of the mountain, they deny the Son of God and refuse to follow Him to Calvary. They not only desire delights, but they seek enlightenment also. The mind is curious to behold, while the heart requires it be filled with soft and flattering emotions. Is this dying to self? Is this the way in which "the just shall live by faith"?[159]

They desire to have extraordinary revelations, which may be regarded as supernatural gifts and a mark of the special favor of God. Nothing is so flattering to self-love [as this]. All the greatness of the world combined could not so inflate the heart. These supernatural gifts nourish in secret the life of nature. It is an ambition of the most refined character, as it is wholly spiritual. But it is merely ambition. Merely a desire to feel, to enjoy, to possess God and His gifts, to behold His light, to discern spirits, to prophesy. In short, to be an extraordinarily gifted person. For the enjoyment of enlightenments and delights leads the soul little by little toward a secret coveting of all these things.

Yet the apostle shows us "a more excellent way,"[160] for which he inspires us with a holy ambition. It is the way of love that "does not seek its own,"[161] and desires not to be clothed upon, if we may adopt the apostle's language, but suffers itself to be unclothed.[162] Love is less in search of pleasure than of

God, whose will it longs to fulfill. If it finds pleasure in devotion, it does not rest in it, but makes [that pleasure] serve to strengthen her weakness. Just as a convalescent uses a cane or crutch to aid in walking, but throws it aside when restored [to health]. In the same way, the tender and childlike soul that God fed with milk in the beginning, allows itself to be weaned when He sees it is time for it to be nourished with strong meat.[163]

We must not forever be children, always hanging upon the breast of heavenly comforts. We must put away childish things with Paul.[164] Our early joys were excellent to attract us, to detach us from gross and worldly pleasures by those of a purer kind, and to lead us into a life of prayer and reflection. But to be constantly in a state of enjoyment that takes away the feeling of the cross, and to live in an intensity of devotion that continually keeps paradise open, this is not dying upon the cross and becoming nothing.

This life of enlightenment and sensible delights is a very dangerous snare if we become so attached to it as to desire nothing further. For those who have no other attraction to prayer will quit both it and God whenever this source of gratification is dried up. St. Theresa says, "You know that a vast number of souls stop praying at the very moment that their devotion is beginning to be real."

There are many who, because of too tender rearing in Jesus Christ, and too great fondness for the milk of His word, go back and abandon the interior life as soon as God undertakes to wean them! We need not be astonished at this, for they mistake the portico of the temple for the very sanctuary itself. They desire the death of their gross external passions so that they may lead a pleasurable life of self-satisfaction within.

Therefore, [there is] so much unfaithfulness and disappointment, even among those who appeared the most fervent and the most devoted. Those who have talked the loudest of abandonment, of death to self, of the darkness of faith, and of desolation, are often the most surprised and discouraged when they really experience these things and their consolation is taken away. Oh how excellent is the way pointed out by John of the Cross, who would have us believe without seeing, and love without desiring to feel

This attachment to sensible delights is the prolific source of all our illusions. Souls that desire something tangible before they can feel secure are earthly. But this is all wrong. It is these very things of sense that produce wavering. While the pleasure lasts, we think that we will never desert God. We say in our prosperity that we will never be moved.clxv But the moment our intoxication is over, we give up all for lost. [This shows that we have] substituted our own pleasure and imagination for God. Naked faith, alone, is the only sure guard against illusion.

To prevent our being subject to illusion, our foundation must not rest upon any imagination, feeling, pleasure, or extraordinary enlightenment. We must rest upon God only in pure and naked faith. Receive in the simplicity of the gospel the consolations that He sends, but dwell in none [of them]. We must abstain from judging, and always be obedient. We must believe that it is easy to be deceived, and that others may be able to set us right. In short, we must act every moment with simplicity and an upright intention, following the light of the faith of the present moment. [If we do this,] then we are indeed [walking] in a way that is little subject to illusion.

Experience will demonstrate better than anything else, how much more certain this path is than that of enlightenments and sensible delights. Whoever will try it, will soon find that when this way of naked faith is rigidly followed it is the profoundest and most complete death of self. Internal delights and revelations reward our self-love for all its external sacrifices, and cherish a secret and refined life. But to allow ourselves to be stripped internally and externally at the same time— externally by Providence, and internally by the night of pure faith, is a total sacrifice, and a state [that is] the furthest possible from self-deception.

Those who seek to guard against being deceived by a constant succession of emotions and certainties, are by that very course exposing themselves most surely to such a result. On the other hand, those who follow the leadings of the love that strips them, and the faith that walks in darkness, without seeking any other support, avoid all the sources of error and illusion.

The author of the Imitation of Christ[166]tells you that if God takes away your inward delights, it should be your pleasure to remain pleasureless. Oh how beloved of God is a soul crucified in this way that rests calmly upon the cross, and desires only to expire with Jesus! It is not true to say that we are afraid of having lost God because we have been deprived of feeling. It is impatience under the trial, the restlessness of a pampered and fragile nature, a search for some support for self-love, a weariness of abandonment, and a secret return to self after our consecration to God.

Oh God, where are they who do not stop on the road to death? If they persevere to the end they will receive a crown of life.[167]

25
The presence of God

The true source of all our perfection is contained in the command of God in Abraham, "Walk before me, and be thou perfect."[168]

The presence of God calms the soul, and gives it quiet and rest even during the day, and in the midst of [our daily activities]—but we must be given up to God without reserve.

When we have once found God, we have nothing to seek among people. We must make the sacrifice of our dearest friendships, for the best of friends has entered into our hearts, that jealous Bridegroom who requires the whole of it for Himself.

It takes no great time to love God, to be refreshed by His presence, to elevate our hearts to Him, or to worship Him in the depths of our soul. To offer to God all we do and all we suffer; this is the true kingdom of God within us,[169] which cannot be disturbed.

When the distraction of the senses and the liveliness of the imagination hinder the soul from a sweet and peaceful state of meditation, we should at least be calm with regard to the state of our will. [The will that is fastened upon God regardless of external distractions] is sufficient for the time being. [When the distractions have passed,] we must return toward God, and do everything that He would have us do with a right intention.

From time to time, we must try to awake within ourselves the desire of being devoted to God in all the extent of our powers. In our intellect, to know Him and think on Him—in our will, to love Him. We must desire, too, that our outward senses are consecrated to Him in all their operations.

Let us be careful how we voluntarily engage, either externally or internally, in matters that cause such distraction of the will and intellect, and so draw them out of themselves, that they find difficulty in re-entering and finding God.

The moment we discover that any [object—thing or person—] causes excessive pleasure or joy within us, let us separate our heart from it. To prevent [our heart] from seeking its rest in the object, let us present it to God, the true object of love, the sovereign good. If we are faithful in breaking up all attachment to the object—that is, if we prevent the object from entering into those depths of the soul that our Lord reserves for Himself, to dwell there and to be there respected, adored, and loved, we will soon experience the pure joy that He never fails to give to a soul freed and detached from all human affections.

Whenever we perceive within us anxious desires for anything, whatever it may be, and find that nature is hurrying us with too much haste to do what is to be done, whether it be to say something, see something, or to do something, let us stop short, and suppress the impulsiveness of our thoughts and the agitation of our actions—for God has said that His Spirit does not dwell in disquiet.[170]

Be careful not to take too much interest in what is going on around you, or to be much engaged in it—it is a prolific source of distraction. As soon as we have found what it is that God requires of us in anything that comes up, let us stop there and separate ourselves from all the rest. By that means we will always preserve the depths of the soul free and steady, and rid ourselves of many things that hinder our hearts and prevent them from turning easily toward God.

An excellent means of preserving our internal solitude and liberty of soul is to make it a rule to not reflect upon every action after they have ended, and neither to indulge in self-love, whether of a proud joy or sorrow. Happy are those whose mind contains only what is necessary, and who think of nothing except when it is time to think of it. In this way it is God who creates the impression by calling us to perform His will as soon as it is exhibited, rather than the mind laboriously foreseeing and seeking it. In short, let us make it a habit to recollect ourselves during the day in the midst of our activities by a simple view of God. By that means let us silence all the movements of our heart when it appears in the least agitated. Let us separate ourselves from all that does not come from God. Let us suppress our superfluous thoughts and amusements. Let us speak no useless word. Let us seek God within us, and we will not fail to find Him, and with Him joy and peace.

While outwardly busy, let us be more occupied with God than with everything else. To be rightly engaged, we must be in His presence and employed for Him. At the sight of the Majesty of God, our interior should become calm and remain peaceful. Once a single word of the Savior suddenly calmed a furiously agitated sea.[171] One look of His at us, and of ours toward Him, should always perform the same miracle within us.

We must often raise our hearts to God. He will purify, enlighten, and direct them. This was the daily practice of the sacred Psalmist: "I have set the Lord always before me."[172] Let us often employ the beautiful words of the same holy prophet, "Whom have I in heaven but Thee? and there is none upon earth that I desire beside Thee! . . . God is the strength of my heart, and my portion forever!"[173]

We must not wait for a leisure hour when we can shut our doors [and be alone with God]. The moment we use in regretting that we have no opportunity to be recollected, might be profitably spent in recollection.[174] Let us turn our hearts toward God in a simple, familiar, spirit, full of confidence in Him. The most interrupted moments, such as while eating or listening to others, are valuable. Tiresome and idle talk in our presence, instead of annoying, will afford us the delight of employing the interval in seeking God. Thus "all things work together for good to them that love God."[175]

We must read [our Bible and spiritual material] according to our necessity and desire, but with frequent interruptions, for the purpose of recollection. A word or two that is simple and full of the Spirit of God will be to us as hidden manna. We forget the words, but the effect remains. They operate in secret, and the soul is fed and enriched.

26
Conformity to the will of God

The essence of virtue consists in the attitude of the will. This is what the Lord would teach us when He said, "The kingdom of God is within you."[176] It is not a question of extensive knowledge, of splendid talents, or even of great deeds. It is a simple matter of having a heart and loving. Outward works are the fruits and consequences of loving, and the spring of all good things is at the bottom of the soul.

There are some virtues that are appropriate to certain conditions, and not to others. Some are good at one time, and some at another. But an upright will is profitable for all times and all places. That kingdom of God that is within us consists in our willing whatever God wills—always, in everything, and without reservation. It is in this way that His kingdom comes. For His will is then done as it is in Heaven,[177] since we will nothing but what is dictated by His sovereign pleasure.

Blessed are the poor in spirit![178] Blessed are they who are stripped of everything, even of their own wills, that they may no longer belong to themselves! How poor in spirit those become who have given up all things to God! But how is it that our will becomes right when it unreservedly conforms to that of God? We will whatever He wills. What He does not will, we do not. We attach our feeble wills to that all-powerful one that regulates everything. Therefore nothing can ever come to pass against our wishes. For nothing can happen contrary to the will of God, and we find in His good pleasure an inexhaustible source of peace and consolation.

The interior life is the beginning of the blessed peace of the saints, who eternally cry, "Amen, Alleluia!"[179] We adore, we praise, we bless God in everything. We see Him continually, and in all things His paternal hand is the sole object of our contemplation. There are no longer any evils. For as the Apostle Paul wrote, even the most terrible things that come upon us work together for good to those that love God. Can the suffering that God destines to purify and make us worthy of Himself, be called an evil?

Let us, therefore, cast all our cares into the bosom of so good a Father, and allow Him to do as He pleases. Let us be content to adopt His will in all points, and to abandon our own absolutely and forever. How can we retain anything of our own when we do not even belong to ourselves? The slave has nothing. How much less, then, should we own anything, who in ourselves are but nothingness and sin, and who are indebted for everything to pure grace! God has only bestowed upon us a will that is free and capable of self-possession so that we may the more generously recompense the gift by returning it to its rightful owner.

We have nothing but our wills. All the rest belongs elsewhere. Disease removes life and health, riches disappear faster than they come, intellectual talents depend upon the state of the body. The only thing that really belongs to us is our will. It is of this, therefore, that God is especially jealous. For He gave us our will, not so that we would retain it, but that we would return it to Him—as whole as we received it, and without the slightest reservation.

If the least desire remains, or the smallest hesitation, it is robbing God, and is contrary to the order of creation. For all things come from Him, and to Him they are all due.

Alas, how many souls are full of self, and desire doing good and serving God, but in such a way as to suit themselves. They desire to impose rules upon God concerning His manner of drawing them to Himself. They want to serve and possess Him, but they are not willing to abandon themselves to Him and be possessed by Him.

What a resistance they offer to Him, even when they appear so full of zeal and fervor! It is certain that in one sense their spiritual abundance becomes an obstacle to their progress. For they hold even their virtues aside, and constantly seek self, even in good. Walking always in virtue on a road of their own choice, they nevertheless consider themselves superior to that humble heart that renounces its own life and every selfish movement, and dismisses all will except that which God gives from moment to moment, in accordance with His Gospel and providence!

Herein lies the meaning of those words of the Lord; "If any man will come after me, let him deny himself, and take up his cross, and follow me."[180]

We must follow Jesus Christ step by step, and not open up a path for ourselves. We can only follow Him by denying ourselves, and what is this but unreservedly abandoning every right over ourselves? For this reason, the apostle Paul tells us, "Ye are not your own."[181] Not a thing remains that belongs to us! Alas for those who resume possession of anything after once abandoning it!

To desire to serve God in one place rather than in another, in this way rather than in that, is desiring to serve Him in our own way rather than in His. But to be equally ready for all things, to will everything and nothing, to leave ourselves in His hands, like a toy in the hands of a child, to set no bounds to our abandonment, for the perfect reign of God cannot tolerate them, this is really denying ourselves. This is treating Him like God, and ourselves like creatures made solely for His use.

27
General directions for attaining inward peace

There is no peace for those who resist God.—if there is joy in the world, it is reserved for a pure conscience. The whole earth is full of tribulation and anguish to those who do not possess it.

How different is the peace of God from that of the world! It calms the passions, preserves the purity of the conscience, is inseparable from righteousness, unites us to God, and strengthens us against temptations. The peace of the soul consists in an absolute resignation to the will of God.

"Martha, Martha, thou art careful and troubled about many things; but one thing is needful."[182] The pain we suffer from so many occurrences, arises from the fact that we are not entirely abandoned to God in everything that happens.

Let us, therefore, put all things into His hands, and offer them to Him in our hearts as a sacrifice beforehand. From the moment that you cease to desire anything according to your own judgment, and begin to will everything just as God wills it, you will be free from your former tormenting reflections and anxieties about your own concerns. You will no longer have anything to conceal or take care of.

Until then, you will be troubled, vacillating in your views and enjoyments, easily dissatisfied with others and but little satisfied with yourself, and full of reserve and distrust. Until they become truly humble and simple, your good intentions will only torment you. Your piety, however sincere, will be the occasion of more internal reproach then of support or consolation. But if you will abandon your whole heart to God, you will be full of peace and joy in the Holy Ghost.[183]

Alas for you if you consider people in the work of God! In our choice of a guide, people must be counted as nothing. The slightest respect for their opinion dries up the stream of grace and increases our indecision. We also suffer and we displease God.

How can we refuse to bestow all our love upon God, who first loved us with the tender love of a Father, pitying our frailty, and well knowing the mire from which we have been dragged? When a soul is filled with this love, it enjoys peace of conscience, it is content and happy, it requires neither greatness nor reputation, nor pleasure, nor any of the perishing gifts of time. It desires only the will of God, and watches incessantly in the joyful expectation of its Spouse.

28
Only pure love can suffer rightly and love its sufferings

We know that we must suffer, and that we deserve it. Nevertheless, we are always surprised at affliction, as if we thought we neither merited nor had need of it. It is only true and pure love that delights to endure, for nothing else is perfectly abandoned. Resignation induces us to bear pain, but there is a something in [the resignation itself] that is afflicted in the suffering and resists. The resignation that measures out its abandonment to God with selfish reflection is willing to suffer, but is constantly examining to determine whether it suffers acceptably. In fact, the resigned soul is composed as it were of two persons—one keeping the other in subjection, and watching lest it should revolt.

In pure, unselfish, and abandoned love, the soul is fed in silence on the cross, and on union with the crucified Savior, without any reflections on the severity of its sufferings. There exists but a single, simple, will, which permits God to see it just as it is, without endeavoring to behold itself. It says nothing, does nothing. What then does it do? It suffers. And is this all? Yes, all—it has nothing else to do but to suffer. Love can be heard easily enough without speech or thought. It does all that it is required to do, which is, to have no will when it is stripped of all consolation. The purest of all loves is a will so filled with [the will] of God that nothing remains [of itself].

What a consolation is it to think that we are then rid of so many anxieties about our exercise of patience and the other virtues in the sight of those about us? It is enough to be humbled and abandoned in the midst of suffering. This is not courage—it is something both more and less. Less in the eyes of the ordinary class of Christians, more in the eyes of pure faith. It is a humiliation that raises the soul into all the greatness of God. A weakness that strips it of every resource, to bestow upon it His omnipotence. "When I am weak," Paul said, "then

I am strong. . . . I can do all things through Christ which strengtheneth me."[184]

It is sufficient, therefore, to feed upon some short sentences suited to our state and our taste, with frequent interruptions to quiet the senses and make room for the inward spirit of reflection. We sometimes suffer even though we hardly know that we are in distress. At other times we suffer and know that we bear it poorly, but we carry this second and heavier cross without impatience. True love always goes straightforward, not in its own strength, but considering itself as nothing. Then indeed we are truly happy. The cross is no longer a cross when there is no self to suffer under it, and to appropriate its good and evil.

29
Interested love and disinterested love have their own seasons

Why do the gifts of God confer more pleasure when they exist in us than when they exist in our neighbor, if we are not attached to self? If we prefer to see the gifts of God in our possession rather than in that of those about us, we shall certainly be afflicted when we see the gifts more perfect in them than they are in us. This is envy. What is our duty then? We must rejoice that the will of God is done in us, and that it reigns there not for our happiness and perfection, but for His own good pleasure and glory.

Now, take notice of two matters. The first is, that this distinction is not an empty subtlety. For in God's desire to desolate the soul for its own perfection, He causes it to pass through these trials of self, and never lets it alone until He has deprived its love of selfish reflection and support. There is nothing so jealous, so exacting, and so searching as this principle of pure love. It cannot tolerate a thousand things that were imperceptible in our previous state. Also, what pious persons would call an "unprofitable nicety," seems an essential point to the soul that is desirous of destroying self. The fire in the furnace consumes all that is not gold, so it seems necessary that the heart be melted with fervent heat so that the love of God may be rendered pure.

The second remark is, that God does not pursue every soul in this way in the present life. There is an infinite number of truly pious persons whom He leaves in some degree under the dominion of self-love. These remains of self, help to support them in the practice of virtue, and serve to purify them to a certain point. Hardly anything would be more unwise or more dangerous than to deprive them of the contemplation of the grace of God in them concerning their own personal perfection.

The first exercise disinterested gratitude. They are thankful to God for whatever He does in them, solely because He does it for His own glory. The second are also grateful, but partly because their own perfection is secured at the same time.

If the former try to deprive the latter of this mixed motive and this interior comfort in self in reference to grace, they would cause them as much injury as they would an infant by weaning it before it was able to eat. To take [a child] away the breast would be to destroy it.

We must never seek to deprive a soul of the food that still contains nourishment for it, and that God lets remain as a support for its weakness. To forestall grace is to destroy it.

In the same way, the latter must not condemn the former because they do not see them as much concerned as they are about their own perfection in the grace ministered to them. God works in every one as He pleases: "the wind blows where it wishes,"[185] and as it wishes. Forgetting self in pure contemplation of God is a state in which God can do in our souls whatever most pleases Him.

The important point is that those who are still in a measure supported by self, should not be too anxious about the state of those that are in pure love, nor should these latter try to make the former pass through the trials peculiar to a higher state of grace before God calls them to it.

30
True liberty

When we are no longer hampered by the restless reflections of self, we begin to enjoy true liberty.

But false wisdom that is always on the watch, ever occupied with self, constantly jealous of its own perfection, suffers severely whenever it is permitted to notice the smallest speck of imperfection.

Not that those who are simple minded and detached from self fail to work toward the attainment of perfection. They are successful in direct proportion to the degree that they forget themselves, and never dream of virtue in any other light than as something that accomplishes the will of God.

The source of all our defects is the love of self. We direct everything to that instead of to the love of God. Those who labor to get rid of self, to deny self in keeping with instructions of Jesus,clxxxvi strike at once at the root of every evil. And in this simple abandonment of self, they find the germ of every good. It is then that those words of Scripture are heard within and understood, "where the Spirit of the Lord is, there is liberty."clxxxvii

We neglect nothing to cause the kingdom of God to come both within and without; but in the midst of our frailties we are at peace. We would rather die than commit the slightest voluntary sin, but we have no fear for our reputation in the judgment of people. We court the reproach of Christ Jesus, and dwell in peace though surrounded by uncertainties. The judgments of God do not frighten us, for we abandon ourselves to them, imploring His mercy according to our attainments in confidence, sacrifice, and absolute surrender. The greater the abandonment, the more flowing the peace. [Our abandonment] sets us in such a large place that we are prepared for everything. We will everything and nothing. We are as open as babes.

Our enlightenment from God discovers the lightest transgressions, but never discourages. We walk before Him. But if we stumble, we swiftly resume our way, and have no watchword but Onward!

If we would find God, we must destroy the remains of the old Adam within. The Lord held a little child in His arms and declared, "of such is the kingdom of Heaven."[188]

The sum of the principal directions is this: Do not reason too much, always have an upright purpose in the smallest matters, and pay no attention to the thousand reflections by which we wrap and bury ourselves in self, under pretence of correcting our faults.

31
The employment of time

I understand perfectly well that you do not ask me for any proof that we are obliged to employ all our time to good purpose—grace has long since convinced you of this. It is a pleasant thing to come in contact with those who can meet us half way. But, notwithstanding this, much remains to be done, and there is a wonderful distance between the conviction of the intellect, even combined with the good intention of the heart, and a faithful and exact obedience.

Nothing has been more common in ancient and modern times then to meet souls who were perfect and holy, theoretically. "Ye shall know them by their fruits," says the Savior.[189] This is the only rule that never deceives us when it is properly understood. It is by this rule that we must judge ourselves.

There is a time for everything in our lives. But the principle that governs every moment is that none of them should be useless. They should all enter into the order and sequence of our salvation. They all should be accompanied by duties that God has allotted with His own hand, and for which He will demand an account.

From the first instant of our existence to the last, God has never assigned us a barren moment, or one that we can consider as given up to our own discretion. The great thing is to recognize His will in relation to them. This is to be brought about not by an eager and restless seeking that is much more likely to spoil everything rather than reveal out duty to us, but by a true submission to those whom God has set over us. Also by a pure and upright heart that seeks God in its simplicity, and heartily opposes all the duplicity and false wisdom of self as fast as it is revealed.

We misuse our time not only when we do wrong or do nothing, but also when we do something other than what was required of us at the moment, even though [that other something] may be the means of good. We are strangely clever in perpetually seeking our own interest. What the world does nakedly and without shame, those who desire to be devoted to God do also. But they do it in a refined manner under cover of some pretext that serves as a veil to hide from them the deformity of their conduct.

The best general means to ensure the profitable employment of our time is to accustom ourselves to living in continual dependence upon the Spirit of God and His law. [All the while] receiving whatever He is pleased to bestow, consulting Him in every emergency requiring instant action, having recourse to Him in our weaker moments when virtue seems to fail, invoking His aid. We must especially raise our hearts to Him whenever we are solicited by sensible objects, and find ourselves surprised and estranged from God and far from the true road.

Happy is the soul that commits itself by a sincere self-abandonment into the hands of its Creator, ready to do all His will, and continually crying, "Lord, what wilt Thou have me to do? . . . Teach me to do Thy will, for Thou art my God!"[190]

During our necessary activities, we need only pay a simple attention to the leadings of divine providence. Since they are all prepared for us, and presented by Him, our only care should be to receive them with a childlike spirit, and submit everything absolutely to Him—our temper, our own will, our misgivings, our restlessness, our self-reflections, our overflowing emotions of hurry, and our excessive joy or other passions that assault us according to the degree that we are pleased or displeased with the different events of the day. Let us be careful, however, not to allow ourselves to be overwhelmed by the variety [and number] of our exterior activities, whatever they might be.

Let us endeavor to begin every activity with a pure view to the glory of God, continue it without distraction, and finish it without impatience.

The intervals of relaxation and amusement are the most dangerous seasons for us, and perhaps the most useful for others. We must, therefore, be on our guard that we are as faithful as possible to the presence of God. We must make use of all that Christian vigilance so much recommended by our Lord, raise our hearts to God in the simple view of faith, and dwell in sweet and peaceful dependence upon the Spirit of grace as the only means of our safety and strength. This is especially necessary for those who are looked up to as being in authority, and whose words may be the cause of so much good or evil.

Our leisure hours are ordinarily the sweetest and pleasantest for us. We can never use them better than in refreshing our spiritual strength by a secret and intimate communion with God. Prayer is so necessary, and the source of so many blessings, that those who have discovered the treasure cannot be prevented from having recourse to it, whenever they have an opportunity.

I could add much more concerning these matters, and I may perhaps do so, if my present views do not escape me. But, if they do, it is of little consequence. God gives others when He pleases. If He does not, it is a proof that they are not necessary; and if so, we should be well satisfied with their loss.

End Notes

1 Revelation 3:18

2 Isaiah 55:8-9

3 Genesis 1:3-19

4 Probably used in the sense of being capable of initiating, sustaining, or supporting reproduction-having within it the power or ability to create.

5 Spoken out loud

6 or substance

7 loved us

8 or received

9 Grace starts with God in eternity and is received by us in time.

10 John 6:35, 48

11 1 John 4:8, 16

12 Paraphrase summary of God's words of creation.

13 disinterest: freedom from selfish bias or self-interest

14 Ephesians 3:17

15 Genesis 5:1-3

16 Isaiah 14:14

17 Matthew 28:20

18 Philippians 2:13

19 Psalm 139:8

20 John 4:23-24

21 John 3:12

22 Ecclesiastes 1:14

23 Ephesians 5:18

24 1 Corinthians 4:9

25 Matthew 11:7

26 Philippians 1:6

27 2 Corinthians 5:17, Galatians 6:15 (NKJV)

28 Romans 9:20-23

29 Acts 9:6

30 Luke 1:38

31 Acts 2:38, 3:19, 17:30, 26:20

32 Matthew 11:25, Luke 10:21

33 Exodus 34:14, Deuteronomy 4:24

34 Romans 8:28

35 Proverbs 16:4

36 John 6:60

37 Matthew 6:8

38 Romans 8:26

39 Romans 8:27

40 Romans 8:26

41 Song of Solomon 5:2

42 Luke 12:37

43 Luke 13:6-9

44 Romans 1:18

45 John 3:8

46 2 Corinthians 3:17

47 Without sensing what is happening.

48 Psalm 66:20

49 Romans 8:29

50 Psalm 119:37

51 1 Corinthians 11:1 (NKJV)

52 Philippians 4:13

53 John 13:28, 1 Corinthians 4:10, 2 Corinthians 4:11

54 1 Peter 5:5

55 John 6:26

56 Matthew 7:17

57 What can be felt by the senses.

58 1 Peter 3:4

59 Isaiah 5:1 (NKJV)

60 Hebrews 11:8

61 Matthew 6:11, Luke 11:3

62 Exodus 16:19-20

63 Matthew 6:34

64 John 1:18

65 Exodus 13:21-22

66 Hebrews 11:8

67 Ephesians 1:9, Philippians 2:13

68 Luke 9:23

69 Isaiah 14:14

70 Luke 14:33

71 1 Corinthians 7:31

72 Luke 14:26

73 Matthew 10:34

74 Deuteronomy 4:24

75 For more on this subject, see the Pure Gold Classic, *The Practice*

of the Presence of God by Brother Lawrence. Published by Bridge-Logos Publishers.

76 Philippians 1:8

77 2 Corinthians 12:9

78 1 Thessalonians 4:1

79 Luke 10:41-42

80 Matthew 6:34

81 Luke 17:21

82 Matthew 6:11, Luke 11:3

83 For a similar, but more detailed teaching on this method, see *The Practice of the Presence of God* by Brother Lawrence, a Pure Gold Classic published by Bridge-Logos Publishers.

84 2 Corinthians 12:10

85 Isaiah 48:18

86 sensible: 1. Perceptible by the senses or by the mind. 2. Readily perceived; appreciable. 3. Having the faculty of sensation; able to feel or perceive.

87 Revelation 2:7; 22:2, 14

88 Psalm 25:15

89 Genesis 17:1

90 disinterested: free of self-interest or concern.

91 John 14, Romans 8

92 1 Corinthians 6:17

93 1 Kings 19:11-12 - My King James Version of the Bible has this marvelous marginal reading of the words "still small voice": That is, a delicate whispering, as of the breeze among the trees.

94 2 Corinthians 3:6

95 John 6:68

96 Hebrews 4:12

97 Luke 10:21

98 John 13:23

99 Proverbs 3:32 - Fénelon quoted the scripture from the Vulgate, which is the Latin edition or translation of the Bible made by St. Jerome at the end of the fourth century A.D. and now used in a revised form as the Roman Catholic authorized version. The King James Version translates the last word of the quotation as "righteous," and the New King James Version translates the word as "upright."

100 Paraphrase of John 14:23

101 Song of Solomon 2:14

102 Genesis 22:2

103 Job 9:4

104 2 Corinthians 12:9

105 occasion: an event or a happening - an incident

106 piety: the state or quality of being pious-especially: (1) religious devotion and reverence to God - (2) devotion and reverence to parents and family.

107 Zechariah 4:10

108 Hebrews 12:10

109 recollect: to summon back to awareness of the subject or situation at hand.

110 Joshua 3:1-4

111 Exodus 40:36-37

112 Matthew 12:32

113 2 Samuel 6:22 (KJV has it "more vile than thus")

114 Isaiah 49:15

115 Philippians 2:13

116 Hebrews 5:12-13

117 privation: lack of the basic necessities or comforts of life-or, the condition resulting from such lack

118 Original words: rendered hardy

119 Psalm 51:19

120 Luke 18:27

121 Hebrews 11:6

122 Matthew 7:14

123 In Fénelon's day there were no anesthetics, and so the patient was operated on while fully conscious and feeling all the pain of the surgery.

124 Matthew 10:30, Luke 12:7

125 Revelations 3:7-8

126 Matthew 26:38, Mark 14.34

127 1 Corinthians 2:11, 10

128 Job 9:4

129 prevenient: preceding, coming before — when used in relation to God, always means that God moves first, for example, He loves us before we love Him.

130 Joshua 5:13-14

131 As noted previously, in Fénelon's day there were no anesthetics, and so the patient was operated on while fully conscious and feeling all the pain of the surgery.

132 Fénelon is, of course, referring to that interior part of us called self, and not to our physical body.

133 Numbers 13:26 - 14:4, Deuteronomy 34:1-4

134 John 4:23-24

135 Ephesians 3:11

136 Isaiah 64:8

137 Matthew 19:29, Mark 10:30

138 1 Timothy 1:1, Hebrews 6:18-19

139 2 Corinthians 1:3

140 Psalm 34:8

141 Matthew 16:24

142 Matthew 7:13-14

143 Matthew 11:12

144 John 3:3, 7; 1 Peter 1:23

145 2 Chronicles 7:14

146 Luke 18:17

147 Matthew 5:3

148 Matthew 5:4

149 John 15:19; 17:14, 16

150 Genesis 3:17

151 Matthew 11:28-30

152 John 1:18

153 Luke 10:27

154 Revelation 3:16

155 Fénelon wrote that statement nearly 500 years ago. What would he think of the condition of our world today?

156 1 Corinthians 7:31

157 John 6:26

158 Mark 9:5

159 Hebrews 10:38

160 1 Corinthians 12:31

161 1 Corinthians 13:5 (NKJV)

162 2 Corinthians 5:2-4 — This appears to be a paraphrase and reversal of Paul's statement in the referenced verses.

163 Hebrews 5:12-14

164 1Corinthians 13:11

165 Psalm 30:6

166 See *The Imitation of Christ* by Thomas à Kempis in modern English, a Pure Gold Classic published by Bridge-Logos Publishers.

167 1 Timothy 4:6-8, Revelation 3:10

168 Genesis 17:1

169 Luke 17:21

170 1 Corinthians 14:33171

171 Mark 4:39

172 Psalm 16:8

173 Psalm 73:25, 26b

174 Bringing our thoughts and feelings inwardly toward God and away from outward distractions.

175 Romans 8:28

176 Luke 17:21

177 Matthew 6:10

178 Matthew 5:3

179 Revelation 19:4

180 Matthew 16:24, Luke 14:33

181 1 Corinthians 6:19

182 Luke 10:41-42a

183 Romans 14:17

184 2 Corinthians 12:10, Philippians 4:13

185 John 3:8 (NKJV).

186 Matthew 16:24, Mark 8:34, Luke 9:23

187 2 Corinthians 3:17

188 Matthew 19:14

189 Matthew 7:16

190 Acts 9:6, Psalm 143:10

SECTION II
SPIRITUAL COMPATRIOTS

FENELON
1651 - 1715

Revised from the biography by T.C. Upham:
The Story of Madame Guyon's Life
Originally printed by Sampson and Low, Inc., England

1

Fénelon
and Mme. Jeanne Guyon Meet

In 1688, Fénelon's history became interwoven with that of Madame Jeanne Guyon in a remarkable way. Because of the great controversy that arose because of their spiritual and intellectual relationship, we should consider some of the things that Fénelon's peers wrote about him.

In the *Memoirs of the Life of My Father*, the Chancellor D'Aguesseau wrote this about Fénelon.

> Fénelon was one of those uncommon men who are destined to give luster to their age, and who do equal honor to human nature by their virtues, and to literature by their superior talents. He was pleasant in his social behavior, and illuminating in his conversation. His peculiar qualities in this were a rich, delicate, and powerful imagination, but one which never let its power be felt. His eloquence had more of mildness in it than of forcefulness, and he triumphed

as much by the charms of his conversation as by the superiority of his talents.

He always brought himself to the level of his company. He never entered into arguments, and he sometimes appeared to yield to others at the very time that he was leading them. Grace dwelt upon his lips. He discussed the greatest subjects with ease, the most trifling [subjects] were ennobled by his pen, and upon the most barren [subjects] he scattered the flowers of rhetoric.

The peculiar, but unaffected mode of expression that he adopted, made many persons believe that he possessed universal knowledge, as if by inspiration. It might, indeed, have been almost said, that he rather invented what he knew than learned it. He was always original and creative, imitating no one, and impossible of being imitated. A noble distinctiveness pervaded his whole person, and a certain indefinable and sublime simplicity gave to his appearance the air of a prophet.

The account that is given of Fénelon by his contemporary, the Duke de St. Simon, is also striking.

Fénelon was a tall man, thin, well made, and with a large nose. From his eyes issued the fire and animation of his mind like a torrent. His countenance was such that I never saw one similar to it, and it could never be forgotten if once seen. It combined everything, and yet with everything in harmony. It was grave and yet alluring, it was solemn and yet gay, it portrayed equally the theologian, the bishop, and the nobleman. Everything that was visible in it, as well as in his whole person, was delicate, intellectual, graceful, becoming, and, above all, noble. It required an effort to cease looking at him.

All the portraits [of him] are strong resemblances, though they have not caught that harmony that was so striking in the original, and that individual delicacy that characterized each feature. His manners were answerable to his countenance. They had that air of ease and refinement that can be derived only from association with the best society, and which diffused itself over all his conversations.

Fénelon, who added fervent piety to the highest order of talents, and to the graces of expression and manner, had formed the purpose to live and act solely for the cause of God. His first plan was to go as a missionary to Canada, which at that time was ruled by France. Such a endeavor could not possibly furnish any attractions to a person of his turn of mind apart from religion. In the simplicity and love of his heart, he was willing to spend the splendid powers that God had given him in instructing a few ignorant savages in the Way of life.

Disappointed in this, he next turned his attention to Greece. He indulged the hope that he might be permitted to preach the gospel in a land that could not fail to be endeared to him by many classical and historical writings. There is a letter written by Fénelon that is still in existence. It is interesting if for no other reason than as a memorial of the young Fénelon, and one in which the warmth of his heart blends with the vividness of his imagination. It is dated at Sarlat, and was probably addressed to Bossuet.[1] The following is a part of it.

Several trifling events have hitherto prevented my return to Paris. But I shall at length set out, sir, and I shall almost fly [in that direction]. But, compared with this journey, I meditate [upon] a much greater one. The whole of Greece opens before me, and the Sultan flies in terror. The Peloponnesus[2] breathes again in liberty, and the Church of Corinth shall flourish once more— the voice of the apostle shall be heard there again. I seem to be transported among those enchanting places and those inestimable ruins, where, while I collect the most curious relics of antiquity, I imbibe also its spirit.

I seek for the Areopagus,[3] where St. Paul declared to the sages of the world the unknown God.[4] I kneel down, 0 happy Patmos![5] upon thy earth, and kiss the steps of the apostle—and I shall almost believe that the heavens are opening on my sight.

Once more, after a night of such long darkness, the dayspring dawns in Asia. I behold the land that has been sanctified by the steps of Jesus, and crimsoned with His blood. I see it delivered from its profaneness, and clothed anew in glory. The children of Abraham are once more assembling together from the four quarters of the earth, over which they have been scattered, to acknowledge Christ whom they pierced, and to show forth the Lord's resurrection to the end of time.

In this plan also Fénelon was disappointed, for there was work for him in France.

It was a part of the system of Louis XIV[6] to establish uniformity of religion, and he had the wisdom to see that in carrying out this difficult plan he needed the aid of distinguished men. As a preliminary step, Louis had revoked the edict of Nantes. This edict, promulgated in 1598 by Henry IV, embodied principles of toleration, which furnished a considerable degree of protection to the French Protestants for many years. Intoxicated with power, and ignorant of that sacred regard that is owed to the religious rights and principles of others, Louis began, even before revocation of the edict, a series of hostile acts that were entirely inconsistent with the terms and principles of Henry's edict.

The sword was drawn in aid of the mystical Church, blood had already been shed in some places, and it is stated that soon after the evocation of the protecting edict, no less than fifty thousand families left France. To do so, many of them were forced to leave behind everything, but they considered their belief in Christ more precious to them than worldly prosperity.

Louis XIV was so intent on making Roman Catholicism the exclusive religion of his kingdom, that he united together different and discordant systems of proselytism,[7] and added the milder methods of persuasion to the argument of the sword. There were men among the Protestants who could never be terrified, but might possibly be convinced. Knowing their tenacity of opinion, if not the actual strength of their theological position, Louis sent religious teachers among them, who were distinguished for their ability, mildness, and prudence. Under these circumstances, he cast his eye upon the Abbé de Fénelon.

The young Abbé was summoned before the king. He received from the king's lips the commission that indicated the field and the nature of his labors. The labor assigned to him was the difficult one of showing to the Protestants, whose property had been pillaged, whose families bad been scattered, and whose blood had been shed like water, the truth and excellencies of the religion of their persecutors.

Fénelon, who understood the tyrannical disposition of Louis, and at the same time felt an instinctive aversion to the violent course he was pursuing, saw the difficulty of his position. He consented, however, to undertake this trying and almost hopeless embassy on one condition only. Namely, that the armed force be removed from the province to which he was sent as a missionary, and that military coercion cease.

It was In Poitou, which Louis had assigned to him as the field of his missionary labors, that Fénelon first heard of Madame Guyon. He became acquainted with the remarkable story of her missionary labors, of her writings on religion and religious experience, and of the high and somewhat peculiar character of her piety.

After nearly three years, Fénelon completed his mission work in Poitou. During those years he had secured the respect and affection of those from whom he differed in opinion, and his desire to know something more about Madame Guyon had grown stronger.

On his return [to Paris] in the latter part of 1688, he passed through Montargis, the early scene of Madame Guyon's life. Thinking it proper to learn all that be conveniently could of her character before be formed a closer acquaintance with her, which he evidently intended to do after his return to Paris, be made all the inquiries necessary. " Questioning several persons about her," says M. de Bausset, "who had witnessed her conduct during her early years, and while she was married, he was interested by the unanimous testimonies that he heard of her piety and goodness."

At Paris, he learned more distinctly [about her] the facts that had been told him while in Poitou. He also learned that she was in disgrace with the king. Knowing as he did the jealous and tyrannical tendencies of the mind of Louis, if he consulted merely worldly interest he would have avoided her. But following the suggestions of his own benevolent heart, and of that silent voice that God utters in the souls of those who love Him, he did otherwise.

Fénelon met Madame Guyon for the first time at the house of the Duchess of Charost, who had a retired establishment at the village of Beine, a few miles beyond Versailles[8] and St. Cyr, where Madame Guyon made frequent visits.

It somewhat saved appearances for Fénelon to meet her here, and so their meeting at this place seems to have been the result of a private arrangement. They talked together for a long time. Not on worldly subjects, for that was foreign to their feelings. Not on the external arrangements and progress of the Church, for that was a subject that had been familiar to them from childhood. But on a subject vastly more important than either—the inward religion of the heart and soul.

The immense importance of the subject, the relation between the doctrines of a transforming and sanctifying spirituality and the deeply felt needs of his own soul, the presence and fervid eloquence of a woman whose rank, beauty, and afflictions could not fail to excite an interest exceeded only by that of her evangelical simplicity and sanctity, made a deep impression on the mind of Fénelon.

After spending a part of the day, they both returned to Paris in the same carriage, accompanied by a young female attendant, whom Madame Guyon kept with her. This gave them further opportunity to explore their subject, and for Madame Guyon to explain more specifically her views of religious experience and growth. From that time they were intimate friends.

In later writings, Madame Guyon wrote:

Some days after my release from prison,[9] having heard of the Abbé de Fénelon, my mind was taken up with him with much force and sweetness. It seemed to me that the Lord would make me an instrument of spiritual good to him, and that, in the experience of a common spiritual advancement, He would unite us together in a very intimate manner.

I inwardly felt, however, that this interview, without failing to increase his interest in the subject of the Interior Life, did not fully satisfy him. And I, on my part, experienced something that made me desire to pour out my heart more fully into his. But there was not as yet an entire harmony in our views and experience, which made me suffer much on his account.

It was in the early part of the next day that I saw him again, (at the house of the Duchess of Bethune [in Paris]. My soul desired that he might be all that the Lord would have him to be. We remained together for some time in silent prayer; and not without a spiritual blessing. The obscurity that had hitherto rested upon his spiritual views and exercises began to disappear; but still he was not yet such as I desired him to be.

During eight whole days he rested as a burden on my spirit. During that time my soul suffered and wrestled for him; and then, the agony of my spirit passing away, I found inward rest.

Since that time, looking upon him as one wholly given to the Lord, I have felt myself united to him without any obstacle. And our union of spirit with each other has increased ever since, after a manner pure and ineffable. My soul has seemed to be united to his in the bond of Divine love, as was that of Jonathan to David. The Lord has given me a view of the great designs He has upon this person, and how dear he is to Him.

The following letter appears to have been the first that passed between them:

Paris, November 1688.

To the Abbé de Fénelon — I take the liberty to send you some of my writings. It is my desire that you should act the part of a censor in regard to them. Mark with your disapproval everything in them that comes from the imperfections of the creature rather than from the Spirit of God. I have other writings, which, if I did not fear to tire you, it would please me much to bring under your notice, to be preserved or to be destroyed as you might think them worthy of preservation or otherwise.

If I should learn that you do not consider those which are now sent as unworthy of your attention, I may send the others at some future time. Since I send them in the spirit of submission to your theological and critical

judgment, and with entire sincerity, I count upon it that
you will spare nothing that ought not to be spared.
When you shall have read the sheets that I have sent to
you, you will do me a favor by returning them with
your corrections.

Permit me to expect that you will deal with me without
ceremony. Have no regard to me, separate from what
is due to truth and to God's glory. God has given me
great confidence in you, but He does not allow me to
cause you trouble. And you will tell me frankly when I
do so.

I am ready to keep up some correspondence with you.
If God inspires you with different views, let me know
without hesitation. I readily submit myself to you. I
have already followed your advice in the matter of
confession.[10]

And now I will turn to another subject. For seven days
past I have been in a state of continual prayer for you.
I call it prayer, although the state of mind has been
somewhat peculiar. I have desired nothing in
particular; have asked nothing in particular. But my
soul, presenting continually its object before God, that
God's will might be accomplished and God's glory
might be manifested in it, has been like a lamp that
burns without ceasing. Such was the prayer of Jesus
Christ. Such is the prayer of the Seven Spirits who
stand before God's throne, and who are well compared
to seven lamps that burn night and day.[11]

It seems to me that the designs of mercy, which God
has upon you, are not yet accomplished. Your soul is
not yet brought into full harmony with God, and
therefore I suffer. My suffering is great. My prayer is
not yet heard.

The prayer that I offer for you is not the work of the creature. It is not a prayer self-made, formal, and outward. It is the voice of the Holy Ghost uttering itself in the soul, an inward burden that man cannot prevent nor control. The Holy Ghost prays with effect. When this inward voice ceases, it is a sign that the grace that has been supplicated is sent down.

I have been in this state of mind before for other souls, but never with such struggle of spirit, and never for so long a time. God's designs will be accomplished upon you. I speak with confidence, but I think it cannot be otherwise. You may delay the result by resistance, but you cannot stop it. Opposition to God, who comes to reclaim the full dominion of the heart, can have no other effect than to increase and prolong the inward suffering. Pardon the Christian plainness with which I express myself.

J. M. B. de la Mothe Guyon

Fénelon and Madame Guyon had opportunities to see each other both at Paris and Versailles. But still it was not convenient, and perhaps not proper, that they should see each other very often. But the deep interest felt by Madame Guyon, and the many questions that Fénelon found it necessary to propose to her higher experience, rendered it necessary that they should correspond. The very next day she wrote another letter, which is here given in part .

Paris, November 1688.

To the Abbé de Fénelon — The application of my soul to God on your account has been so deeply absorbing that I have slept but little during the past night. And at this moment I can give an idea of my state only by saying that my spirit, in the interest that it feels for your entire renovation, burns and consumes itself within me.

I have an inward conviction that the obstacle that has to this time separated you from God, is diminishing and passing away. [This conviction is so] certain that my soul begins to feel a spiritual likeness and union with yours, which it has not previously felt. God appears to be making me a medium of communicating good to you, and to be imparting to my soul graces that are ultimately destined to reach and to bless yours.

It may not be improper to say, however, that while He is blessing and raising you in one direction, He seems to be doing that which may be the means of profitable humiliation in another. That is, by making a woman, and one so unworthy as myself, the channel of communicating His favors. But I too must be willing to be where God has placed me, and not refuse to be an instrument in His hands. He assigns me my work. And my work is to be an instrument. And it is because I am an instrument, which He employs as He pleases, that He will not let me go.

Nevertheless, He makes me happy in being His prisoner. He holds me incessantly, and still more strongly than ever, in His presence. And my business there is to present you before Him, that His will may be accomplished in you. And I cannot doubt that the will of God is showing itself in mercy and that you are entering into union with Him, because I find that my own soul, which has already experienced this union, is entering into union with you through Him. It doing this in such a manner that no one can well explain who has not had the experience of it. . . . So easy, so natural, so prompt are the decisions of the sanctified soul on all moral and religious subjects that it seems to reach its conclusions intuitively . . .

Be so humble and childlike as to submit to the dishonor, if such it may be called, of receiving blessings from God through one so poor and unworthy as myself. By this, the grace that God has imparted to my own heart flowing instrumentally into yours, and producing a similarity of dispositions, our souls shall become like two rivers mingling in one channel and flowing on together to the ocean. Receive, then, the prayer of this poor heart, since God wills it to be so.

The pride of nature, in one in your position,[12] will cry out against it. But remember that the grace of God is magnified through the weakness of the instrument He employs.[13] Accept this method in entire contentment and abandonment of spirit—as I have no doubt that you will, simply because God wills it. And be entirely assured that God will bless His own instrument in granting everything that will be necessary to you.

I close by repeating the deep sympathy and correspondence of spirit which I have with you.

Jeanne Marie B. de la Mothe Guyon

2

Fénelon's Spiritual Condition

Those who are acquainted with the personal history of Fénelon, know how fully he combined greatness of intellect with humility and benevolence of temper. Thus it was not difficult for him to associate with others, or even to receive instruction in those particulars in which his own experience was defective. Accordingly, he did not hesitate to state frankly those points in which he needed advice. He was already a religious man in a high sense, but still it seemed to him that he was not all that he should be, and not all that with divine aid he could be. He panted for higher advancements. He could not rest until he possessed victory over the natural evils of the heart and had become one with God in freedom from selfishness, and in purity and perfection of love.

The first struggle of his mind seemed to turn upon the point of whether he should make to God that essential entire and absolute consecration of himself in all things. He realized that without this consecration, the higher results to which his mind was directed would be impossible.

Having taken this first and great step, he awaited the dealings of God with submission, but not without some degree of perplexity. The way was new, and it baffled in his case, as it generally does in others, all the conjectures of merely human wisdom. The matter of forgiveness through Jesus Christ as our Savior from the penalty of violated law, was easily understood. But the matter of holy living, of being kept moment by moment in distinction from forgiveness in the first instance, presented itself as a problem attended with different incidents, and perhaps involving new principles.

For two years Fénelon and Madame Guyon wrote frequently to each other. In her letters, it is easy to see her untiring patience and her deep religious insight. It was hard for him at first to understand, and to realize in practice, the great lesson of living by faith alone. Even at the end of some six or eight months after their correspondence began, he had questions to ask and difficulties to be resolved.

In this state of things she wrote him a long letter, in which she gives a general view of the process in which the soul, that is entirely consecrated to God, undergoes the successive steps of inward crucifixion and of progressive conformity, until it realizes the highest results. She took great pains with it. It is entitled, A Concise View of the Soul's Return to God, and of its Reunion with Him.[14]

To this we find a well-digested answer of some length from Fénelon, which is here summarized.

Paris, August 11, 1689.

To Madame De La Mothe Guyon — I think, Madame, that I understand, in general, the statements in the paper that you had the kindness to send to me, in which you describe the various experiences that characterize the soul's return to God by means of simple or pure faith. I will endeavor, however, to summarize some of your views, as they present themselves to me, that I may learn whether I correctly understand them.

1. The first step that is taken by the soul that has formally and permanently given itself to God, would be to bring what may be called its external powers—that is, its natural appetites and propensities, under subjection. The religious state of the soul at such times is characterized by that simplicity that shows its sincerity, and that it is sustained by faith. So that the soul does not act of itself alone, but follows and cooperates, with all its power, with that grace that is given it. It gains the victory through faith.

2. The second step is to cease to rest on the pleasures of inward sensibility. The struggle here is, in general, more severe and prolonged. It is hard to die to these inward tastes and relishes, which make us feel so happy, and which God usually permits us to enjoy and to rest upon in our first experience. When we lose our inward happiness, we are very apt to think that we lose God—not considering that the moral life of the soul does not consist in pleasure, but in union with God's will, whatever that may be. The victory here also is by faith—acting, however, in a little different way.

3. Another step is that of entire crucifixion to any reliance upon our virtues, either outward or inward. The habits of the life of self have become so strong, that there is hardly anything in which we do not take a degree of complacency. Having gained the victory over its senses, and having gained so much strength that it can live by faith, independently of inward pleasurable excitements, the soul begins to take a degree of satisfaction, which is secretly a selfish one, in its virtues, in its truth, temperance, faith, benevolence,

and to rest in them as if they were its own—and as if they gave it a claim of acceptance on the ground of its merit. We are to be dead to them, considered as coming from ourselves, and alive to them only as the gifts and the power of God. We are to have no perception or life in them, in the sense of taking a secret satisfaction in them, and are to take satisfaction in the Giver of them only.

4. A fourth step consists in a cessation or death to that revulsion that people naturally feel to those dealings of God that are involved in the process of inward crucifixion. The plows that God sends upon us are received without the opposition that once existed, and existed oftentimes with great power. So clear is the soul's perception of God's presence in everything, and so strong is its faith, that those apparently adverse dealings, once exceedingly trying, are now received not merely with acquiescence,[15] but with cheerfulness. It kisses the hand that smites it.

5. When we have proceeded so far, the natural man is dead. And then comes, as a fifth step in this process, the new life—not merely the beginning, but a new life in the higher sense of the terms, the resurrection of the life of love. All those gifts that the soul before sought in its own strength, and perverted and rendered poisonous and destructive to itself, by thus seeking them out of God, are now richly and fully returned to it, by the great Giver of all things. It is not the design or plan of God to deprive His creatures of happiness, but only to pour the cup of bitterness into all that happiness, and to smite all that joy and prosperity that the creature has in anything out of himself.

6. And this life, in the sixth place, becomes a truly transformed life, a life in union with God, when the will of the soul becomes not only conformed to God

practically and in fact, but is conformed to Him in everything in it, and in the relations it sustains, which may be called a disposition or tendency. It is then that there is such a harmony between the human and Divine will, that they may properly be regarded as having become one. This, I suppose, was the state of St. Paul, when he says, "I live; yet not I, but Christ liveth in me."[16]

It is not enough to be merely passive under God's dealings. The spirit of entire submission is a great grace. But it is a still higher attainment to become flexible—that is to say, to move just as He would have us move. This state of mind might perhaps be termed the spirit of cooperation, or of Divine cooperation. In this state the will is not only subdued, but, what is very important, all tendency to a different or rebellious state is taken away. Of such a soul, which is described as the Temple of the Holy Ghost,[17] God Himself is the inhabitant and the light.

This transformed soul does not cease to advance in holiness. It is transformed without remaining where it is—new without being stationary. Its life is love, all love, but the capacity of its love continually increases.

Such, Madame, if I understand them, are essentially the sentiments of the letter that you had the kindness to send me.

I wish you to write me whether the statement that I have now made corresponds with what you intended to convey.

I would make one or two remarks further in explanation of what has been said. One of the most important steps in the process of inward restoration is to be found in the habits of the will. This I have already alluded to, but it is not generally well understood. A person may, perhaps, have a new life, but it cannot be regarded as a perfectly transformed life, a life brought into perfect harmony with God, until all the evil influences of former habits are corrected. When this takes place, it is perhaps not easy to determine, but must be left to each one's consciousness. This process must take place in the will, as well as in other parts of the mind. The action of the will must not only be free and right, but must be relieved from all tendency in another direction resulting from previous evil habits.

Another remark that I have to make, is in relation to faith. That all this great work is by faith, is true. But I think we should be careful, in stating the doctrine of faith, not to place it in opposition to reason. On the contrary, we only say what is sustained both by St. Paul and St. Augustine, when we assert that it is a very reasonable thing to believe. Faith is different from mere physical and emotive[18] impulse, and it would be no small mistake to accuse those who walk by faith as being thoughtless and impulsive persons and enthusiasts.

Faith is necessarily based upon preceding acts of intelligence. By the use of those powers of perception and reasoning, which God has given us, we have the knowledge of the existence of God. It is by their use also, that we know that God has spoken to us in His revealed Word. In that Word, which we thus receive and verify by reason, we have general truths laid down, general precepts communicated, applicable to our situation and duties. But these truths, coming from Him who has a right to direct us, are authoritative. They command. And it is our province and duty, in the exercise of faith in the goodness and wisdom of Him who issues the command, to yield obedience, and to go wherever it may lead us, however dark and mysterious the path may now appear. Those who walk by faith walk in obscurity, but they know that there is a light above them, which will make all clear and bright in its appropriate time. We trust—but, as St. Paul says, we know in whom we have trusted.[19]

I illustrate the subject, Madame, in this way. I suppose myself to be in a strange country. There is a wide forest before me, with which I am totally unacquainted, although I must pass through it. I accordingly select a guide, whom I suppose to be able to conduct me through these ways never before trodden by me. In following this guide, I obviously go by faith. But as I know the character of my guide, and as my intelligence or reason tells me that I ought to exercise such faith, it is clear that my faith in Him is not in opposition to reason, but is in accordance with it. On the contrary, if I refuse to have faith in my guide, and undertake to make my way through the forest by my own shrewdness and wisdom, I may properly be described as a person without reason, or as unreasonable. And I would probably suffer for my lack of reason by losing my way. Faith and reason, therefore, if not identical, are not in disagreement.

Fully subscribing, with these explanations, to the doctrine of faith as the life and guide of the soul, I remain, Madame, yours in our common Lord, Francis S. Fénelon.

3

The Inward Life

The principles of the inward life commended themselves entirely to Fénelon. It is true that these principles, to say nothing of the support they have in the Scriptures, are found with slight variations in many of the Mystic writers— Kempis,[20] Thauler, Ruysbroke, Cardinal Bona, Catherine of Genoa, John of the Cross, Brother Lawrence,[21] and others. But Fénelon does not appear to have been familiar with these writers at this time.

Although the principles were introduced to Fénelon through the instrument of a woman, who, though greatly accomplished in other respects had but a limited knowledge of theological writings, and had learned the principles not so much from books as from the dealings of God with her personally, they were nevertheless sustained by an inward conviction of their soundness. His enlightened and powerful mind, uninfluenced by the various prejudices that often prevent a correct perception, saw at once that they bore the signatures of reason and truth. So by letting them have their full power upon him, and endeavoring with divine assistance to be what he felt that he should be, he stood forth to the world as not merely a man, but a man in the image of Christ. He was a man more commended by his simplicity of spirit, his purity, and benevolence, than by the powers of his intellect and the perfection of his taste.

It is in this inward operation that we find the secret spring of that justice and benevolence that impart unspeakable attractions and power to his writings. They seem to be entirely exempted from the spirit of selfishness, and to be bathed in purity and love. It is generally accepted that no person reads the writings of Fénelon without feeling that he was an eminently good and holy man.

On receiving the letter from Fénelon, summarized in the previous chapter, Madame Guyon wrote a letter in reply. Here is the substance of that letter.

To the Abbé de Fénelon — It gives me great pleasure to perceive, sir, that you have a clear understanding of the sentiments that I wished to convey. I agree with you entirely that faith and reason, although different principles of action, are not opposed to each other. He, however, who lives by faith, ceases to reason on selfish principles and with selfish aims. Rather he submits his reason to that higher reason that comes to man through Jesus Christ, the true conductor of souls. He who walks in faith, walks in the highest wisdom, although it may not appear such to the world.

The world does not more clearly understand the truth and beauty of the life of faith, than the ancient Jews understood the divine but unpretentious beauty that shone in the life of Christ. A worldly mind that is full of the maxims of a worldly life is not in a condition to estimate the pure and simple spirit of one whose heart is conformed to the precepts of divine wisdom.

You will notice, that I use the term is appropriation,[22] and entire disappropriation, as convenient expressions for freedom from all selfish bias whatever. I perceive that you understand and appreciate entirely the idea that I endeavored imperfectly to express. Namely, that the misappropriation or unselfishness of the will is not to be regarded as perfect, merely because the will is broken down and submissive to such a degree as to have no repugnance whatever to anything that God in His providence may see fit to send.

It is true, this is a very great grace. In a mitigated sense, under such circumstances the will may be regarded as dead. But in the true and absolute sense, there is still in it a lingering life. There still remains a secret tendency, resulting from former selfish habits, that causes it to look back, as it were, with feelings of interest upon what is lost.

In other words, the will puts forth its purposes a little less promptly and powerfully in some directions than it would have done if it had been required to act in others. Thus Lot's wife had determined to leave the city of Sodom. She vigorously purposed, in going forth from the home where she had long dwelt, to conform to the decrees of Providence, which required her departure. But as she passed on in her flight over the plain there was a lingering attachment, a tendency to return, which induced her to look back. Her will, though strongly set in the right direction, did not act in perfect freedom and power because of certain latent reminiscences and attachments that operated as a hindrance.

In like manner the Jews, when they left the land of Goshen and were on their way to the better country that the Lord had promised them, often thought with complacency o! their residence in Egypt, and of what they enjoyed there.

In regard to the principle of FAITH, it sometimes lies latent, as it were, and concealed in the midst of discomfort and sorrow. I recollect that in the former periods of my experience I once spent a considerable time in a state of depression and deep sorrow, because I supposed I had lost God, or at least had lost His favor.[23] My grief was great and without cessation. If I had seen things as I now see them, and had understood them then as I now understand them, I would have found a principle of restoration and of comfort in the very grief that overwhelmed me.

How could I have mourned the loss of God's presence, or rather what seemed to me to be such loss, if I did not love Him? And how could I love Him, without faith in Him?

In my sorrow, therefore, I might have found the evidence of my faith. And it is a great truth that in reality, whatever may at times be the appearance, God never does desert, and never can desert, those who believe.

Desiring to receive from you, from time to time, such suggestions as may occur, and believing that your continued and increased experience in religious things will continually develop to you new truth, I remain, yours in our Lord,

Jeanne Maria B. de la Mothe Guyon

About this time, Fénelon, who had been selected in preference to able competitors, was appointed by Louis XIV as tutor to his grandson, the Duke of Burgundy, the heir-apparent to the throne of France. Fénelon was recommended to this position by the Duke de Beauvilliers, governor to the grandchildren of the king, of whom the Duke of Burgundy was the eldest.

About the appointment, Madame de Bausset wrote, "Louis XIV did not hesitate for a moment as to whom he should select as a governor for his grandson. Nor did Monsieur Beauvilliers hesitate a single moment as to the choice of a preceptor.[24] He nominated Fénelon to that office on the 17th of August 1689, the very day after his own appointment." The king apparently approved the nomination with entire cordiality, and the choice was greatly applauded in France. We have the testimony of Bossuet, who subsequently came into painful collision with Fénelon, how satisfactory and gratifying it was to him.

The appointment seems to have been unexpected by Fénelon, and certainly received without any solicitation. The duty especially assigned to him was to train up the young prince. He could not be ignorant of the vast responsibility of such an undertaking, but he did not see fit to decline it. He entered upon his duties in September 1689.

His pupil, the Duke of Burgundy, had but few of the elements required in someone destined to be the ruler of a great people. In his natural dispositions he was proud, passionate, and unpredictable. He was also tyrannical to his inferiors, and haughty and disobedient to those who had the control of him.

"The Duke of Burgundy," says Monsieur de St. Simon, "was by nature terrible. In his earliest youth he gave occasions for fear and dread. He was unfeeling and irritable to the last excess, even against inanimate objects. He was furiously impetuous, and incapable of enduring the least opposition, even of time and the elements, without breaking forth into such intemperate rage that it was sometimes to be feared that the very veins in his body would burst. This excess I have frequently witnessed."

These unhappy traits of disposition were made even more dangerous by being found in combination with a considerable powers of intellect. It was such a character that was committed to Fénelon to be trained, corrected, and remodeled.

To this great task, whose success apparently determined the hopes and happiness of France, Fénelon brought great powers of intellect, a finished education, and above all the graces of a pure, humble, and believing heart. It was this last trait, perhaps, more than the others that have been mentioned, that had recommended him to the Duke de Beauvilliers. It was natural for him to desire that the young prince, while he had other advantages and means of culture, should not be deprived of those connected with a religious example and with religious impressions. Fénelon undertook this difficult task, which he knew required something more than mere intellectual culture, as a man of faith and prayer.

In all her labors, Madame Guyon appreciated relations and effects. The soul of Fénelon in itself was not more dear than that of any other person. But when she considered the relations in which he stood, and the influence that he was capable of exerting, she felt how necessary it was that he be delivered from inferior motives, and act and live only in the Lord.

It is not surprising, therefore, that on the very day after his appointment she wrote a letter to him.

Paris, August 18, 1889.

To the Abbé de Fénelon — I have received without surprise, but not without sincere joy, the news of your appointment, in which it seems to me his Majesty has done no more than respond to your just claims. For some time past I have had but little doubt that the position would be given to you.

The last time in which I attended the mass,[25] at which you administered, I had an impression, without being able to tell why, that I might not hereafter have so frequent opportunities to unite with you in this service. The secret prayer arose from my heart — O that, amid the artifices of the world to which he is exposed, he may ever be a man of a simple and childlike spirit! I understand now, better than I did then, why it was that the Lord gave me such earnest desires in your behalf.

I should not be surprised, sir, if you experience some degree of natural distaste to the office, but you will commit yourself to the Lord who will enable you to overcome all such trials. Act always without regard to self. The less you have of self, the more you will have of God. Great as are the natural talents that God has given you, they will be found to be useful in the employment to which you are now called only in proportion as they move in obedience to divine grace.

You are called in God's providence to aid and to superintend in the education of a prince—whom, with all his faults, God loves, and has, it seems to me, designs to restore spiritually to Himself. And I have the satisfaction of believing that, in this important office, you will feel it your duty to act in entire dependence, moment by moment, on the influences of the Holy Spirit.

God has chosen you to be His instrument in this work, and He has chosen you for this purpose, while He has passed by others, because He has enabled you to recognize and appreciate in your own heart the divine movement. Although you may not, on account of the extreme youth of the prince, see immediately those fruits of your labors that you would naturally desire, still do not be discouraged.

Die to yourself in your hopes and expectations, as well as in other things. Leave all with God. Do not doubt that the fruit will come in its season; and that God, through the faith of those that love Him and labor for Him, will build up that which is now in ruins. Perhaps you will be made a blessing to the king, his grandfather, also.

This morning in particular, my mind was greatly exercised. And as I was thinking, in connection with your character and your position in society, of the deep interest that I had felt and continue to feel, the thought arose in my heart: Why is it so? Why does the heavy responsibility of watching and praying for you rest upon me, and consume me? I am but a little child, an infant. But a voice seemed to utter itself in my heart, and to reply: "Say not that thou art a little one. I have put my word in thy mouth. Go where I shall send thee, and speak what I shall command."[26]

I speak, then, because I must do what the Lord has appointed me to do, and because the Lord employs me as an instrument and speaks in me. Already my prayer is in part answered. When the work is completed, and when I see, in the full sanctification of a soul that is so dear to me, all that I have looked for and all that I have expected, then shall I be able to say, `Now, Lord, let thy servant depart in peace; for mine eyes have seen thy salvation."[27] — I remain yours in our Lord, Jeanne Marie B. de la Mothe Guyon

In the early part of 1689, a few months before the above events, some Roman Catholic priests and theological doctors made a visit to Dijon[28] and its neighborhood. To their great surprise, they found a considerable religious movement in progress, based upon the teachings of Madame Guyon.

In her return from Grenoble[29] to Paris in 1686, she passed through Dijon on her way and spent a day or two there. She left a deep impression on a few persons, especially Monsieur Claude Guillot, a priest of high character in the city. The seed thus sown in conversations, enforced by a single sermon from La Combs,[30] sprang up and bore fruit.

So much so, that in 1689 the new religious principles were creating a great deal of excitement.

The persons who visited Dijon at this time had some degree of ecclesiastical authority from Rome, and forcefully opposed this new religious activity. Among other things, they collected three hundred copies of the work of Madame Guyon on prayer, and had them publicly burned in the town square.[31]

The letters that passed between Madame Guyon and Fénelon over a period of two to three years, occupy nearly a full volume of her printed correspondence. The same great objects led them also to seek each other's company, with a view to a more direct interchange of opinions. These interviews at one period were frequent.

Madame Guyon resided with her daughter until the year 1692. Here, more than anywhere else, Fénelon had conversations with her, which she referred to in the following passage from her writings.

> The family into which my daughter married were
> numbered among the Abbé Fénelon's friends, so I had
> frequent opportunities of seeing him. Our
> conversations turned upon the inward and spiritual life.
> From time to time he expressed objections to my
> views and experience, which I endeavored to answer
> with sincerity and simplicity of spirit. The doctrines of
> Michael de Molinos[32] were so generally condemned
> that the plainest things began to be distrusted, and the
> terms used by writers on the spiritual life were for the
> most part regarded as objectionable and were set aside.
> But regardless of these unfavorable circumstances, I
> was enabled to explain everything to Fénelon so fully,
> that he gradually entered into the views that the Lord
> had led me to entertain, and finally gave them his
> unqualified agreement. The persecutions that he has
> suffered since are an evidence of the sincerity of his
> belief.

4

Bossuet and Fénelon

Over the years, Bossuet, Bishop of Meaux, and the recognized leader of the French Roman Catholic Church, became increasingly concerned about the teachings of Madame Jeanne Guyon and her effect upon so many people, most especially her effect upon Fénelon. A prior work, entitled, A History of the Variations of the Doctrines of the Reformed Church, in which he had subjected the doctrines of Martin Luther and the other Protestant reformers to a severe scrutiny, had earned Bossuet the reputation of defender of the faith. It was a reputation he cherished and a position he gladly and enthusiastically accepted.

The case of Fénelon particularly troubled him—for this was someone whose talents he knew, whose friendship he valued, and whose piety and influence he had the highest hopes. He determined, therefore, through with some reluctance, to put forth his own great strength, and to risk his own splendid reputation, in the attempt to extinguish this new heresy. But he had known Madame Guyon only by report, and he thought that charity and truth required him to form a personal acquaintance with her as a means of distinctly determining her views.

Accordingly, he visited her at her residence in Paris in September 1693, accompanied by the Duke of Chevreuse. In this first meeting, both he and the Duke expressed agreement with some of the things in her writings, but stated that there were things in her treatise, Spiritual Torrents, that needed explanation on her part. They parted amicably with Bossuet telling her that he would examine her works more closely at his leisure and make known more definitely his opinions of them.

They met again in January 1694, and this time Bossuet questioned her extensively about her teachings over a period of several hours, from early afternoon until mid-evening. Madame Guyon later wrote that Bossuet "spoke almost with violence and very fast, and hardly gave me time to explain some things that I wished to explain. He was evidently unfavorably affected toward me by the secret efforts of some persons. We parted late in the evening, and I returned home so wearied and overcome with what had passed between us, that I was sick for several days."

By the following year, Bossuet had determined that he must destroy Madame Guyon's influence in general and particular her influence over Fénelon. During 1695 and the early part of 1696, he wrote a remarkable ten-book treatise entitled Instructions on the States of Prayer. In it, he touched upon both the character and writings of Madame Guyon, but being offended by her doctrines, he was more critical and condemning than just. He then sent the manuscript to the Bishop of Chartres and the Archbishop of Paris for their approval, which they heartily gave. Having their approval, he sent the manuscript to the recently appointed Archbishop of Cambray, Fénelon, thinking that Fénelon would also approve the book and in so doing condemn the character and doctrines of Madame Guyon.

Fénelon refused to do either. In a letter to Madame de Maintenon, he wrote —

August, 2, 1898

Madame — When the Bishop of Meaux proposed to me to approve of his book, I expressed to him, with tenderness, that I would be delighted to give such a public testimony of the conformity of my sentiments with those of a prelate whom I had ever regarded, from my youth, as my master in the science of religion. I even offered to go to Germigny to compose, in conjunction with him, my approbation.[33]

I said, at the same time, to the Archbishop of Paris, to the Bishop of Chartres, and to Monsieur Tronson, that I did not, in fact, see any shadow of difficulty between me and the Bishop of Meaux on the fundamental questions of doctrine. But, if he personally attacked Madame Guyon in his book, I could not approve of it. This I declared six months ago.

The Bishop of Meaux gave me his book to examine. At the first opening of the leaves, I saw that it was full of personal refutation.[34] I immediately informed the Archbishop of Paris, the Bishop of Chartres, and Monsieur Tronson, of the perplexing situation in which the Bishop of Meaux had placed me.

After adding that be could not approve of a book in which many unfavorable things are said of Madame Guyon, without doing an injury to himself as well as injustice to her, he proceeds in the same letter to give his reasons.

I have often seen her. Every one knows that I have been closely acquainted with her. I may say further, that I have esteemed her, and that I have experienced her also to be esteemed by illustrious persons, whose

reputation is dear to the Church and who had
confidence in me. I neither was nor could be ignorant
of her writings, although I did not examine them all
accurately at an early period. I knew enough of them,
however, to perceive that they were liable to be
misunderstood. And must confess that I was induced
by some feelings of early distrust to examine her with
the greatest rigor.

I think I can say I have conducted this examination
with greater accuracy than her enemies, or even her
authorized examiners, can have done it. And the
reason of my saying this is that she was much more
candid, much more unconstrained, much more open
toward me at a time when she had nothing to fear.

I have often made her explain what she thought
respecting the disputed points. I have frequently
required her to explain to me the meaning of
particular terms in her writings, having relation to the
subject of inward experience, which seemed to be
mystical and uncertain. I clearly perceived, in every
instance, that she understood them in a perfectly
innocent and universal sense.

I followed her even through all the details of her
practice, and of the counsels that she gave to the most
ignorant and least cautious persons. But I could never
discover the least trace of those wrong and injurious
maxims that are attributed to her. Could I then
conscientiously impute them to her by my approbation
of the work of the Bishop of Meaux, and thus strike
the final blow at her reputation, after having so clearly
and so accurately ascertained her innocence?

Let others, who are acquainted with her writings only,
explain the meaning of those writings with rigor, and
censure them. I leave them to do it if they please. But,

as for myself, I think I am bound in justice to judge of
the meaning of her writings from her real opinions,
with which I am thoroughly acquainted. And not judge
her opinions by the harsh interpretations that are given
to her expressions, and which she never intended.

The work of Bossuet, although not yet published, was
spoken of everywhere. It was generally understood also, that it
did not meet with the official approval of Fénelon. Bossuet and
Fénelon were, therefore, at odds. Two men who embodied more
of public thought and public attachment than any other two men
in France. And, strange as it may seem, the object of
controversy between them was a poor captive woman, who was
at this very time shut up in the fortress of Vincennes, and
employed in writing religious songs.

It was not possible for a man of Fénelon's reputation and
standing, toward whom so many eyes were now turned, to
remain silent. Under these circumstances, enlightened by his
own experience as well as by history, he gave to the world his
now classical work, The Maxims of the Saints, in January 1697.

In this celebrated work, it was his object to state some
of the leading principles found in the most devout
writers on the higher inward experience. The work of
Bossuet, although it embraced a multitude of topics,
might be justly described as an attack upon Madame
Guyon. The work of Fénelon, without naming her, was
designed to be her defense. It was an exposition of her
views as Fénelon understood them, and as she had
explained them to him in private.

5

The Battle Rages

During the contest that arose between Fénelon and Bossuet, Madame Guyon was comparatively forgotten. Publication of the *Maxims of the Saints* had immediately turned all thoughts and eyes to Fénelon. His high ecclesiastical rank made his theological and controversial position more important, and consequently attracted more attention.

Fénelon had not used the name of Madame Guyon in the Maxims of the Saints, but his work so clearly recognized the doctrine of pure love that she taught, that he was naturally regarded as her expounder and defender. The doctrines she advocated had given great offense to many in her church, and the public feelings against her, which were heightened and encouraged by prominent ecclesiastics, could not be satisfied with permitting her to remain at large. If the views of Madame Guyon were heretical and her personal efforts dangerous, the heresy was not diminished or the danger lessened under Fénelon's support.

Was it right that Madame Guyon be condemned and the Archbishop of Cambray, who had added the authority of his great learning and influence to her opinions, be approved? Was it right that one be imprisoned and the other escape without notice? These were questions that naturally arose at that time.

The position of Fénelon was no longer a matter of uncertainty. On the great question of the fact and of the mode of present sanctification, he had spoken in a manner too clear to be mistaken. And those who understood his character knew that without a change in his convictions he was too conscientious to abandon his position or be unfaithful in defending it. Naturally mild and forbearing in his dispositions, he was inflexible in his principles. Incapable of being influenced by flatteries on the one hand or threats on the other, he asserted only what he believed. And he felt himself morally bound to defend the ground he had taken, although he had no disposition to do it otherwise than in the spirit of humility and candor.

It became necessary, therefore, on the part of his opponents, either to concede that he was right, or to show that be was wrong. Either to admit that the alleged heresy was not heresy, or to include a highly distinguished name in the category of those who had deviated from the strictness of the Roman Catholic faith.

Some of the leading men in France, De Noaillus, Pirot—a theologian of great eminence, Tronson, and some others gave early attention to Fénelon's book and examined it carefully. The spirit of piety that pervaded it was so pleasing to some of them that they seemed unwilling to condemn it. In particular, Monsieur de Noailles, Archbishop of Paris and a cardinal, and Godet-Marais, Bishop of Chartres, men whose opinions could not fail to have great weight, saw so much truth and merit in the work that they were inclined to let it pass in silence. But it was not so with Bossuet, whose feelings seem to have become somewhat exasperated toward the new sect.[35]

"Take your own measures," Bossuet wrote. "I will raise my voice to the heavens against those errors so well known to you. I will complain to Rome, to the whole earth. It shall not be said that the cause of God is weakly betrayed. Though I should stand alone in it, I will advocate it."

The courage of Bossuet had a support that was better known to him than to others, for he knew that in attacking the doctrines of Fénelon he would be considered a defender of the opinions of Louis XIV.

If Louis XIV had no love for Madame Guyon, he had as little or less for Fénelon. Their minds were differently constituted. There was no common bond of sympathy. In obedience to public sentiment, and in accordance undoubtedly with his own convictions of duty, he had nominated Fénelon to the archbishopric of Cambray. But his lack of personal interest in him was so strong as to be noticed and mentioned both by the Duke of St. Simon and the Chancellor D'Aguesseau.

There was something peculiarly commanding in the personal appearance of Fénelon. His mind possessed that moral simplicity and strength that he demonstrated in his writings, left its impression of calm and dignified serenity in his countenance, and gave a high character to his manners. Vice withdrew from him, and hypocrisy stood abashed in his presence. These writers observe that Fénelon, while he possessed a great superiority of genius, exhibited also an elevation of moral and personal character that awed the king of France.

Bossuet, aroused once more to a sense of his position as the guardian of the Roman Catholic Church, and strong also in the favor of the king, no longer concealed his intentions. Fénelon, on the other hand, although he foresaw what it would cost him, was equally ready to defend a doctrine that he believed to be in accordance with the Scriptures, and sanctioned by the opinions of many authorized writers.

The distinguished character of the combatants gave increased interest to the controversy. People looked on with a sort of awe as they beheld this conflict of the two great minds of France. About them, the Chancellor D'Aguesseau wrote:

> Then were seen to enter the lists[36] two combatants, rather equal than alike. One of them of consummate skill, covered with the laurels he had gained in his combats for the Church, an indefatigable warrior. His age and repeated victories might have dispensed him from further service. But his mind, still vigorous and superior to the weight of years, preserved in his old age a great portion of the fire of his early days. The other, in the strength and manhood of earlier life, was not as yet much known by his writings. But, enjoying the highest reputation for his eloquence and the loftiness of his genius, he had long been familiar with the subject that came under discussion. A perfect master of its facts and language, there was nothing in it which he did not comprehend, nothing in it which he could not explain, and everything he explained appeared plausible.

This was in reality the great question between them: Can we be holy in this life or not? Can we love God with all our heart or not? Can we "walk in the Spirit;" or must we be more or less immersed in the flesh?

Fénelon very correctly said when he was charged by Bossuet with introducing a new spirituality, "It is not a new spirituality that I defend, but the old." There probably has not been any period in the history of the Church in which the doctrine of present sanctification has not stirred up Church interest. Not a period in which, while the great mass of Christians have complained of the " body of sin" that they have carried about with them, there have not been some who have been deeply conscious of the constant presence and indwelling of the Holy Ghost, and of their entire union with God.

At one time the views and feelings of Bossuet and Fénelon on this subject were much the same. Fénelon would have cheerfully agreed to a considerable portion of Bossuet's work, Instructions on Prayer. In repeated instances, Bossuet spoke favorably of the doctrines of Madame Guyon, except for a few peculiarities of expression. But new influences had arisen. Strongly marked parties had made their appearance. New causes of distrust and alienation had presented themselves. What at first seemed a harmless exaggeration of the authorized doctrines of the Church, had assumed the form of an odious heresy.

The publications in this controversy occupy more than two large volumes of the writings of these distinguished men.

The advocates of Fénelon and of Madame Guyon maintained that the doctrines found in their writings were supported by a continuous succession of testimonies from the time of the apostles down to that period.

In answer, Bossuet published his work, titled, *The Traditional*[37] History of the New Mystics. This treatise does not enter into the subject in its full extent, being occupied chiefly with an examination of the opinions of Clement of Alexandria, and of passages that are found in the works circulated under the name of Dionysius the Areopagite.[38] Soon after, another work appeared, entitled, A Memoir of the Bishop of Meaux, addressed to the Archbishop of Cambray, on the Maxims of the Saints. Five distinct papers or articles appeared, at different times, under this title. The first is dated July 15, 1697.

The doctrine of Fénelon may be reduced to three leading propositions.

1. The provisions of the Gospel are such, that Christians may gain entire victory over their sinful propensities, and live in constant and accepted communion with God.

2. Persons are in this state when they love God with all their heart—in other words, with pure or unselfish love.

3. There have been Christians, though probably few in number, who, so far as can be decided by our imperfect judgment, have reached this state. And it is the duty of all, encouraged by the ample provision that is made, to strive to attain to it.

Perhaps the difference between the two men is well shown in a statement Bossuet made about Fénelon in one of his letters, and Fénelon's reply to that statement.

Bossuet wrote, "His friends say everywhere that his reply [to one of Bossuet's letters] is a triumphant work, and that he has great advantages in it over me. We shall see hereafter whether it is so."

Fénelon's replied to this in a letter addressed to Bossuet. "May Heaven forbid that I should strive for victory over any person, least of all, over you. It is not man's victory, but God's glory, that I seek. And happy, thrice happy, will I be, if that object is secured, though it should be attended with my confusion and your triumph. There is no occasion, therefore, to say, 'We shall see who will have the advantage.' I am ready now, without waiting for future developments, to acknowledge that you are my superior in science, in genius, in everything that usually commands attention. And in respect to the controversy between us, there is nothing that I wish more than to be vanquished by you, if the positions that I take are wrong. Two things only do I desire: TRUTH and PEACE. Truth that may enlighten, and peace that may unite us."

Bossuet, surprised at the strength and skill of his antagonist, and exposed to defeat after fifty years of victory, made a renewed and still more vigorous effort in a new work that he titled The History of Quietism. In his biography of Fénelon, Charles Butler said about this new work:

In composing it, Bossuet availed himself of some secret and confidential writings that he had received from Madame Guyon, also of private letters written to him by Fénelon during their early friendship, and a letter of friendship that Fénelon had written to Madame de Maintenon. In this difficult hour, she unfeelingly sent the letter to Bossuet.

Bossuet connected together the substance of these different pieces with great skill—he interwove in them the mention of many curious facts, gave an entertaining account of Madame Guyon's visions and pretensions to inspiration, and related many interesting anecdotes of the conduct of Louis XIV and of Madame de Maintenon during the controversy. This was not all. He dignified his narrative from time to time with bursts of lofty and truly episcopal[39] eloquence. He feelingly deplored the errors of Fénelon, presented his own conduct during their disputes in a highly favorable, put the whole together with exquisite skill, and expressed it with so much elegance and even brilliancy of language that it excited universal admiration, and attracted universal favor to its author.

In one part of it he assumed a style of mystery, and announced "that the time was come when it was the Almighty's will that the secrets of the union (that is to say, of the undue intimacy between La Combs, Fénelon, and Madame Guyon) should be revealed." A terrible revelation was then expected. It seemed to dismay every heart, and bring concern to many that the existence of virtue itself would become problematical, if it should be proved that Fénelon was not virtuous.

This work of Bossuet could not fail to excite universal attention. There is a letter of Madame de Maintenon still in existence that shows the eagerness with which it was read. "They talk here (at Versailles) of nothing else. They lend it;

they snatch it from one another, they devour it." There was a natural desire on the part of cultured people to read anything that came from the hand of Bossuet. But under the existing circumstances, religious zeal, more than anything else, instigated the principle of curiosity. When the Church was in danger, how was it possible to remain indifferent? There were some also who were wearied with what was constantly said of the disinterestedness and virtue of Fénelon, who seized with eagerness upon everything that promised to smear the luster of his character.

When this remarkable work appeared, the consternation of the friends of Fénelon was very great. Strong in the confidence of his own integrity, and never doubting the care of an overruling Providence, Fénelon, who wished to retain a Christian spirit in the bitterness of controversy, had at first no intention of answering it. But his friends, particularly the Abbé de Chanterac whose opinions he strongly trusted, informed him that the impression against him was so strong it absolutely necessary that he fully refute it. On further reflection, therefore, he wrote the reply under the title of an Answer to the History of Quietism in about six weeks. The work of Bossuet appeared in the middle of June—the reply of Fénelon was published on the third of August.

If the work of Bossuet was ingenious and eloquent, the reply of Fénelon was not less so. "Eloquence has never produced" says Butler, "a nobler outpouring of the indignation of insulted virtue and genius. In the very first lines of it, Fénelon placed himself above his antagonist, and to the last word preserves his elevation."

> Notwithstanding my innocence, I was always
> apprehensive that the controversy might take the shape
> of a dispute in relation to facts. I well knew that such a
> dispute between persons who held the office of Bishop
> must occasion no small degree of scandal. If, as the
> Bishop of Meaux has a hundred times asserted, my

work on the Maxims of the Saints in relation to the Interior Life, considered in its theological and experimental aspects, is full of the most extravagant contradictions and the most monstrous errors, why does he introduce other topics, and have recourse to other discussions that must be attended with the most terrible of scandals? Why does he reveal to libertines[40] what he terms, speaking of myself, a woeful mystery, a prodigy of seduction? Why, when the propriety of censuring my book is the sole question, does he travel out of its text and introduce other matters?

The reason of this course is here. The Bishop of Meaux begins to find it difficult to establish the truth of his accusations of my doctrine. In his inability to convict me of theological error, be calls to his aid the personal history of Madame Guyon, and lays hold of it as he would of some amusing romance, which he thought would be likely to make all his mistakes of my doctrine disappear and be forgotten. Not only this, he attacks me personally. No longer satisfied with unfavorable insinuations, he boldly publishes on the housetop what be formerly only ventured to whisper. In doing this, I am obliged to add, he has taken recourse to a mode of proceeding that human society condemns not only as wrong but as odious.

The secret of private letters, written in intimate and religious confidence (the most sacred after that of confession), has nothing sacred, nothing inviolable to him. He produces my letters to Rome, and prints letters that I wrote to him in the strictest confidence. But all will be useless to him. He will find that nothing that is dishonorable ever proves serviceable.

In some passages of Bossuet's work, he complains that improper influences had been used, that conspirators and contentious groups were active in Fénelon's favor. Fénelon replied by asserting if such were the case it could not be ascribed to him personally, for he was at that time banished from the court in a state of exile. "The Bishop of Meaux," he wrote, " complains that conspirators and factions are in action, and passion and interest divide the world. Be it so. But what interest can any person have to stir in my cause? I stand alone, and am wholly destitute of human help. No one that has a view to his interest dares look upon me. 'Great bodies, great powers,' says the bishop, 'are active.' But where are the great bodies, the great powers that stand up for me? These are the excuses the Bishop of Meaux gives for the world's appearance of being divided on his charges against my doctrine, which at first he represented to be so completely abominable as to admit of no fair explanation. This division in public opinion on a matter that he represented to be so clear, makes him feel it advisable to shift the subject of dispute from a question of doctrine to a personal charge.

"If the Bishop of Meaux has any further writing, any further evidence to produce against me, I urge him not to do it by halves. Such a proceeding, which leaves a part untold, is worse than any full and open publication. Whatever he has against me, I urge him to announce it, and to forward it instantly to Rome. I thank God that I fear nothing that will be communicated and examined judicially. I fear nothing but vague report and unexamined allegation."

He concludes by saying, "I cannot here forbear from calling to witness the adorable Being whose eye pierces the thickest darkness, and before whom we must all appear. He reads my heart. He knows that I adhere to no person, and to no book. That I am attached to Him alone and to His Church. That in His holy presence I continually beseech Him with sighs and tears to shorten the days of scandal, to bring back the shepherds to their flocks, and to restore peace to His Church.

And, while He once more reunites all hearts in love, to bestow on the Bishop of Meaux as many blessings as the Bishop of Meaux has inflicted crosses on me."

"Never did virtue and genius," says Butler, "obtain a more complete triumph. Fénelon's reply, by a kind of enchantment, restored to him every heart. Crushed by the strong arm of power, abandoned by the multitude, there was nothing to which he could look but his own powers. Obliged to fight for his honor and not willing to passively sink under the accusation, it was necessary for Fénelon to assume a position more imposing than that of his mighty antagonist. Much had been expected from him. But none had supposed that he would raise himself to so great a height as would not only repel the attack of his antagonist, but actually reduce him to the defensive."

Much to the credit of Fénelon, he seemed entirely willing that his own high character should stand or fall with that of Madame Guyon. The king of France had shown himself decidedly hostile to her. Madame de Maintenon, once her warm friend, had either adopted new views or fallen under unfavorable influences. The prominent men of the Church were almost all united against her. Her character, as well as her opinions, had been assailed. And, apparently deserted by everyone, she was at the present time shut up in prison. Fénelon, who had a mind too pure to measure virtue by the public favor or the lack of public favor that attended it, was not a person to forsake her at this trying time.

Bossuet attacked her by secret insinuations. Fénelon defended her by facts and arguments. He not only produced the honorable testimonials both in respect to her piety and morals that had been given her by Bishop D'Aranthon some time before, but he drew a strong argument in her favor from the conduct of Bossuet himself. Bossuet had repeatedly examined her in relation to her opinions, and had expressed himself in a favorable manner toward her on more than one occasion. Just before her imprisonment at Vincennes, he had administered the Eucharist to her, and given her an honorable written testimonial.

In the second century during the reign of Marcus Aurelius, a religious sect sprang up called the Montanists, from Montanus, a Phrygian by birth. He was probably a man of piety, whose speculative opinions on religion were corrupted by a mixture of error. His doctrines attracted the attention of the churches of that period, and were condemned as heretical. His reputation for piety, however, was so great that he drew after him many followers. Among others were two distinguished Phrygian ladies, Priscilla and Maximilla, whose zeal was such that they were willing to become his disciples at the great and perhaps criminal expense of leaving their families. Priscilla, in particular, became one of the active teachers and leaders of the sect.

Bossuet compared Fénelon and Madame Guyon to Montanus and his friend and prophetess Priscilla. Fénelon exclaimed against the comparison as calculated to bring contempt upon him. Bossuet, in justifying what he had said, admitted that though Montanus and Priscilla were closely connected with each other in their religious views and efforts, there never had been any reason to suspect any improper intimacy between them, and that the relation between them was nothing more than a community and interaction of mere mental illusion. And in making reference to them, be wished to be understood as merely saying that the relation of Madame Guyon and Fénelon was of the same nature.

This partial retraction did not entirely satisfy Fénelon.

Does my illusion, even in the modified form in which you now present it, resemble that of Montanus? That enthusiastic and deluded man separated two wives from their husbands, and they followed him everywhere. The result of his instructions and example was to inspire in them the same false spirit of prophecy with which he himself was actuated. And it cannot be unknown to you, that, in the unhappy and wicked excitements to which their system led, two of them, Montanus and Maximilla, strangled themselves. And such is the man on whom succeeding ages have looked with disapprobation, and even with horror, to whom you think it proper to compare me. And you say further that I have no right to complain of the comparison. And I say in reply that I have undoubtedly less reason to complain for myself, than I have to grieve for you. You, who can coolly say that you accuse me of nothing and cast no improper reflection upon me when you make such a comparison. I repeat that you have done a greater injury to yourself than to me. But what a wretched comfort is this, when I see the scandal it brings into the house of God! I can rejoice in no dishonor that you may incur by such attempts to injure me. Such joy belongs only to heretics and libertines.

"The scandal was not so great," says the Chancellor D'Aguesseau, "while these great antagonists confined their quarrel to points of doctrine. But the scene was truly afflicting to all good people when they attacked each other on facts. They differed from each other so much in their statements that it seemed impossible that both of them should speak the truth. So the public saw with great concern that one of the two prelates must be guilty of prevarication. Without saying on which side the truth lay, it is certain that the Archbishop of Cambray contrived to obtain, in the opinion of the public, the advantage of probability."

At this time, among the distinguished men of France, was the Abbé de Rancè. In early years a man of the world and devoted to its pleasures and honors, his conversion was remarkable. But from the day that his eye was opened to the truth of God and his heart felt its influences, he left no doubt of his purpose to live to God alone. From the rocks and forests of his almost impenetrable seclusion, the keen eye of this remarkable man watched with great attention the contest between Fénelon and Bossuet.

De Rancè distinctly acknowledged the importance of the principle of faith. But he attached great importance to those physical restraints, humiliations, and sufferings, that go under the name of austerities. He was alarmed at the diminished importance in which they appeared to be held in the writings of Madame Guyon and Fénelon, which he seems to express in this letter to Bossuet.

La Trappe, March 1697

To the Bishop of Meade — I confess, sir, that I cannot be silent. The book of the Archbishop of Cambray has fallen into my hands. I am unable to conceive how a man like him could be capable of indulging in such fantasies, so opposite to what we are taught by the gospel, as well as by the holy tradition of the Church. I thought that all the impressions that might have engendered in him this ridiculous opinion were entirely effaced, and that be felt only the grief of having listened to them. But I was much deceived. It is known that you have written against this monstrous system—that is, that you have destroyed it. For whatever you write, sir, is decisive. I pray to God that He may bless your pen, as He has done on so many other occasion, and that He may gift it with such energy that not a stroke it makes but what shall be a blow. While I cannot think of the work of the Archbishop of Cambray without indignation, I implore of our Lord Jesus Christ that He will give him grace to be sensible of his errors."

In a letter to Bossuet on the following 14th of April, the Abbé de Rancè expresses himself still more harshly concerning the book of the Archbishop of Cambray.

If the illusions of these fanatics were to be received, we must close the book of God—we must abandon the gospel, however holy and necessary may be its practices, as if they were of no utility. We must, I say, hold as nothing the life and actions of Jesus Christ, adorable as they are, if the opinions of these madmen are to find any credence in the mind, and if their authority is not entirely removed from it. It is, in short, a consummate impiety, hidden beneath singular and unusual phrases, beneath affected expressions and extraordinary terms, all of which have no other end than to impose upon the soul and to delude it.

The letters of the Abbé de Rancè contrary in all probability to his own expectations, were made public, and great efforts were made to circulate them. As the letters were not addressed to Fénelon, and were apparently written with no design of their being published, he did not make any formal reply to them. A few months afterwards, however, he had occasion to address a Pastoral Letter to the clergy of his own diocese. The letter, while it did not entirely exclude some other appropriate topics, was a learned and eloquent defense of the doctrine of PURE LOVE, as expressing a true, desirable, and possible form of Christian experience.

This letter seemed to Fénelon to be a suitable opportunity to open a correspondence with De Rancè. He accordingly sent to the Abbé a copy of it, accompanied by the following letter, addressed to the Abbé himself:

Cambray, October 1697.

To the Abbé de Rancè — I take the liberty, my reverend father, of sending you a Pastoral Letter that I have issued respecting my book. This explanation seemed to me to be necessary as soon as I perceived from your letters, which were made public, that so enlightened and experienced a man as yourself had conceived me in a manner very different from my meaning. I am not surprised that you believed what was said to you against me, both with regard to the past and the present. I am not known to you, and there is nothing in me that can render it difficult to believe the evil that is reported of me.

You have confided in the opinion of a prelate whose acquirements are very vast. It is true, my reverend father, that if you had done me the honor to write to me respecting anything that may have displeased you in my book, I would have endeavored either to remove your displeasure, or to correct myself. In case you should be thus kind, after having read the accompanying pastoral letter, I shall still be ready to profit by your knowledge, and with deference.

Nothing has occurred to alter in me those sentiments that are due to you, and to the work that God has performed through you. Besides, I am sure you will not be hostile to the doctrine of disinterested love, when that which is equivocal in it shall be removed, and when you are convinced how much I should abhor to weaken the necessity of desiring our beatitude in God.

On this subject I wish for nothing more than what St. Bernard has taught with so much sublimity, and which you know better than I do. He left this doctrine to his children as their most precious inheritance. If it were lost and forgotten in the whole world beside, it is at La Trappe, where we would still find it in the hearts of your pious ascetics. It is this love that gives their real value to the holy austerities that they practice. This pure love that leaves nothing to nature by referring everything to grace, does not encourage illusion, which always springs from the natural and excessive love of ourselves. It is not in yielding to this pure love, but in not following it sufficiently, that we are misled.

I cannot conclude this letter without soliciting of you the aid of your prayers, and of those of your community. I have need of them. You love the Church—God is my witness that I wish to live but for her, and that I should abhor myself if I could account myself as anything on this occasion. I shall ever be, with sincere veneration, yours, Francis, Archbishop of Cambray.

Such was the reputation for piety of the Abbé de Rancè, that perhaps no one else in France at that time could have done Fénelon so much injury. But how calmly and triumphantly the gentle and purified spirit of Fénelon carries him above the violence that issued from the solitude of La Trappe. De Rancè had faith, but not enough to subdue the fears, the agitations, and the injustice of nature.

The faith of Fénelon was of that triumphant kind that can forgive its enemies and turn the other cheek to those who smite us. " We do not know," says M. de Bausset, in his Life of Fénelon, "whether the Abbé de Rancè replied to this letter. It must have caused him some regret for having expressed himself with so much harshness concerning a bishop who wrote to him with such mildness and esteem. It is certain, however, that the name of the Abby of La Trappe was heard no more in the course of this controversy."

6

Controversy Brought Before the Pope

It was seen at an early period of the controversy, that there was no probability of its being settled by any tribunal short of the highest authority of the Roman Catholic Church,. Innocent XII, a man of a benevolent and equitable spirit, filled the papal chair. The subject was pressed upon him with great earnestness by persons apparently acting in accordance with the wishes of Louis XIV, the Roman Catholic king of France.

It was a matter of great grief to the Pope that so strong a controversy on such a subject should be brought before him. He had indulged the hope that the business might be settled in France by mild and conciliatory measures, and went so far as to order his nuncio[41] to express this wish. The suggestion was entirely useless. Louis was certain that the doctrine of Fénelon was heretical, and it had caused great discussions and divisions in France. It had been brought to his attention in so many ways, and had so implicated itself in his various relations, that it had become a personal concern to him. Nothing would satisfy him but its formal condemnation.

The position of Pope Innocent was a trying one. The relations between him and the king of France were of such a nature that it would probably have caused great difficulty between them if be had declined to give attention to this matter.

The Pope appointed a commission of twelve persons, called consultors,[42] to examine the book of Fénelon and give an opinion upon it. They were directed to hold their meeting in the chamber of the master of the Sacred Palace. Having discussed the principles and expressions of the book in twelve successive sittings, they found themselves so divided in opinion that no satisfactory result could reasonably be anticipated. They were accordingly dissolved.

His next step was to select a commission or congregation of cardinals, in the hope that they would be able to come to some conclusion. This body also had twelve sittings. They found themselves, however, greatly divided, came to no conclusion, and were dissolved.

He then appointed a new congregation of cardinals. They met in consultation no less than fifty-two times. Though it was by no means unanimous, the result of their deliberations was that they extracted from Fénelon's work a number of propositions that they regarded as censurable, and reported them to the Pope. After they had advanced so far, they held thirty-seven meetings to settle the form of the censure. In addition to these more formal meetings, private conferences on the subject were frequently held at the Pope's direction, and sometimes in his presence.

The cardinals Alfaro, Fabroni, Bouillon, and Gabriellio, and some others of perhaps less note, took the side of Fénelon. Men of no ordinary learning and power, they maintained with great ability that the doctrine in question had authority and support in many approved Roman Catholic writers. They did not hesitate in the least to defend the statements repeatedly made by Fénelon in his arguments with Bossuet and on other occasions, that it was a doctrine not only received but greatly cherished by many pious and learned people in all ages of the Church. By Clement, Cassian, Dionysius, Thauler, Gerson, De Sales, John of the Cross, St. Theresa, the Bishop of Bellay, and others. To this they were willing to add that there was not more of such learned and pious authority in its favor than there was of Scripture and reason. On one occasion, Cardinal Gabriellio expressly said that it was a doctrine that conformed to the Scriptures, the Church Fathers, and the Mystics.

They did not, however, in maintaining the doctrine of pure love, exclude the idea of a suitable regard to our own happiness. They seem to have taken the ground that God and ourselves, considered as objects of love, are impossible to measure or compare. Consequently, the motive of God's love, exceeding our love beyond all comparison, practically absorbs and annihilates it. So that a soul wholly given to God may properly be said to love God alone. But the doctrine of GOD ALONE does not exclude other things, since God is All in All.

In other words, by loving God, who is the sum of all good, for Himself alone, we cannot help loving ourselves, our neighbor, and everything else in their proper place and degree. In concluding some remarks at one of these meetings, Cardinal Alfaro read a letter that was written many ages before by St. Louis of France to one of his daughters, in which he advised her to do everything from the principle of pure love.

Among other things, the cardinals expressed a large degree of dissatisfaction with the course the controversy had taken in certain respects. They protested strongly against the attempt to confound doctrines with men, to implicate the permanency of truth with the imperfections of character, and to support a doubtful argument by personal defamation. When they saw the efforts constantly made in high places and low to destroy the character of Fénelon, it was much to their credit that they gave their opinions freely and boldly in his favor.

"Consider a moment," said Cardinal Bouillon, "who it is that you propose to condemn—a distinguished Archbishop, prudent and wise in the government of his diocese, who combines with a literary taste and power not exceeded by that of any other person in the kingdom, and having the utmost sanctity of life and manners."

They went so far as to proclaim that if the doctrine of PURE LOVE were condemned, sustained as it was by such a weight of authority and argument, and encircled as it was by so many strong affections, it could hardly fail to produce a schism in the Church.

The leading men on the other side were the Cardinals Massoulier, Pantiatici, Carpegna, Casanata, and Granelli. Their arguments were directed against the doctrine, partly in its general form, and partly against particular expressions and views that characterized it in the writings of Fénelon. So far as their arguments were general, they were very much the same as are employed against it at the present day. They maintained that it was a state too high to be possessed and maintained in the present life. That there were many things in the Scriptures against it, that the exaggerated expressions in the mystical or experimental writers of the Roman Catholic Church ought to be received in a modified sense. That it was either modified or rejected by a great majority of their theological writers and other writers not of the mystical class. That it had been accompanied in a number of instances with practical disorders.

The contest between the two parties was animated, and sometimes violent. For a time it seemed doubtful what the result would be. The discussion continued this way from 1697 to 1699, a period of nearly two years, under the eye and in the presence of the Pope. The king of France, who was in frequent communication with Bossuet, became impatient on learning of doubts that he did not himself entertain, and a delay that he did not anticipate.

In order to hasten an issue, he had a letter written in 1697 to the Pope, in which he denounced the book of the Archbishop of Cambray as erroneous and dangerous, and as already censured by a great number of theological doctors and other learned persons. He stated that the explanations more recently given by the Archbishop were inadmissible, and concluded by assuring the Pope that he would employ all his authority to obtain the due execution of his Holiness's decree.

This letter, drawn up by Bossuet, was dated the 26 July 1697.

The desires and feelings of the king were made known in other ways still more painful. When Fénelon was first appointed Archbishop of Cambray in 1695, his character was so much esteemed and his services were regarded so important, that the king insisted he should spend three months in the year at Versailles in the instruction of the young princes.

Six days after the date of the letter to the Pope, the king wrote a letter or order to Fénelon, which might properly be designated an order of banishment, in which he required him to leave Versailles and go to the diocese of Cambray, and commanded him not to leave it. It was added further that be was not at liberty to delay his departure any longer than was absolutely necessary to arrange his affairs.

Those principles of inward experience, which so triumphantly sustained Madame Guyon in her imprisonment, received a new confirmation in the victory that they now achieved in Fénelon.

The very moment he received from the king the order that effectively banished him from all places outside his own diocese, he wrote the following letter to Madame de Maintenon. (In his biography of Fénelon, Bausset says that he copied it from the original manuscript in Fénelon's handwriting)

Versailles, August 1, 1897.

In obedience to the king's commands, Madame, I shall depart from this place tomorrow. I would not pass through Paris, did I not feel it difficult to find anywhere else a man fit to attend to my affairs at Rome, and who would be willing to make the journey there. I shall return to Cambray with a heart full of submission, full of zeal, of gratitude, and of the greatest attachment toward the king. My greatest grief is, that I have harassed and displeased him. Not a day of my life shall pass over, that I will not pray to God to bless him. I am willing to be still more humbled.

The only thing that I would implore of his Majesty is, that the diocese of Cambray, which is guiltless, may not suffer for the faults that are imputed to me. I solicit protection only for the Church, and I limit this protection to the circumstance of being free to perform the little good that my situation will permit me to perform as part of my duty.

It only remains, Madame, that I request your forgiveness for all the trouble I may have caused you. God knows how much I regret it; and I will unceasingly pray to Him until He alone shall occupy your whole heart. All my life I shall be as sensible of your past goodness as though I had never forfeited it, and my respectful attachment towards you, Madame, will never diminish.

"We may easily conceive," says Bausset, "what an effect this letter—every line of which breathes nothing but mildness, affection, and serenity—had upon Madame de Maintenon. Recalling all her former friendship for Fénelon, she could not conceal from herself the active part that she had taken in his present disgrace. It cannot, indeed, be doubted, that this letter left a painful and durable impression upon her heart. She tells us, herself, that her health was impaired in consequence, and that she did not conceal the cause of her illness from Louis XIV.

The monarch himself seemed, at first, to be a little hurt, and could not help peevishly exclaiming to her as he marked her affliction—'So it seems, Madame, we are to see you die in consequence of this business.'"

The Duke of Burgundy, who had owed so much to Fénelon was no sooner informed of the order of exile than he hastened to throw himself at the feet of the king, his grandfather. He appealed to himself and to the renovation of his own heart and life as a proof of the purity of the life and maxims of his faithful and affectionate instructor. Louis was touched by an attachment so open and generous. But fixed in his principles of belief, and invariable in whatever he had decided, he merely replied to the young prince, "My son, it is not in my power to make this thing a matter of favor. The purity of religious faith is concerned in it. And Bossuet knows more on that subject than either you or I"

On the second of August, Fénelon departed from Versailles, never to return again. He remained at Paris only twenty-four hours. He cast a tender and last look towards the seminary of St. Sulpitius, in which he had spent the peaceful and happy years of his youth. A motive of delicacy, nevertheless, forbade his entering its walls. He feared that he might involve in his own sorrow and disgrace his former friend and instructor, Monsieur Tronson, who had charge of it. He, however, wrote him a few lines in which he expressed his veneration and gratitude. He also asked the continuance of that good man's prayers, of which he said he had much need in his sufferings, and then went on his way.

It was but a few months after he had reached Cambray, and was unceasingly engaged in his religious duties among his own people, when he received information that the way was open for his return on certain conditions. To this he refers in a letter to the Abbé de Chanterac, dated December 9, 1697.

It is reported that the only means by which I can appease the king, obtain my return to court, and prevent all scandal, is to remove the present unfavorable opinions by a humble acknowledgment of error. But I assure you that I have no present nor future idea of returning to court. If I am in error, it is my desire to be undeceived. But as long as I am unable to perceive my error, it is my purpose to justify my position with unceasing patience and humility. Be assured that I will never return to court at the expense of truth or by a compromise, which would leave the purity either of my doctrine or of my reputation in doubt.

The friends of Fénelon were, to some extent, involved in his calamities. Foremost among them was the Duke of Beauvilliers. He believed in the doctrine of pure love, originated and sustained by faith in the Son of God. He had experienced in his own renovated heart the effects that this doctrine, more than any other, is calculated to produce. He was the avowed and known friend of Madame Guyon, as well as of Fénelon, The king was offended with him. Taking Beauvilliers aside soon after the banishment of the Archbishop of Cambray, he told him how much he was dissatisfied at his connection with a person whose doctrines were so much suspected. He made it known distinctly to him that his continuance in such a course would be likely to be attended with the most unpleasant consequences.

Beauvilliers assured him of his entire conviction that the princes who had been under the care of the Archbishop of Cambray had not been infected with any erroneous or dangerous doctrine. He then proceeded to say, " I remember, Sire, that I recommended to your Majesty the appointment of Fénelon to be the preceptor[43] of the Duke of Burgundy. I can never repent that I did so. I have been the friend of Fénelon. I am his friend now. I can submit to whatever your Majesty may impose upon me, but I cannot eradicate the sentiments of my heart. The power of your Majesty has raised me to my present position, the same power can degrade me. Acknowledging the will of God in the will of my king, I shall cheerfully withdraw from your court whenever you shall require it; regretting that I have displeased you, and hoping that I may lead hereafter a life of greater tranquility."

The king, overawed by the nobleness of his sentiments, or fearing the rashness of the course that he had threatened, permitted him to remain in his place.

On the June 2, 1698, the king removed from the Abbé Beaumont and the Abbé de Langeron their title of sub-preceptors. Bausset wrote:

The former was Fénelon's nephew, the latter was his
most tender and faithful friend. Messieurs M. Dupuy
and De Leschelle, gentlemen who held positions about
the person of the young prince, were dismissed on the
same day and ordered to leave the court. The pretext
for their dismissal was their partiality for the spiritual
maxims of the Archbishop of Cambray. The real
motive was their affectionate and inviolable fidelity
toward him.

All of them had been involved in the education of the
Duke of Burgundy for nine years, and the excellence
of this education has been detailed. They were
dismissed without receiving the slightest reward for
their services. Thus the men who had transformed the
vices of the Duke of Burgundy into virtues were
severely punished, a severity that could have been
justified only if they had changed his virtues into
vices.

Fénelon felt more deeply the disgrace and suffering of his friends than his own, but he maintained the same calmness and triumphant faith that had supported him up to this time. In a letter that he wrote at this time to the Duke of Beauvilliers, we find the following expressions, which indicate very clearly how patient and lovely is the heart that is wholly given to God:

I cannot avoid telling you, my good duke, what I have at heart. Yesterday I spent the day in devotion and prayer for the king. I did not ask for him any temporal prosperity, for of that he has enough. I only begged that he might make a good use of it, and that, amidst such great success he might be as humble as if he had undergone some deep humiliation. I begged that he might not only fear God and respect religion, but that he might also love God, and feel how easy and light His yoke is to those who bear it less through fear than love. I never found in myself a greater degree of zeal or, if I may venture to use the expression, of affection to his person.

Far from being under any uneasiness at my present situation, which might have suggested unpleasant feelings against him, I would have offered myself with joy to God for the sanctification of the king. I even considered his zeal against my book as a commendable effect of his religion, and of his just abhorrence of whatever has to him the appearance of novelty. Desirous that he might be an object of the Divine favor, I called to mind his education without solid instruction, the flatteries which have surrounded him, the snares laid for him in his youth, the profane counsels that were given him, the distrust that was with so much pains instilled into him against the excesses of certain professors of devotion, and, lastly, the perils of greatness, and so great a multiplicity of pleasant affairs.

I admit that with all these things in view, I had great compassion for a soul so much exposed. I judged his case deserved to be lamented, and I wished him a more plentiful degree of mercy to support him in so formidable a state of prosperity. In all this I had not, as I had feared, the least interested view. For I would

have consented to a perpetual disgrace, provided I
knew that the king was entirely after God's own heart.

As far as relates to me, all I can say is that I am at
peace in the midst of almost continual sufferings.
Trusting in God's assistance to sustain me, the
scandals that my enemies cast upon me shall neither
exasperate nor discourage me.

One object of these actions of the king of France was to
make an impression at Rome. They were a part of a plan of
intimidation, but they did not have the immediate effect
anticipated. Public opinion was still divided. There had been a
lack of total agreement in the debates and decisions of the
congregation of the cardinals at Rome, and the Pope himself
hesitated to give a decision.

Under these circumstances, Louis, near the end of 1698,
wrote another letter, which was dispatched to the Pope by an
extraordinary courier. It was as follows:

Most Holy Father — At the time when I expected
from the zeal and friendship of your Holiness, a
prompt decision upon the book of the Archbishop of
Cambray, I could not learn without grief that this
decision, so necessary to the peace of the Church, is
still retarded by the craftiness of those who think it
their interest to delay it. I see so clearly the fatal
consequences of this delay, that I could not consider
myself as duly supporting the title of eldest son of the
Church, were I not to reiterate the urgent entreaties
that I have so often made to your Holiness, and to beg
of you to calm, at length, the anxieties of conscience
that this book has caused. Tranquility can now be
expected only from the decision that shall be
pronounced by the common father—but let it be clear
and precise, and capable of no misinterpretations—
such a decision, in fact, as is necessary to remove all

doubt with regard to doctrine, and to eradicate the very root of the evil. I demand, most holy Father, this decision for the good of the Church, the tranquility of the faithful, and for the glory of your Holiness. You know how truly sensible I am, and how much I am convinced of your paternal tenderness.

To such powerful and important motives, I would add the attention that I entreat you to pay to my request, and the filial respect with which I am,

Most holy Father, your truly devoted Son, Louis.

Under such circumstances as these, on March 12, 1699, a decree was issued under the signature of the Pope condemning Fénelon's book, The Maxims of the Saints, or perhaps more properly condemning twenty-three propositions, purporting to be extracted from it. The Pope, however, took the pains to say, and to have it understood, that they were condemned in the sense that they might bear, or that they were actually regarded as bearing in the view of others, and not in the sense in that they were explained by Fénelon himself.

"The Pope," says Monsieur de Bausset, "had openly declared on many occasions that neither he nor the cardinals had intended to condemn the explanations that the Archbishop of Cambray had given of his book."

To such a condemnation Fénelon could have comparatively little objection. It was really not a condemnation of him, but of others who undertook to speak and to interpret for him. While be was sincere and firm in his own belief, be had no disposition to defend the misconceptions and perversions of other people. To what extent, however, he availed himself of the statement from the Pope, we have no means of knowing. It is certain, however, that whatever view he took of the act of condemnation, he made no complaint. He thought it his duty to be submissive to the higher authorities of his Church. He received the news of his condemnation on the Sabbath, just as he was about to ascend his pulpit to preach. He delayed a few moments, changed the plan of his sermon, and delivered one upon the duty of submission to the authority of superiors.

From that time, he ceased to write controversially upon the subject. But, without regarding what was said by others, and in the discharge of his own duties among his own people, he never ceased to advocate in his life, his conversations, and his practical writings, the doctrine of pure love. He thought it his duty to avoid certain forms of expression, and certain illustrations that had been specifically condemned in the papal decree, and which were liable to misconception. But nothing shows that he went further.

In other words, he condemned sincerely what he understood the Pope to condemn, and he did this without any change, further than has already been indicated, either in his life or opinions.

7

Fénelon's Character

Early in his career, Fénelon had devoted himself to the ministry of Jesus Christ. After he was appointed Archbishop of Cambray, he had but one object, that of benefiting his people. This was particularly the case after he was confined by the royal order to his own diocese. It wasn't that he then had a more benevolent disposition, but he had a better opportunity to exercise it. With a heart filled with the love of God, which can never be separated from the love of God's creatures, it was his delight to do good.

He was very diligent in visiting all parts of his diocese. He preached by turn in every church in it, and with great care and faithfulness examined, instructed, and exhorted both priests and people.

In his preaching, he was affectionate and eloquent, but still very plain and intelligible. Excluding from his sermons superfluous ornaments as well as obscure and difficult reasoning, he was said to preach from the heart rather than from the head. He generally preached without notes, but not without premeditation and prayer. Before be preached, it was his custom to spend some time in the retirement of his closet, so that he could be sure that his own heart was filled from the divine fountain before he poured it forth upon the people. One great topic of his preaching was the doctrine that was so dear to him, and for which he had suffered so much, of PURE LOVE.

He was very temperate in his habits, eating and sleeping but little. He rose early and devoted his first hours to prayer and meditation. His chief relaxation was walking and riding. He loved rural scenes, and it was a great pleasure to him to go out in the midst of them. "The country," he says in one of his letters, "delights me. In the midst of it, I find God's holy peace." Everything seemed to him to be full of infinite goodness, and his heart glowed with the purest happiness as he escaped from the business and cares that took so much of his time into the air and fields, flowers and sunshine, of the great Creator.

But the first principle of Christianity is that we should forget ourselves and our own happiness in order that we may do good to others, so he felt it a duty to make even this sublime pleasure subservient to the claims of benevolence. He improved these opportunities to form a personal acquaintance with some of the poor peasants and their families in his diocese, and to counsel and console them. Sometimes, when he met them, he would sit down with them upon the grass and ask familiarly about the state of their affairs. He gave them kind and suitable advice—but above all things, he affectionately recommended to them to seek salvation in the Savior, and to lead a religious life.

He went into their cottages to speak to them of God, and to comfort and relieve them under the hardships they suffered. If these poor people presented him with any refreshments in their unpretending and unpolished manner, he pleased them much by seating himself at their simple table, and partaking cheerfully and thankfully of what was set before him. He showed no false delicacy because they were poor, and because their homes had little of the conveniences and comforts of those who were more prosperous. In the fullness of his benevolent spirit, which was filled with the love of Christ and of all for whom Christ died, he became one of them, as a brother among brothers and sisters, or as a father among his children.

In one of his rural excursions, he met with a peasant in much distress. Inquiring the cause of his grief, he was informed by the man that he had lost his cow. Fénelon attempted to comfort him, and gave him money enough to buy another. The peasant was grateful for the kindness of the archbishop, but still he was very sad. The reason was that although the money given him would buy a cow, it would not buy the cow he had lost— to which he seemed very much attached. Continuing his walk, Fénelon found the man's cow at a considerable distance from the place of his conversation with him. The sun had set, and the night was dark, but the good archbishop drove her back himself to the poor man's cottage.

The revenues that he received as Archbishop of Cambray were very considerable, but he had learned the difficult though noble art of being poor in the midst of plenty. He kept nothing for himself. His riches were in making others rich—his happiness, in making the poor and suffering happy.

While he was at Versailles instructing the young princes, the news came that a fire had burned to the ground the archiepiscopal palace at Cambray, and consumed all his books and writings. His friend, the Abbé de Langeron, seeing Fénelon conversing with a number of persons, and apparently much at his ease, supposed he had not heard this unpleasant news, and began with some formality and caution to inform him of it. Fénelon, perceiving the solicitude and kindness of the good Abbé, interrupted him by saying that he was acquainted with what had happened. Then he said that although the loss was a very great one, that he was really less affected in the destruction of his own palace than be would have been by the burning of a cottage of one of the peasants.

So elevated and diffusive were his religious principles, that they rendered him the friend of all humanity. It was not necessary for him to stop and inquire a person's creed or nation before benefiting them. There are an abundance of occasions that illustrate this.

The war, which raged near the commencement of the eighteenth century, between France and Bavaria on the one side, and England, Holland, and Austria on the other, drew near to the city where Fénelon lived.[44] Cambray is not far from the Netherlands, which has sometimes been called the battlefield of Europe. During the war, large armies met in its vicinity, and battles were fought near it.

At this difficult time, not only the residence of Fénelon, but other houses beside, hired by him for the purpose, were filled with the sick and wounded, and poor people driven from the neighboring villages. The expense he thus incurred used up all his revenues, but he had no inclination to spare either time, money, or personal effort in these acts of benevolence—acts that were shown as kindly and as freely to the enemies of his country who were taken prisoners in the war, as to those of his own nation.

The sight of the wretched condition of the refugees in his palace was painful to him. Many were suffering from lack of proper clothing. Others were in agony from their wounds, and others were afflicted with infectious diseases. But nothing lessened Fénelon's zeal. He appeared among them daily with the kindness of a parent, dropping words of instruction and consolation, and testifying by his tears how much he was moved with compassion.

The marked respect in which he was held was not confined to the French army alone. He was held in equal veneration by the enemy. The distinguished commanders opposed to France, the Duke of Marlborough, Prince Eugene, and the Duke of Ormond, embraced every suitable opportunity of showing their esteem. They sent detachments of their men to guard his meadows and his corn, and had it transported to Cambray with a military escort so that it would not be seized and carried off by their own foragers.

In the discharge of his religious duties in his diocese, Fénelon went abroad among the people without regard to the hostile armies that occupied the territory. As he traveled in the discharge of these duties in the spirit of Christ, he had faith in God's protection. So far from any violence being offered to him, when the English and Austrian commanders heard that he was to take a journey in that part of the diocese where their armies were, they sent him word that he had no need of a French escort, that they would furnish an escort themselves. It is said that even the hussars[45] of the Imperial troops did not hesitate to do him service.

At this time, Cambray was visited by the celebrated Cardinal Quirini, whose whole life, as remote as possible from the pursuits of war, was devoted to learned researches and useful studies. In the prosecution of literary objects, he visited almost all parts of Europe, and became acquainted with the most distinguished literary people. In the account of his travels, which he wrote in Latin, be speaks very particularly of his interview with Fénelon.

> I considered Cambray as one of the principal objects of my travels in France. I will not even hesitate to confess that it was toward this single spot, or rather toward the celebrated Fénelon who resided there, that I was most powerfully attracted. With what emotions of tenderness I still recall the gentle and affecting familiarity with which that great man deigned to discourse with me. He even sought my conversation, though his palace was then crowded with French generals and commanders-in-chief, toward whom he displayed the most magnificent and generous hospitality. I have still fresh in my recollection all the serious and important subjects that were the topics of

our discourse. My ear caught with eagerness every word that issued from his lips. The letters that he wrote me, from time to time, are still before me—letters that are an evidence alike of the wisdom of his principles and of the purity of his heart. I preserve them among my papers, as the most precious treasure that I have in the world.

It is evidence of both the kindness and faithfulness of Fénelon that he endeavors in these very letters to turn Cardinal Quirini from a too eager and exclusive pursuit of worldly knowledge, to that knowledge of Jesus Christ that renews and purifies the soul.

Strangers from all parts of Europe came to see him. Although the duties of hospitality became a laborious work to him, amid the multiplicity and urgency of his other employments, he fulfilled them with the greatest attention and kindness. He readily allowed himself to be interrupted in his important duties in order to attend to any who might call upon him, whatever might be their condition and their needs. He did not hesitate to drop his eloquent pen, with which he conversed with all Europe, whenever Providence called him to listen to the imperfect utterance of the most ignorant and degraded among his people. In doing this, he acted on religious principle. He would rather suffer the greatest personal inconvenience than injure the feelings of another person.

Wrote the Chevalier[46] Ramsay:

I have seen him in the course of a single day, converse with the great and speak their language in all his episcopal dignity, and then talk with the simple and the little like a good father instructing his children. This sudden transition from one extreme to the other was without affectation or effort, like one who, by the extensiveness of his genius, reaches to all the most opposite distances. I have often observed him at such conferences, and have as much admired the evangelical condescension by which he became all things to all people, as the sublimity of his discourses.

While he watched over his flock with a daily care, he prayed in the deep retirement of internal solitude. The many things that were generally admired in him, were nothing in comparison to that divine life by which he walked with God like Enoch, and was unknown to men.

In the language of those who knew Fénelon's virtue, but still were willing to say something to his discredit, he was termed a Quietist. This term is can have both a good and a bad meaning. Quietude is bad when it is the result of the ignorant and unbelieving pride of self. Quietude is good, even sublime, when it is the quietude that is the result of an intelligent and believing abandonment to the will of God. The quietude that was ascribed to Fénelon was that inward rest the Savior calls peace, and of which it is declared there is no peace to the wicked. It was that state of mind that the Savior not only called peace, but which He describes as "My peace."[47] In other words, Christ's peace—"the peace of God, which passeth all understanding."[48] It was this peace that supported and sustained the Archbishop of Cambray in the trials he endured, and in the duties of humanity and religion that he was called to discharge.

An anonymous writer wrote, "As fast as they arose, he dismissed all useless ideas and disquieting desires, to the end that he might preserve his soul pure and in peace—taken up with God, detached from everything not divine. This brought him to such a simplicity as to be far from valuing himself for his natural talents, accounting all but dross, that he might win Christ, and be found in Him."[49]

Among his written religious meditations we find this one.

I adore thee, Oh infant Jesus!—naked, weeping, and
lying in the manger. Thy childhood and poverty are
become my delight. Oh that I could be thus poor, thus
a child, like thee! Oh Eternal Wisdom, reduced to the
condition of a little babe, take from me the vanity and
presumptuousness of human wisdom. Make me a
child with thee. Be silent, ye teachers and sages of the
earth! I wish to know nothing, but to be resigned, to
be willing to suffer, to lose and forsake all, to be all
faith. The WORD made flesh! Now silent, now He
has an imperfect utterance, now weeps as a child.
And shall I set up for being wise? Shall I take a
complacency in my own schemes and systems? Shall
I be afraid lest the world should not have an opinion
high enough of my capacity? No, no! All my pleasure
shall be to decrease, to become little and obscure, to
live in silence, to bear the reproach of Jesus crucified,
and to add thereto the helplessness and imperfect
utterance of Jesus a child.

The anonymous writer just quoted also wrote: "To die to
all his own abilities must have been a thing more painful to
him than any other. He understood thoroughly the principles of
almost all the liberal sciences. He had studied the ancients of
all kinds, poets, orators, and philosophers. He was well
acquainted both with their faults and with their beauties. Yet
he rejected that pompous erudition that so powerfully tends to
swell the mind with pride. He thought it his duty to renounce
all the false riches of the mind. and to be wise with sobriety.
This is what those learned men and teachers, who are always
contending about frivolous questions, will never be able to
comprehend."

It was one characteristic of this remarkable and deeply
pious man that he bore the passions and faults of others with
the greatest calmness. He was faithful without ceasing to be

patient. Believing that the providence of God has to do with time as well as to things, and that there is a time for reproof as well as for everything else, a time that may properly be called God's time, he waited calmly for the proper moment of speaking. Thus keeping his own spirit in harmony with God, he was enabled to administer reproof and to utter the most unpleasant truths without a betrayal of himself, and without giving offence to others.

" It is often," he said, " our own imperfection that makes us reprove the imperfections of others—a sharp-sighted self-love of our own that cannot pardon the self-love of others. The passions of others seem insupportable to him who is governed by his own. Divine charity makes great allowances for the weaknesses of others, bears with them, and treats them with gentleness and condescension. It is never over-hasty in its proceeding. The less we have of self-love, the more easily we accommodate ourselves to the imperfections of others, in order to cure them patiently when the right season arrives for it. Imperfect virtue is apt to be sour, severe, and implacable. Perfect virtue is meek, affable, and compassionate. It thinks of nothing but doing good, bearing others' burdens. It is this principle of disinterestedness with regard to ourselves, and of compassion for others, that is the true bond of society."

When Fénelon was appointed a missionary among the Protestants of Poitou, he accepted this difficult and delicate office only on the condition that the king remove all the troops and all appearance of military coercion from those places to which he was sent. In 1709, during the latter period of his life, he was visited by a young prince at the episcopal residence. The Archbishop recommended to him very emphatically never to compel his subjects to change their religion. "Liberty of thought," he said, "is an impregnable fortress that no human power can force. Violence can never convince, it only makes hypocrites. When kings take it upon themselves to direct in matters of religion, instead of protecting it, they bring it into bondage. You should, therefore, grant to all a legal toleration.

Not as approving everything indifferently, but as tolerating with patience what God tolerates. Endeavor in a proper manner to restore such as are misled, but never by any measures but those of gentle and benevolent persuasion."

Fénelon had many friends affectionately attached to him in Versailles, Paris, and other parts of France, but in his banishment he seldom saw them. Many of them were persons of eminent piety. In one of his letters to them he wrote the following.

Let us all dwell in our only CENTER, where we continually meet and are all one and the same thing. We are very near, though we see not one another. Whereas others, who even live in the same house, yet live at a great distance. God reunites all, and brings together the remotest points of distance in the hearts that are united to Him. I am for nothing but unity, that unity that binds all the parts to the center. That which is not in unity is in separation, and separation implies a plurality of interests, which in each self is too much fondled. When self is destroyed, the soul reunites in God, and those who are united in God are not far from each other. This is the consolation that I have in your absence, and which enables me to bear this affliction patiently, however long it may continue.

Oh what a beautiful sight to see all kinds of goods in common, nobody looking on his own knowledge, virtue, joys, riches, as his peculiar property. It is thus that the saints in heaven possess everything in God, without having anything of their own. It is the flow and ebb of an infinite ocean of good, common to all, which satiates their desires and completes their happiness. Perfectly poor in themselves, they are perfectly rich and happy in God, who is the true source of riches. If this poverty of spirit, which in depriving us of self fills us with love, prevailed here below as it should, we would hear no more those cold words of mine and yours. Being one in the abandonment of self, and one in harmony with God, we would be all at the same time rich and poor in unity.

After Fénelon left Versailles, he never had the opportunity of seeing his beloved pupil, the Duke of Burgundy; and it was a number of years before they had the means of even corresponding with each other. But the Duke never forgot him, and Fénelon, on his part, never ceased to counsel and encourage.

In one of his letters written a short time before the death of the prince,[50] he wrote: "Offspring of Saint Louis, be like him, mild, humane, easy of access, affable, compassionate, and liberal. Let your grandeur never hinder you from condescending to the lowest of your subjects, yet in such a manner that this goodness may never weaken your authority, nor lessen their respect. Do not allow yourself to be surrounded by insinuating flatterers, but value the presence and advice of those of virtuous principles. True virtue is often modest and retired. Princes have need of her, and therefore ought to seek her out. Place no confidence in any but those who have the courage to contradict you with respect, and who love your prosperity and reputation better than your favor. Make yourself to be loved by the good, feared by the bad, and esteemed by all. Hasten to reform yourself so that you may labor with success in the reformation of others."

The effect of the correspondence of Fénelon with the Duke of Burgundy may be seen from the following letter.

To the Archbishop of Chambray.

My Dear Archbishop — I will endeavor to make use of the advice you give me. I ask an interest in your prayers, that God will give me His grace to do so. I desire of God more and more that He will grant me the love of Himself above all other things, and that I may love my friends and love my enemies IN Him and FOR Him. In the situation in which I am placed, I am obliged to listen to many remarks, and sometimes to those which are unfavorable. When I am rebuked for taking a course that I know to be a right one, I am not disquieted by it. When I am made to see that I have done wrong, I readily blame myself. And I am enabled sincerely to pardon all, and to pray for all, who wish me ill or who do me ill.

I do not hesitate to admit that I have faults. But I can also add that I have a fixed determination, whatever may be my failings, to give myself to God. Pray to Him without ceasing that He will be pleased to finish in me what He has already begun,[51] and to destroy in me those evils that proceed from my fallen nature. In respect to yourself, you may be assured that my friendship is always the same.

Fénelon died in 1715, at the age of sixty-five. His work was finished. It was found after his death that he was without property and without debts. United to Christ, be had no fear. As he had the spirit, so he delighted in the language of the Savior. His dying words were, "THY WILL BE DONE."[52]

Here is a final word on Fénelon and his burial place by a women who visited Cambray in the mid-nineteenth century.

I visited Cambray in 1841. The Revolution had done its perfect work in his palace, cathedral, and first tomb! His memory is revered as the good and great Fénelon. Rue Fénelon, Place Fénelon, and his name given as the Christian name in the families of the citizens, shows the estimation he is yet held in. The people spoke of him as if he had lived but yesterday. His present tomb was raised by the venerable Louie Belmas, who was lying in state twenty-four hours after his death when we visited the palace—it was designed by David,[53] in 1825, and is simple and truthful to history.

The Revolutionists in 1783 destroyed the venerable cathedral, in which lay the remains of its venerable Archbishop. Their embarrassed posterity have, by way of making some atonement for their lawless violence, erected a monument to the memory of a man whose name is Immortalized by his talents in the literary world, and in the Christian world. All due to a Christian piety that will shed its sweet Influence forever on the hearts of those who believe that God is Love!

Endnotes

1 Jacques Bénigne Bossuet - 1627-1704. French Roman Catholic bishop and historian noted for his funereal orations and a philosophical treatise on history.

2 Peloponnesus (formerly Morea), A peninsula forming the southern part of Greece south of the Gulf of Corinth. Probably named for Pelops, mythical founder of Pelopid dynasty at Mycenae. It was dominated by Sparta until the fourth century B.C. (Sparta was a city-state of ancient Greece in the southeast Peloponnesus. Settled by Dorian Greeks, it was noted for its militarism and reached the height of its power in the sixth century B.C. A protracted rivalry with Athens led to the Peloponnesian Wars (460-404) and Sparta's hegemony over all of Greece. Its ascendancy was broken by Thebans in 371.)

3 The highest judicial and legislative council of ancient Athens.

4 Acts 17:23

5 Revelation 1:9

6 Louis XIV (born 1638, ruled 1643-1715) inherited this power from his father and carried it further. He was styled the Grand Monarch, and his brilliant court at Versailles became the model and the despair of other less rich and powerful princes, who accepted his theory of absolute monarchy (L'etat c'est moi, "I am the state"). Until 1661 the government was largely in the hands of the wily Italian Cardinal Mazarin. At the cardinal's death Louis declared that he would be his own prime minister. From then on he worked faithfully at his "trade of a king."

7 The practice of using various means to induce someone to convert to one's own religious faith.

8 A city of north-central France west-southwest of Paris. It is best known for its magnificent palace, built by Louis XIV in the mid-17th century, where the treaty ending World War I was signed in 1919.

9 Louis XIV imprisoned her in the convent of St. Maria on 29 January 1688.

10 In the time of this writing, certain levels of Roman Catholics had priests or bishops assigned to them as their Confessor - one to whom they confessed their sins.

11 Revelation 4:5

12 Fenelon at this time was high in ecclesiastical, political, and social circles in Rome and France.

13 2 Corinthians 12:9

14 See Book 2 in the Pure Gold Classic Madame Jeanne Guyon, published by Bridge-Logos Publishers.

15 acquiescence: passive assent or agreement without protest.

16 Galatians 2:20

17 1 Corinthians 6:19

18 emotive: of or relating to emotion.

19 2 Timothy 1:12

20 See the Imitation of Christ by Thomas à Kempis, a Pure Gold Classic published by Bridge-Logos Publishers.

21 See *The Practice of the Presence of God* by Brother Lawrence, a Pure Gold Classic, published by Bridge-Logos Publishers

22 A word coined by Madame Guyon, which is something she often did to explain her difficult concepts of the inner life. See the Pure Gold Classic, Madame Jeanne Guyon, published by Bridge-Logos Publishers.

23 This "considerable time" lasted for seven years according to her autobiography.

24 A teacher, an instructor, a tutor.

25 A Roman Catholic mass, which is a public celebration of the Eucharist.

26 Paraphrase of Jeremiah 1:7

27 Luke 2:29-30

28 A city of eastern France, north of Lyons. Lyons, in turn, is a city of east-central France at the confluence of the Rhone and Saône rivers south of Mâcon. Founded in 43 B.C. as a Roman colony, it was the principal city of Gaul and an important religious center after the introduction of Christianity. Its silk industry dates to the 15th century.

29 A city of southeast France on the Isère River, south-southwest of Chambéry. An ancient Roman city, Grenoble is today a noted tourist and skiing center and was the site of the 1968 Winter Olympics.

30 La Combs was a Roman Catholic priest who counseled Madame Guyon in spiritual matters for many years.

31 See the Pure Gold Classic *Madame Jeanne Guyon*, published by Bridge-Logos Publishers. This book contains the prayer teaching that was burned in Grenoble.

32 Michael de Molinos, (1628 - 1696), came from a respectable Spanish family and led a blameless life. He first made his appearance in Italy as a religious teacher and reformer. He published his views in a work titled, *The Spiritual Guide*, which in a few years passed through twenty editions in different languages.

Molinos maintained the high doctrine of present and effective sanctification. He attached comparatively little value to ceremonial observances, but insisted strongly upon the religion of the heart, and upon faith as its constituting principle. His doctrines were received with great joy by many people in various parts of Italy, including Rome.

But his popular doctrines and their effects upon the people soon came under the scrutiny of the Roman ecclesiastical authorities, and the Inquisition was assigned to investigate him. He was seized and shut up in prison with several hundred of his followers, some them noted for their learning and piety and others high in social ranks. Some of the latter, who protested strongly at the injustice, were allowed to escape the Inquisition, but not Molinos.

Though his irreproachable life and profound piety had made a highly favorable impression on many people, he was kept in prison and tried by the Inquisition. The doctrines of *The Spiritual Guide* were condemned as heretical, and he was sentenced to prison. Efforts were made to save him, but were ineffective. He died in the dungeons of the Inquisition after many years of close confinement, during which he exhibited the greatest humility and peace of mind.

33 Official approval.

34 Arguments against Madame Guyon's doctrines.

35 A group of people forming a distinct unit within a larger group by virtue of certain refinements or distinctions of belief or practice.

36 Used in a way seldom used today: 1. An arena for jousting tournaments or other contests. 2. A place of combat. 3. An area of controversy.

37 The word in the text we used was "Traditionary," but there is no such word in the dictionary, and so it may have been misspelled at some time in past years.

38 A member of the Council of the Areopagus. The Areopagus was the highest judicial and legislative council of ancient Athens. (Latin, from Greek Areios pagos, Areopagus, hill of Ares - where the tribunal met).

39 episcopal: related to a bishop or the office of a bishop.

40 1. One who acts without moral restraint; a dissolute person. 2. One who defies established religious precepts; a freethinker.

41 Papal representative or ambassador.

42 consultor: a priest or religious appointed to assist and advise a bishop.

43 Teacher or instructor.

44 1701: War of the Spanish Succession, continuation of the War of the League of Augsburg, lasted from 1701 - 1714. It was occasioned by the eagerly awaited death of Charles II, last of the Hapsburg kings of Spain, who died in 1700.

Because England, France, and the Dutch Republic were all pressing claims to Spain, a Treaty of Partition was drawn up in 1698, giving the kingship to the elector of Bavaria, Joseph Ferdin. His death in February 1699 made a second treaty necessary. Holy Roman Emperor Leopold I would not agree to it, nor did the Spanish nobility. Charles II himself had decided to will the succession to the House of Bourbon. This would give Spain to the grandson of Louis XIV of France, Philip of Anjou.

Philip was proclaimed Philip V by Louis, who then launched an invasion of the Netherlands to secure it for Spain. An anti-French alliance was immediately formed by England, the Dutch Republic, the Holy Roman emperor, Prussia, Portugal, and some German states. Due to the outstanding generalship of the Duke of Marlborough for England and Eugene of Savoy for Austria, France lost the war. Nevertheless, Philip V was able to maintain himself on the throne of Spain. When Leopold I died in 1711, his son inherited all the Hapsburg possessions.

Then rivalries broke out in the alliance. England especially was unwilling to see Charles, the new Holy Roman emperor, get Spain. As the alliance collapsed, each party negotiated separately with France, and the war ended in 1714. The North American part of the conflict was called Queen Anne's War.

45 Horsemen of the Hungarian light cavalry organized during the 15th century.

46 1. A member of certain male orders of knighthood or merit, such as the Legion of Honor in France. 2. A French nobleman of the lowest rank, also used as a title for such a nobleman.

47 John 14:27

48 Philippians 4:7

49 Philippians 3:7-9

50 Louis XIV had the distinction of ruling longer than any other European king. Seventy two years passed between the time he ascended the throne, as a child of less than 5, until his death in 1715. The Grand Monarch, who had outlived both his son and his son's son (the Duke of Burgundy), was succeeded by his 5-year-old great-grandson, Louis XV, the last son of the duke of Burgundy.

51 Philippians 1:6

52 Matthew 6:10, 26:42

53 Unknown

Index

To LanzhuGaichia